SEMEIA 14

Apocalypse: The Morphology of a Genre

Guest Editor:
John J. Collins

© 1979
by The Society of Biblical Literature

SEMEIA 14

Copyright © 1979 by the Society of Biblical Literature

All rights reserved. No part of this work may be reproduced or transmitted in any form or by any means, electronic or mechanical, including photocopying and recording, or by means of any information storage or retrieval system, except as may be expressly permitted by the 1976 Copyright Act or in writing from the publisher. Requests for permission should be addressed in writing to the Rights and Permissions Office, Society of Biblical Literature, 825 Houston Mill Road, Atlanta, GA 30329, USA.

ISSN 0095-571X
ISBN 1-58983-114-4

Printed in the United States of America
on acid-free paper

CONTENTS

Contributors to this Issue iv

Preface v

Introduction: Towards the Morphology of a Genre
    John J. Collins 1

The Jewish Apocalypses
    John J. Collins 21

The Early Christian Apocalypses
    Adela Yarbro Collins 61

The Gnostic Apocalypses
    Francis T. Fallon 123

Greek and Latin Apocalypses
    Harold W. Attridge 159

Apocalypses and "Apocalyptic" in Rabbinic Literature and Mysticism
    Anthony J. Saldarini 187

Persian Apocalypses
    John J. Collins 207

Index of Works Discussed 219

CONTRIBUTORS TO THIS ISSUE

Harold W. Attridge
    Perkins School of Theology
    Southern Methodist University
    Dallas, TX   75275

Adela Yarbro Collins
    McCormick Theological Seminary
    5555 South Woodlawn Avenue
    Chicago, IL   60637

John J. Collins
    DePaul University
    2323 North Seminary Avenue
    Chicago, IL   60614

Francis T. Fallon
    University of Kansas
    Lawrence, KS   66044

Anthony J. Saldarini
    Boston College
    Chestnut Hill, MA   02167

PREFACE

The essays in this volume represent the first stage of the work of the Apocalypse Group of the SBL Genres Project. They attempt to provide a comprehensive survey of all the texts which might be or have been classified as apocalypses and can be dated with any plausibility in the period 250 BCE-250 CE, with the purpose of establishing how far they can purposefully be regarded as members of one genre. We do not attempt to provide a full analysis of these texts, still less an interpretation. The question of function, which is obviously essential to interpretation, is not taken up here, but will be pursued at a later stage of the Project. These essays do, however, claim to provide the basis for further analysis and interpretation by defining the extent of the genre, determining its constitutive elements and showing the different types that must be distinguished within the genre.

The decision to publish at this stage rather than wait until a full analysis and interpretation could be offered was determined primarily by the unwieldly bulk of material involved. A full analysis of all the works surveyed here would be impossible within a single volume, and would require an indefinite period to complete. Yet it was felt to be necessary that at least a skeletal analysis of *all* the works in question be presented rather than a more detailed study of a few select examples with a mere list of other texts. Previous studies of apocalypses and apocalypticism have relied on the detailed study of a few works which were then used as the basis for broad generalizations. The validity of such generalizations has been doubtful, however, in the absence of a comprehensive survey. The present volume attempts to lend perspective to the view of apocalypses which is based on the few better known examples, by showing the extent and the limits of the similarities which are found throughout the apocalyptic corpus. The argument that it is in fact possible to recognize a coherent genre "apocalypse" does not then rest on the assumption that selected works are typical, but on the cumulative weight of the entire survey. Inevitably, any attempt to specify the members of a genre will encounter border-line cases whose inclusion is disputable (e.g. the book of Jubilees). What is essential to our thesis is that a substantial number of works do in fact fit the definition we have proposed. We hope to have shown that the genre so defined is well established in Jewish, Christian and Gnostic literature and has at least some representatives in Greco-Roman, Persian and the later Jewish rabbinic literature. While an attempt has been made to synthesize the surveys of all these areas, the individual essays are essentially independent. So, for example, the survey of the Gnostic apocalypses stands in its own right and does not depend on the accuracy of the analysis of the Jewish apocalypses.

Since the object of the essays is to demonstrate a recurring pattern in the individual texts, the discussion is inevitably repetitive. Accordingly, to facilitate the reader, each essay is divided into a synopsis, which provides a compact overview of the material, and a survey which shows the data on which the synopsis is based and can be checked by those who wish to pursue the details on a particular work. An index to the surveys and bibliographies of the texts discussed can be found at the end of the volume.

The identification of a genre "apocalypse" is an attempt to bring some order into a rather chaotic area of study. The genre is regarded here as essentially a heuristic device which can operate in two ways. On the one hand, it shows the recurrent features which we may expect to encounter in this literature. On the other hand, it provides a foil which can highlight the distinctive features by which a particular work deviates from the generic pattern. No individual apocalypse can be adequately understood by reference to its generic characteristics alone. Hence it should be clear that the identification of the common elements of the genre is not intended to reduce the apocalypses to that common core. Rather it is an attempt to provide perspective on the individual works by which both the typical and the distinctive elements can be more fully appreciated. Ultimately any study of apocalypses and apocalypticism must rest on the detailed study of individual texts. However, it should be apparent that individual texts cannot be studied in isolation. Interpretation involves recognition of the appropriate context in which to view the work, of the conventions which are operative and the parallels which are relevant. In short, interpretation already involves an implicit notion of genre. The present attempt to clarify the nature of the genre should, then, be understood as a first step towards the process of interpretation.

John J. Collins
DePaul University
Chicago, June 1978

INTRODUCTION:
TOWARDS THE MORPHOLOGY OF A GENRE

John J. Collins
DePaul University

The purpose of this volume is to identify and define a literary genre "apocalypse." Since neither "genre" nor "apocalypse" has a precise, universally accepted connotation, it is necessary to begin by stating what we mean by these terms.

Literary Genre

By "literary genre" we mean a group of written texts marked by distinctive recurring characteristics which constitute a recognizable and coherent type of writing. The texts which make up the genre must be intelligible as independent units. This does not necessarily mean that they have ever existed as independent works. In many cases recognizable units are embedded in larger works and we cannot be sure whether they ever circulated independently. If they constitute coherent wholes which are intelligible without reference to their present context, they can qualify as members of a genre.

While the study of a genre inevitably involves a diachronic, historical dimension (Fowler), its identification and definition are independent of historical considerations. A genre is identified by the recognizable similarity among a number of texts. Similarity does not necessarily imply historical relationships. It is important to emphasize that when we list a number of texts from diverse sources as "apocalypses" we are not implying that they are all historically related or derived from a common prototype. Our concern in this volume is with phenomenological similarity, not historical derivation, although some implications for the history of the genre will emerge from the discussion.

Further, while a complete study of a genre must consider function and social setting, neither of these factors can determine the definition. At least in the case of ancient literature our knowledge of function and setting is often extremely hypothetical

and cannot provide a firm basis for generic classification. The
only firm basis which can be found is the identification of recurring elements which are explicitly present in the texts. (For a
compact review of diverse recent discussions of "genre" see Doty;
on the theory of genre, see further, Gerhart.)

Apocalypse

The term "apocalypse" is simply the Greek word for revelation. However, it is commonly used in a more restricted sense,
derived from the opening verse of the book of Revelation (The
Apocalypse of John) in the NT, to refer to "literary compositions
which resemble the book of Revelation, i.e., secret divine disclosures about the end of the world and the heavenly state" (Koch:
18). However, the word is used loosely and is frequently interchanged with the related terms "apocalyptic" and "apocalypticism."
In the words of Koch (13): "Generally speaking, apocalyptic is
understood to mean a complex of writings and ideas which were widespread about the turn of the era in Palestine, in the Israelite
diaspora and in early Christian circles; but which can also appear
in similar form in other religious situations and mental climates."
While the best-known apocalypses are Jewish and Christian, we cannot ignore the possibility that writings of the same type were produced independently in other traditions in ancient or in modern
times.

It is important to note that the classification "apocalyptic" or "apocalypse" is a modern one. Some ancient Jewish,
Christian and Gnostic works are entitled *Apokalypsis* in the manuscripts (e.g. 3 Baruch, the Apocalypse of the Holy Mother of God,
the Apocalypse of Adam). However, the title is not a reliable
guide to the genre. The so-called "Apocalypse of Moses" (a variant
of the Life of Adam and Eve) is quite different from the main bulk
of apocalypses. On the other hand, several works which are not
called "apocalypses" in the mss. must be included in any discussion
of the genre.

It is obvious then that the identification of a genre
"apocalypse" is not a simple matter of collecting texts which bear
this label or have already been otherwise clearly identified. An
"apocalypse" is simply that which scholars can agree to call an
"apocalypse." The purpose of this volume is to attain consistency
and clarity in the use of the term on the assumption that the
single name "apocalypse" should refer to a single coherent and

recognizable type of writing. The choice of the name "apocalypse" is influenced by the use of that word in some ancient works, and more immediately by current scholarly usage. We therefore begin from the current, loose and inconsistent scholarly use of "apocalypse" and "apocalyptic" and inquire which works can meaningfully be classified together as one coherent genre.

The Need for a Literary Definition

There is a general consensus among modern scholars that there is a phenomenon which may be called "apocalyptic" and that it is expressed in an ill-defined list of writings which includes (on any reckoning) the Jewish works Daniel (chaps. 7-12), 1 Enoch, 4 Ezra and 2 Baruch and the Christian book of Revelation. The list is generally agreed to be more extensive than this but its precise extent is a matter of dispute. Despite the consensus that "apocalyptic" can be found in specific books there is a widespread opposition to any attempt to define it as a literary genre. So Gerhard von Rad insists: "die Apokalyptik in literarischer Hinsicht keine besondere 'Gattung' repraesentiert. Sie ist im Gegenteil in formgeschichtlicher Hinsicht ein mixtum compositum" (330). Von Rad's assertion is misleading in two respects. First, it is true that every apocalypse contains a number of smaller recognizable forms-- such as visions, prayers or exhortations. This fact, however, cannot preclude the possibility that the larger frameworks, within which these elements are held together, are also marked by distinctive recurring characteristics which constitute an equally recognizable type of writing. Second, von Rad's discussion suffers from semantic confusion since the abstraction "apocalyptic" hovers vaguely between literature, sociology, and theology. The confusion latent in the term "apocalyptic" has been highlighted in the discussion after von Rad, especially by M. Stone (439) and P. D. Hanson (29-30). These scholars distinguish between "apocalypse" as a literary genre, "apocalyptic eschatology" as a particular religious perspective and structure of thought, and "apocalypticism" as a sociological ideology. While these three concepts are closely related to each other, their referents do not necessarily coincide exactly. Not every writing which expresses apocalyptic eschatology can be classified as an apocalypse. Much of the confusion which currently reigns results from a failure to observe these distinctions.

In his review of the status of "apocalyptic," Klaus Koch reflected an awareness of the difference between "apocalypse" as a literary type and the broader dimensions of apocalyptic eschatology and apocalypticism, but was also concerned with the relationship between these phenomena. This awareness led him to formulate a principle of fundamental importance: "If we are to succeed at all in the future in arriving at a binding definition of apocalyptic, a starting-point in form-criticism and literary and linguistic history is, in the nature of things, the only one possible" (23). In the interests of terminological consistency and clarity, the label "apocalyptic eschatology" should be reserved for the eschatology found in apocalypses or recognized by analogy with them. Furthermore, the sociological study of apocalypticism depends almost entirely on evidence of a literary nature. If apocalypticism is assumed to be at all related to apocalypses, then the analysis of the literary genre must cast some light on the social phenomenon, even if they cannot be directly correlated. It should be noted, however, that our analysis of the genre does not presuppose that all the works identified as "apocalypses" have a common social milieu. The use to which a genre is put may vary widely. Even an individual work may be re-interpreted in various settings or employed for different purposes. Conversely, a given sociological movement may find expression in several different genres. The study of the social settings and functions of this literature is a highly complex undertaking which lies beyond the scope of the present volume.

The Scope of this Study

The study of apocalypses, even from a literary point of view, must eventually address the history and social functions of the genre. However, these questions are consequent to the purely literary description and identification. The present study is restricted in its purpose to the initial stage of literary analysis. Some light is thrown immediately and inevitably on the historical development of the genre, but we do not attempt to discuss historical and sociological questions in detail. We do, however, claim to establish the literary basis on which all historical and sociological studies of this genre must necessarily be built.

The literary genre "apocalypse" was not clearly recognized and defined in antiquity and has not been precisely delineated in modern scholarship. Consequently, the strategy employed in this volume has been to begin by examining all the writings which are either called apocalypses or are referred to as apocalyptic by modern authors, and any other writings which appear to be similar to these. By listing the prominent recurring features in these works it is possible to assess the extent of the similarity between them and decide which writings can meaningfully be classified in the same genre. The material surveyed has been limited to "late Antiquity" (approximately 250 BCE to 250 CE, although some earlier material has been studied for background and some material of uncertain date may be later) and to the area of the eastern Mediterranean. Within this material there is a wide range of revelatory literature which can be classified in various ways according to different degrees of similarity. Some use the term "apocalyptic" very broadly to refer to any type of revelatory literature irrespective of content. Others restrict it to a narrow group of writings (usually Jewish) which contain *ex eventu* prophecies of history and envisage cosmic transformation. Now a study of the inclusive genre of revelatory literature is certainly legitimate and perhaps desirable. Again, the narrow group of historical apocalypses can arguably be treated as a coherent genre. However, in view of the customary usage of the terms "apocalypse" and "apocalyptic" neither of these extremes is satisfactory. The broader view loses all the distinctiveness of apocalypses over against other types of revelation. The narrower view fails to account for too many texts usually regarded as "apocalyptic" and also ignores much material found in all the apocalypses which does not deal with either history or cosmic transformation (see Stone). In fact, our study shows that the genre may be defined more broadly while remaining distinctive over against other types of revelatory literature. The defining characteristics embrace both the manner or form of revelation and the content of the things revealed. The significant recurring elements constitute a paradigm which shows not only the persistent similarities which run throughout the corpus but also the variations which distinguish the different sub-groups and individual works.

The Master-Paradigm

The master-paradigm may be divided into two main sections: the framework of the revelation and its content. The framework in turn involves both the manner in which the revelation is conveyed and the concluding elements. The content embraces historical and eschatological events on a temporal axis and otherworldly beings and places on a spatial axis. Direct exhortation to the recipient in the course of the revelation is rare and plays a significant role only in a few Christian works. The paradigm is as follows:

Manner of Revelation

1. *Medium* by which the revelation is communicated.
1.1 *Visual* revelation may be either in the form of
1.1.1 *Visions*, where the content of the revelation is seen, or
1.1.2 *Epiphanies*, where the apparition of the mediator is described.
1.2 *Auditory* revelation usually clarifies the visual. Epiphanies are always followed by auditory revelation. They may be either in the form of
1.2.1 *Discourse*, uninterrupted speech by the mediator, or
1.2.2 *Dialogue*, where there is conversation between the mediator and recipient, often in the form of question and answer.
1.3 *Otherworldly Journey*, when the visionary travels through heaven, hell or remote regions beyond the normally accessible world. Revelation in the course of a journey is usually predominantly visual.
1.4 *Writing*, when the revelation is contained in a written document, usually a heavenly book.
2. An *Otherworldly Mediator* communicates the revelation. Often the mediation consists of interpreting a vision but it can also take the form of direct speech or simply of guiding the recipient and directing his attention to the revelation. The mediator is most often an angel, or in some Christian texts, Christ.
3. The *Human Recipient*.
3.1 *Pseudonymity*: The recipient is usually identified as a venerable figure from the past. A few Christian apocalypses are not pseudonymous.
3.2 The *Disposition of the Recipient* notes the circumstances and emotional state in which the revelation is received.
3.3 The *Reaction of the Recipient* usually describes the awe and/or perplexity of the recipient confronted with the revelation.

Content: Temporal Axis

4. *Protology*: Matters which deal with the beginning of history or pre-history.

4.1	*Theogony* (in Gnostic texts, describing the origin of the Pleroma) and/or *Cosmogony* (the origin of the world).
4.2	*Primordial events*, which have paradigmatic significance for the remainder of history (e.g. the sin of Adam).
5.	*History* may be reviewed either as:
5.1	*Explicit recollection* of the past, or
5.2	*Ex eventu prophecy* where past history is disguised as future and so associated with the eschatological prophecies.
6.	*Present salvation through knowledge* is a major way of salvation in Gnostic texts and distinguishes them significantly from other apocalypses.
7.	*Eschatological crisis*. This may take the form of
7.1	*Persecution* and/or
7.2	*Other eschatological upheavals* which disturb the order of nature or history.
8.	*Eschatological judgment* and/or *destruction*. This is brought about by supernatural intervention. It comes upon
8.1	*Sinners*, usually oppressors, but in Gnostic texts, the *ignorant*.
8.2	The *world*, i.e., the natural elements.
8.3	*Otherworldly beings*, e.g. the forces of Satan or Belial, or other evil powers.
9.	*Eschatological salvation* is the positive counterpart of eschatological judgment. Like the judgment, it is always brought about by supernatural means. It may involve:
9.1	*Cosmic transformation*, where the whole world is renewed;
9.2	*Personal salvation*, which may be part of the cosmic transformation or may be independent of it. This in turn may take the form of
9.2.1	*Resurrection*, in bodily form or
9.2.2	*Other forms of afterlife*, e.g. exaltation to heaven with the angels.

Content: Spatial Axis

10.	*Otherworldly elements* may be either personal or impersonal and either good or bad.
10.1	*Otherworldly regions* are described especially in the otherworldly journeys but also in lists of revealed things in other contexts. Again they may be evaluated in either a positive or a negative way. The Gnostic texts evaluate the lower heavens negatively.
10.2	*Otherworldly beings*, angelic or demonic.

Paraenesis

11. *Paraenesis* by the mediator to the recipient in the course of the revelation is relatively rare and is prominent only in a few Christian apocalypses.

Concluding Elements

12. *Instructions to the recipient*. These are distinct from Paraenesis (11) and come after the revelation as part of the concluding framework: e.g. they tell the recipient to conceal or publish the revelation.

13. *Narrative conclusion*. This may describe the awakening or return to earth of the recipient, the departure of the revealer or the consequent actions of the recipients. In some Gnostic texts we find reference to the persecution of the recipients because of the revelation.

The particular combination of elements involved here does not necessarily always constitute an entire independent work. It may be a subordinate part of a larger work: e.g. we will distinguish an apocalypse in Test Levi 2-5 although Test Levi as a whole is not an apocalypse. Conversely, an apocalypse may include subsidiary literary forms which are independent of the genre, e.g. the prayer in Daniel 9. Further, the apocalyptic paradigm, either entirely or in part, may be repeated more than once in a single apocalypse. So Daniel 7-12 and Revelation, to take the most familiar examples, juxtapose visions or series of visions which go over the same material in slightly different ways. This repetition does not indicate separate compositions but results from the common apocalyptic technique of "recapitulation" (see Yarbro Collins: 32-44). The repetition of variant formulations draws attention to the underlying structure which is common to all (compare the well-known folkloric device of "tripling").

Now it is apparent that no one apocalypse contains all the elements noted in the paradigm above. (The exact distribution can be seen from a glance at the charts in the individual essays.) Again, not all these elements are equally important. The disposition and reaction of the recipient (3.2 and 3.3) and the concluding elements are by no means constant and obviously are less important than the presence of an otherworldly mediator and human recipient. These less significant elements are noted here because they recur with notable frequency and may be of significance for more detailed study of particular works. However, they are not defining characteristics of either the genre apocalypse or any of its subtypes. Paraenesis by the mediator to the recipient occurs very rarely. It is noted in the paradigm, however, because it is a significant element. There is little doubt that all apocalypses seek to influence the lives of their readers and many imply exhortation to a specific course of action. The hortatory purpose is usually implicit in the work as a whole, but is expressed explicitly in the few works which contain paraenesis.

Definition of the Genre

A few elements are constant in every work we have designated as an apocalypse. These elements pertain to both the framework and the content. There is always a narrative framework in which the manner of revelation is described. This always involves an otherworldly mediator and a human recipient--it is never simply a direct oracular utterance by either heavenly being or human. The content always involves both an eschatological salvation which is temporally future and present otherworldly realities. The eschatological salvation is always definitive in character and is marked by some form of personal afterlife (see Collins, 1974a). Explicit reference to afterlife is lacking in only two Jewish apocalypses, the Apocalypse of Weeks and Test Levi 2-5, and is quite probably implied even there (both are embodied in texts where afterlife is explicit). In all the other Jewish, and in all the Christian, Gnostic and Greco-Roman apocalypses there is clear explicit reference to personal afterlife. This is seldom the only aspect of eschatological salvation: cosmic transformation is very frequently involved. However, personal afterlife is the most consistent aspect of the eschatology of the apocalypses, and it ensures the definitive and transcendent character of that eschatology. The spatial, otherworldly realities always involve the activity of otherworldly, angelic or demonic beings. Heavenly geography is described in detail in many apocalypses. The existence of another world beyond what is accessible to humanity by natural means is a constant element in all the apocalypses.

This common core of constant elements permits us, then, to formulate a comprehensive definition of the genre: *"Apocalypse" is a genre of revelatory literature with a narrative framework, in which a revelation is mediated by an otherworldly being to a human recipient, disclosing a transcendent reality which is both temporal, insofar as it envisages eschatological salvation, and spatial insofar as it involves another, supernatural world.*

This definition marks the boundaries of the genre and enables us to identify it. It is not intended as a complete or adequate description of the constituent works. No individual apocalypse can be adequately understood without reference to some other elements of the paradigm. The fuller paradigm permits us to see the variety within the genre and distinguish different types of apocalypses.

In the light of this definition it is immediately possible to distinguish apocalypses from other closely related categories. While oracles, testaments and revelatory dialogues all frequently contain eschatological material analogous to that found in apocalypses, they all lack some aspect of the apocalyptic manner of revelation. Oracles are not mediated at all, but are uttered directly, testaments are mediated by a human figure, and revelatory dialogues lack the narrative framework which describes the process of revelation. On the other hand, dreams and visions which lack the eschatology or otherworldly dimension of the apocalypses are also excluded from the genre. In this way the term "apocalypse" can be applied to a specific and limited number of texts from the period under consideration.

The Inner Coherence of the Genre

The different elements which make up our comprehensive definition of the genre are not associated at random, but are integrally related by their common implications. The key word in the definition is transcendence. The manner of revelation requires the mediation of an otherworldly being: i.e., it is not given directly to the human recipient and does not fall within the compass of human knowledge. The manner of revelation then already asserts the reality of another world, superior to our own in knowledge, even in the knowledge of human affairs and destiny. The reality of this other world is further affirmed by reference to angelic and demonic beings, and by the descriptions of heavenly geography. Human life is set in a context which is shaped by this otherworldly, supernatural dimension. Finally, the transcendent nature of apocalyptic eschatology looks beyond this world to another. The forms of salvation are diverse, exaltation to the heavens or renewal of the earth, but in all cases they involve a radically different type of human existence, in which all the constraints of the human condition, including death, are transcended. Both the manner of revelation and the eschatological content point beyond this world to another, which is at once the source of revealed knowledge and of future salvation.

There is, then, an intrinsic relation between the revelation which is expressed in an apocalypse as a whole and the eschatological salvation promised in that revelation. This is especially obvious in the Gnostic texts where revealed knowledge already confers salvation in the present. The other apocalypses do not envisage salvation in the present, at least in any full, definitive sense. However, the revelation conveyed by all the apocalypses is presumed to be conducive to salvation for those who accept it. There is a great difference in degree between the Gnostic salvation through knowledge and the understanding and hope to which revelation gives rise in other apocalypses. Nevertheless, in all the apocalypses the expectation of salvation is based on otherworldly revelation.

The emphasis on the transcendent in the apocalypses suggests a loss of meaning and a sense of alienation in the present which tallies well with current views of the social milieu of apocalypticism (Smith; Gager; Collins, 1975a). However, a word of caution is in order here. A given work may be understood quite differently by groups with varying degrees of sophistication and different social circumstances. An account of an otherworldly journey in Plato or Cicero does not necessarily carry the same implications as a similar or even identical account in a Jewish or Gnostic context. As we have noted already, the social functions and implied attitudes of this literature present highly complex problems which lie beyond the range of the present study. Here we only wish to demonstrate that the elements of the definition are integrally related and coherent.

We should also note that the other elements of the paradigm can be seen to be closely related to the elements singled out in the definition. The various media of revelation--visions, auditions, otherworldly journeys, writings--are all qualified by the otherworldly mediator and are in fact diverse kinds of otherworldly revelations. The disposition and reaction of the recipient, and also his awakening or return to earth, all emphasize the unusual and supernatural character of the revelation. Pseudonymity, a feature which is universal in Jewish and Gnostic apocalypses and very common in the Christian ones, is a complex phenomenon which has many implications but it is at least clear that the attribution of a work to an ancient author such as Enoch or Shem effectively removes it from the time and place of the present. In this way the impression of the inadequacy of the present world and the need to derive revelation from elsewhere is confirmed.

The temporal axis of the revelation provides a context in which the transcendent eschatological salvation is seen to contrast sharply with previous history and the afflictions of the eschatological crisis. There is, of course, some variety in the functions of historical material in the apocalypses. Primordial history serves to explain the way reality is structured. History can be regarded as a source of examples or structured to reflect a recurring pattern. *Ex eventu* prophecies which attempt to outline the entire course of history serve to show that the end is near. (For more detailed discussion of the functions of pseudonymity and historical reviews, see Collins, 1977a.) Finally, even paraenesis, when it occurs, only makes explicit what is implied elsewhere: the apocalyptic revelation provides a framework in which humans can decide their commitments in the full knowledge of the nature of reality present and future.

These remarks on the relation of the various elements of the paradigm to each other are of the most preliminary nature. An adequate discussion of these matters can only be achieved through the detailed analysis of individual apocalypses and the examination of the precise ways in which the various elements function (see Collins, 1977b; Yarbro Collins). However, even these preliminary remarks indicate that the paradigm is internally coherent. The common elements singled out in the comprehensive definition of apocalypse are not random but constitute a kernel to which the other elements are integrally related. The formal derivation of revelation from an otherworldly source complements the contentual emphasis on transcendent eschatology and the supernatural world.

The Extension and Typology of the Genre

The corpus of apocalypses which fits the definition given above is drawn heavily from Jewish and Christian literature. Not all the Gnostic apocalypses are necessarily of Jewish or Christian origin, but the majority clearly are. However, we have also identified a number of Greco-Roman apocalypses and found some examples of the genre in Persian literature. There is neither reason nor evidence to argue that all these apocalypses are related historically. While historical connections are certainly important within the various traditions, the genre as a whole is bound together by phenomenological similarity, irrespective of derivation.

Within the framework of the genre there is still considerable variation. In part this is due to the different historical traditions from which the works derive. Reviews of history, and concern for political eschatology, are much more prominent in the Jewish apocalypses than elsewhere. Paraenesis occurs somewhat more frequently in Christian apocalypses although it is rare even there. Historical references to Christ are of course distinctively Christian but they do not modify the apocalyptic paradigm in any significant way. Gnostic apocalypses have several distinguishing features. The visual element in the revelation is very slight and often consists only of the apparition of the mediator. Even more strikingly, the content of the Gnostic apocalypses places its greatest emphasis on salvation through knowledge, which is extended into personal afterlife. There is very little interest in history or eschatological crises. While the Gnostic apocalypses fall within the overall framework of the genre, they show a distinctive shift of emphasis from the temporal axis to the spatial, or rather to interior knowledge which cannot be easily correlated with either space or time. The Greco-Roman apocalypses are distinguished by the fact that they are preserved in the context of philosophical treatises or poetic compositions. In these cases we must reckon with a secondary use of the genre where the apocalypses are deliberately employed in the service of philosophical discussion or literary effect.

However, the variations of the genre apocalypse are not adequately reflected by the distinctions between the different cultural traditions. We have consistently found distinct types of apocalypses which cut across the traditional cultural groups. These types are distinguished by both manner of revelation and eschatological content. The most obvious and fundamental distinction is between apocalypses which do not have an otherworldly journey (Type I) and those that do (Type II). Within each of those types further distinctions can be made in view of eschatological content: (a) the "historical" type which includes a review of history, eschatological crisis and cosmic and/or political eschatology; (b) apocalypses which have no historical review but envisage cosmic and/or political eschatology (this type lacks the review of history which distinguishes type a, but retains some public character in its eschatology as opposed to the purely individual interest in type c); and (c) apocalypses which have neither historical review nor cosmic transformation but only personal eschatology. So we have, in effect, six types within the genre: Ia, b and c and IIa, b and c. The distribution of these types is as follows.

Ia: "Historical" Apocalypses with No Otherworldly Journey

This is perhaps the most widely recognized type of apocalypse and is often the basis for generalizations about "apocalyptic." In fact, however, it is virtually confined to a small group which makes up about one-third of the pseudepigraphical Jewish apocalypses: Daniel 7-12, the Animal Apocalypse, the Apocalypse of Weeks, Jubilees 23, 4 Ezra and 2 Baruch. Significantly, however, the Persian Zand-ī Vonuman Yasn conforms to this type. Only one Christian apocalypse, Jacob's Ladder, should be classified in Type Ia, and it is very probably an adaptation of a Jewish work. In the later Jewish writings, the Hebrew Apocalypse of Elijah also conforms to this type.

Ib: Apocalypses with Cosmic and/or Political Eschatology
(which have neither historical review nor otherworldly journey)

The most obvious example of this type is the Christian book of Revelation. No Jewish or Greco-Roman apocalypse conforms to this type. Other examples are the Christian Apocalypse of St. John the Theologian, Apoc Peter, Shepherd of Hermas, Testament of the Lord 1:1-14 and (tentatively) the book of Elchasai, and the Gnostic 2 Apoc James, Nature of the Archons, Pistis Sophia I-III and Gospel of Mary (the latter has only a slight allusion to cosmic eschatology). It should be noted that the Gnostic texts do not involve cosmic transformation but only judgment and destruction.

Ic: Apocalypses with Only Personal Eschatology (and no otherworldly journey)

Again, this type is found only in Christian and Gnostic works: 5 Ezra 2:42-48, Test Isaac 2-3a, Test Jacob 1-3a, Ques Bart and Resurr (Bart) 8b-14a (all Christian) and Apoc Adam, Sophia Jesu Christi, Apocryphon of John, I Apoc James, Gnostic Apoc Peter, Pistis Sophia IV (all Gnostic). This is the most common type of Gnostic Apocalypse. The Christian Apocryphon of James from Nag Hammadi, which is not clearly Gnostic, also conforms to this type. The Poimandres, from the Corpus Hermeticum, is a further example.

IIa: "Historical" Apocalypses with An Otherworldly Journey

This type is very rare. The historical interest never predominates in an otherworldly journey. An example is found in the Jewish Apocalypse of Abraham, which has a very brief review of history and in the later Jewish work Sefer Hekalot (3 Enoch), where the historical interest is outweighed by the prominence of the heavenly world.

IIb: Otherworldly Journeys with Cosmic and/or Political Eschatology

This type is very widely attested and includes 1 Enoch 1-36, Similitudes of Enoch, Heavenly Luminaries, 2 Enoch and Test Levi 2-5 (all Jewish); Apoc Esdras, Ascension of Isaiah 6-11, the Apocalypse of the Virgin Mary and Apoc Paul (all Christian), Paraphrase of Shem (Gnostic). The apocalypse in Seneca's Ad Marciam de Consolatione fits this type and also the late Jewish works Hekalot Rabbati, Merkabah Rabbah, the Revelation of Joshua ben Levi and the Chronicles of Jerahmeel (in part). There is considerable variation in the degree of prominence of the cosmic/political eschatology in these works.

IIc: Otherworldly Journeys with Only Personal Eschatology

This type is also very widely attested. It includes 3 Baruch, Test Abraham 10-15 (8-12 in Rec. B) and Apoc Zephaniah (Jewish); Test Isaac 5-6, Test Jacob 5, Zosimus, the Apocalypse of the Holy Mother of God concerning the Punishments, the Apocalypse of James the brother of the Lord, the Mysteries of St. John the Apostle and Holy Virgin, Resurr (Bart) 17b-19b and Apoc Sedrach (Christian) and the Gnostic Apoc Paul. The majority of the Greco-Roman apocalypses fall in this category: the "myth of Er" in Plato, Somnium Scipionis in Cicero, the apocalypses in Plutarch and the journey to the underworld in Aeneid VI. The parodies of Lucian are based on this type of apocalypse. The very late Jewish Ascension of Moses and the Persian book of Arda Viraf, which is very late in its present form (ninth century) also conform to this type.

The Christian apocalypses are distributed most widely and are found in every type except IIa. Jewish apocalypses (both early and late) are found in every type except Ib and Ic and Gnostic apocalypses in all but Ia and IIa. (We should note, however, that the Gnostic works are predominantly from Types Ic and IIc and even those that envisage cosmic destruction do not envisage cosmic restoration. The Greco-Roman apocalypses are also predominantly from Type IIc with one representative (Poimandres) in Ic and one (Seneca, Ad Marciam) in IIb. This distribution has obvious implications for the history of the genre.

Implications for the History of the Genre

Within Judaism, both Type Ia (the "historical" apocalypses) and Type IIb (otherworldly journeys envisaging cosmic eschatology) are clearly attested in the second century BCE. Type IIc (otherworldly journeys with only personal eschatology) is found only in works which are probably from the first century CE or later. Outside Judaism, Type Ia is also found in the Persian Zand-ī Vohuman Yasn, which is widely thought to date substantially from the Hellenistic age. Type IIc is found in Greek literature as early as Plato, and Type IIb (otherworldly journey with cosmic eschatology) is found in Seneca. In the light of this evidence from the first century CE and earlier, it seems very unlikely that all apocalypses can be traced to a common origin. Even the types involving an otherworldly journey are not clearly derived from a single historical source. In the Greco-Roman world, otherworldly journeys can be traced back to Parmenides and even to Homer. It is far from evident that the Jewish journeys of Enoch depend on the Greek tradition, and the relation, if any, of the Persian book of Arda Viraf to either Greek or Jewish traditions has not yet been shown (on the diverse traditions of otherworldly journeys, see Colpe).

The question might arise whether we should speak of two originally distinct genres, the "historical" apocalypses and the otherworldly journeys, which came to overlap to some extent in their later development. In fact, no pre-Christian apocalypse combines a review of history with an otherworldly journey and all the pre-Christian apocalypses which do not have an otherworldly journey have an *ex eventu* prophecy of history. This observation is certainly significant for the historical development of apocalypses. However, the question whether we should speak of two genres, or of two strands in a single genre, is a matter of terminological clarity and of finding the classification which deals most adequately with both the similarity and the diversity of the works involved. A sharp distinction between "historical" apocalypses and otherworldly journeys is very difficult to maintain. All are bound together by the common core that we have isolated in the definition of "apocalypse" above. Further, all the pre-Christian Jewish heavenly journeys have some interest in cosmic eschatology. The Similitudes of Enoch, a heavenly journey, is extremely close to Daniel in both manner of revelation and content. The NT book of Revelation, from which the name of the genre "apocalypse" is derived, fits neither the category "historical" apocalypse nor otherworldly journey but is extremely similar to both Daniel and the Similitudes. In view of these close bonds between the types it seems preferable to speak of one genre "apocalypse."

Within this genre we recognize variations and transformations which in some cases are due to historical development. The clear distinction between "historical" apocalypse and otherworldly journey in the earliest Jewish apocalypses, Daniel and 1 Enoch 1-36 may be taken as one stage in the development of the genre. In a later stage, represented by the Similitudes of Enoch and the book of Revelation, this distinction becomes far less clear. In view of the comprehensive definition of "apocalypse" given above, there is sufficient similarity between the different works to warrant their classification in the same genre.

In the apocalypses of the Christian era it is no longer possible to identify a particular kind of eschatology with one manner of revelation. All the same variants of eschatology are found in apocalypses with or without otherworldly journeys. The reviews of history prominent in one group of Jewish apocalypses are almost completely lacking in non-Jewish works, but are reflected in the late Jewish Sefer Hekalot (3 Enoch) and the Hebrew Apocalypse of Elijah. Of course it is important to emphasize that these "historical" apocalypses were never the only, or even the most frequent, type of Jewish apocalypse and are attested at least in some non-Jewish works. Since reviews of history are also found in related literary categories such as oracles, including some Greco-Roman works, there is no reason to conclude that an interest in history was unique to Judaism.

Personal eschatology is an important feature of all types of apocalypses at all stages of the genre. However, the emphasis placed on individual afterlife is modified by the degree to which it is put in the context of cosmic destruction and/or transformation. Both the purely personal eschatology and the expectation of cosmic destruction and/or transformation are found throughout, in Jewish, Christian, Gnostic and Greco-Roman works. The emphasis in the Greco-Roman tradition is predominantly personal at all stages. In the Jewish tradition the purely personal eschatology is characteristic of later works, although cosmic and political eschatology is also found in late texts such as Sefer Hekalot (3 Enoch). In the Gnostic material, cosmic eschatology is relatively minor and involves only destruction, not transformation. It is far less prominent than personal salvation. The Christian evidence is more ambiguous. It has been the policy in this volume to exclude works which are clearly later than 300 CE but include works of uncertain date. Now apocalypses which deal with political and historical events are much more easily dated than those which emphasize otherworldly elements and personal salvation. Accordingly, the proportional emphasis on personal eschatology may be somewhat exaggerated in this review.

In the light of this study there appears to be some shift in emphasis towards personal eschatology and away from historical affairs in the apocalypses of the Christian era. This is most obviously the case in the Gnostic texts. However, we should note that the otherworldly journeys always emphasized the spatial rather than the temporal axis, and that some concern for cosmic eschatology can be found even in the latest stages covered by our study.

One final comment on the history of the genre. The material presented in this volume covers the emergence of the genre, at least in the area bounding the eastern Mediterranean. We have made no attempt to trace it to its historical decline. The genre continues on into the Middle Ages and perhaps beyond.

Related Types

A discussion of related literary categories, such as oracles, testaments and revelatory dialogues, has been appended to each group of apocalypses. These writings overlap with various aspects of the apocalypses, either in manner of revelation or in content, but fail to satisfy the definition at some point. However, this material is extremely important for the broader phenomena of apocalypticism and revelatory literature and for the light it sheds on the function of elements which it shares with the apocalyptic paradigm.

Conclusion

This volume represents only the first stage in the study of the apocalypses and points to the need for much further study. However, it already permits some conclusions which modify widely-held opinions about apocalypses.

1. It is in fact possible to identify a coherent and recognizable literary genre, which may appropriately be labelled "apocalypse" in the light of common scholarly terminology. Our use of this designation is consistent with much scholarly usage although we claim to be more precise and comprehensive.

2. This genre is represented in Jewish, Christian, Gnostic, Greco-Roman and Persian literature. While the great majority of apocalypses come from the Judeo-Christian tradition, it is not

possible to regard the genre as a purely Jewish and Christian phenomenon. The Greco-Roman apocalypses show a well-defined group of otherworldly journeys which appear to have developed independently in the Hellenic tradition.

3. The genre did not entirely die out in Judaism after the first century CE since it is attested in late texts such as Sefer Hekalot (3 Enoch).

4. The "historical" apocalypses which give prominence to reviews of history followed by cosmic transformation and on which many generalizations about "apocalyptic" are based, constitute only about one-third of the Jewish apocalypses and are extremely rare elsewhere. It is significant that the Persian Zand-ī Vohuman Yasn is of this type.

5. The correspondence between the Christian apocalypses and the non-"historical" Jewish apocalypses is very close.

6. Despite the very significant distinctive traits of Gnostic revelatory literature, a substantial group of Gnostic texts fits the definition of "apocalypse."

WORKS CONSULTED

Collins, J. J.
    1974a   "Apocalyptic Eschatology as the Transcendence of Death." *CBQ* 36: 21-43.

    1975a   "Jewish Apocalyptic against its Hellenistic Near Eastern Environment." *BASOR* 220: 27-36.

    1977a   "Pseudonymity, Historical Reviews and the Genre of the Apocalypse of John." *CBQ* 39: 329-343.

    1977b   *The Apocalyptic Vision of the Book of Daniel*. HSM 16. Missoula: Scholars Press.

Colpe, C.
    1967   "'Die Himmelsreise der Seele' ausserhalb und innerhalb der Gnosis." Pp. 429-447 in *Le Origini dello Gnosticismo*. Studies in the History of Religion 12. Ed. U. Bianchi. Leiden: Brill.

Doty, W. G.
    1972   "The Concept of Genre in Literary Analysis." SBL Proceedings 2: 413-448.

Fowler, A.
    1971   "The Life and Death of Literary Forms." *New Literary History* 2: 199-216.

Gager, J. G.
    1975   *Kingdom and Community*. Englewood Cliffs, NJ: Prentice-Hall.

Gerhart, M.
    1977   "Generic Studies: Their Renewed Importance in Religious and Literary Interpretation." *JAAR* 45/3: 309-325.

Hanson, P. D.
    1976a   "Apocalypse, Genre." "Apocalypticism." IDBSup 27-34.

Koch, K.
    1972   *The Rediscovery of Apocalyptic*. SBT 2/22. Naperville, IL: Allenson.

Rad, G. von
    1965   *Theologie des Alten Testaments*. 4th ed. Vol. 2. Munich: Kaiser.

Smith, J. Z.
    1976   "A Pearl of Great Price and a Cargo of Yams: A Study in Situational Incongruity." *HR* 16:1-19.

Stone, M. E.
    1976   "Lists of Revealed Things in the Apocalyptic Literature." Pp. 414-452 in *Magnalia Dei. The Mighty Acts of God*. Eds. F. M. Cross, W. E. Lemke, and P. D. Miller, Jr. Garden City: Doubleday.

Yarbro Collins, A.
    1976   *The Combat Myth in the Book of Revelation*. HDR 9. Missoula: Scholars Press.

THE JEWISH APOCALYPSES

John J. Collins
DePaul University

SYNOPSIS

The Jewish apocalypses have been the subject of a very extensive literature in modern times. This literature has been thoroughly reviewed by Schmidt (1969), Koch (1972) and Hanson (1976b). Much of the discussion has been concerned with the historical origins of "apocalyptic." Some have sought to derive the phenomenon from extra-Israelite sources--e.g. Persian (Bousset) or Hellenistic-Oriental (Betz). Others have looked primarily to Israelite traditions, most recently with a component of ancient Canaanite mythology (Hanson). Within the OT, scholars have most frequently looked to the eschatological aspects of the prophetic books (e.g. Rowley) although the wisdom tradition has recently been invoked (von Rad, 1965; see Collins, 1977c). These diverse suggestions on the origins of "apocalyptic" reflect differing views of the nature of the phenomenon. Scholars who find their sources and parallels in ancient mythology and/or eschatological prophecy usually place greatest emphasis on the temporal axis of the apocalyptic writings. Scholars who look rather to Hellenistic-Oriental syncretism place greater stress on "vertical" aspects--the manner of revelation and spatial symbolism of the heavenly world. While the merit of these diverse suggestions varies widely, none are completely without foundation. All rest on some valid analogies.

In this essay we are not concerned with the historical origin of apocalypticism but the identification of a literary genre "apocalypse" as represented in Jewish literature. Accordingly, we will confine our attention to the analysis of Jewish texts. We will begin with those texts in the prophetic corpus which are most frequently adduced in discussions of "apocalyptic"--Zechariah and the later parts of Isaiah. The two main views of apocalypticism, the "historical" view which emphasizes temporal eschatology and the "vertical" view which stresses the spatial symbolism of the heavenly world, both find analogies and precedents in these books.

We will then proceed to the apocalyptic writings of the Hellenistic and Roman periods.

Definition and Typology

The method of this study has been primarily inductive: the master-paradigm and the definition of the genre have emerged from the observation of the significant recurring features in the literature commonly regarded as "apocalyptic." In this way it has been possible to clarify the common terminology by identifying those works which constitute a coherent and recognizable type of writing as the literary genre "apocalypse." Other types of writing which are commonly included in discussions of "apocalyptic" are noted here as related categories.

In the interest of clarity, the definition and typology which emerge as the result of this study may be set out here at the beginning. As noted in the Introduction to this volume, "Apocalypse" may be defined as *a genre of revelatory literature with a narrative framework, in which a revelation is mediated by an otherworldly being to a human recipient, disclosing a transcendent reality which is both temporal, insofar as it envisages eschatological salvation, and spatial, insofar as it involves another, supernatural world.* In the Jewish literature which can be dated with some plausibility to the period 250 BCE - 150 CE, it is possible to identify fifteen apocalypses by this definition. This corpus can be classified further according to the typology presented in the Introduction.

The most obvious distinction within the Jewish apocalypses is between those that do not have an otherworldly journey (Type I) and those that do (Type II). This distinction coincides strikingly with a distinction in the content of the revelation. All apocalypses which do not have an otherworldly journey contain an *ex eventu* prophecy of history. Only one apocalypse (the Apocalypse of Abraham 15-32) combines an otherworldly journey with a historical review.

Type Ia: "Historical" Apocalypses with No Otherworldly Journey

The "historical" apocalypses constitute a particularly compact group within the Jewish apocalypses. The works in question are Daniel 7-12, the Animal Apocalypse and the Apocalypse of Weeks in 1 Enoch, Jubilees 23, 4 Ezra and 2 Baruch. Within this group, 4 Ezra and 2 Baruch show conspicuously less interest in the heavenly world than the others, but the spatial axis still plays a significant part. While scholarly generalizations about "apocalyptic" are frequently based on this type, it is important to note that it includes less than half the corpus of Jewish apocalypses and excludes several works which are universally regarded as "apocalyptic" (other sections of 1 Enoch, 2 Enoch, Apoc Abraham 15-32, 3 Baruch).

The second type of Jewish apocalypses, those with otherworldly journeys, contains a wider spectrum of revealed material. Here all three sub-types which we have distinguished in the Introduction (IIa,b,c) are found.

Type IIa: Apocalypses with An Otherworldly Journey and a Review of History

This type is represented only by the Apocalypse of Abraham 15-32, and even there the review of history is minimal. However, the fact that some historical review is presented here in the context of a heavenly journey makes a significant bridge between the "historical" apocalypses of Type Ia and the otherworldly journeys of Type IIb and c.

Type IIb: Otherworldly Journeys with Cosmic and/or Political Eschatology

The greater number of the Jewish otherworldly journeys retain some interest in cosmic and/or political eschatology. The works in question are 1 Enoch 1-36, the Similitudes of Enoch, the Book of the Heavenly Luminaries (all in 1 Enoch), 2 Enoch and Test Levi 2-5. The degree of eschatological interest in these works varies considerably. It is very slight in the book of the Heavenly Luminaries. The Similitudes of Enoch, at the other extreme, is dominated by the coming judgment which has a clear cosmic dimension and will destroy the political structures of the present. Even the manner of revelation in the Similitudes involves visions within the heavenly journey which are very similar to what we find in Daniel.

Type IIc: Otherworldly Journeys with Only Personal Eschatology

A small group of Jewish apocalypses have no reference to cosmic or political eschatology but are concerned only with personal afterlife and spatial transcendence. These are 3 Baruch, Test Abraham 10-15 (8-12 in Rec. B) and Apoc Zephaniah. It is noteworthy that none of these works is likely to be earlier than the first century CE.

We have, then, a spectrum ranging from the "historical" apocalypses at one extreme to the purely "personal" apocalypses at the other, while the otherworldly journeys of Type IIa and b occupy mediating positions.

While Type IIc appears to be a late development in the Jewish apocalypses, it is not possible to speak of any simple one-directional historical development in the genre. Both Type Ia and Type IIb include some of the oldest (Daniel, 1 Enoch 1-36) and latest (4 Ezra, 2 Enoch) compositions. The latest "historical" apocalypses, 4 Ezra and 2 Baruch, show a somewhat diminished interest in the heavenly world, but they are roughly contemporary with Apoc Abraham where a historical review is set in the context of a heavenly journey and the spatial axis predominates. The earliest journeys, 1 Enoch 1-36 and the book of the Heavenly Luminaries, are more clearly distinct from the "historical" apocalypses than the later Similitudes of Enoch. However, we should note that already in the Animal Apocalypse, Enoch is taken up "to a lofty place" (1 Enoch 87:3). This does not amount to a heavenly journey (there is no mention of travel through the heavens) but it warns against too hasty a conclusion that "historical" and "heavenly" apocalypses were sharply distinguished in the earliest period. It is certainly possible to distinguish Type I and Type II as two distinct strands throughout the Jewish corpus, but they should not be too sharply separated.

Despite the distinctions between the types, all fifteen Jewish apocalypses fall within the compass of the definition of the genre. The degrees of similarity and variety can be seen more clearly in view of the master-paradigm, as set forth on the chart at the end of this Synopsis.

In every apocalypse the revelation is mediated by an otherworldly, angelic figure. In every case but one the revelation involves visions. The exception is in the book of Jubilees where the revelation of Jubilees 23 is included in the discourse of the angel of the presence to Moses. (One section of Daniel, chaps. 10-12, is also presented as an epiphany and angelic discourse, without a vision.) The visual revelation is supplemented by some form of audition, usually a dialogue in which the visionary asks questions, but sometimes by a discourse of the mediator. The Animal Apocalypse in 1 Enoch is the only one which dispenses with verbal revelation. The dialogue can on occasion become the main medium of revelation in a section of an apocalypse, e.g. 4 Ezra 3-9. The visionary is always pseudonymous. His disposition before the revelation and his reaction to it are frequently, but not consistently, noted.

In every case the content of the revelation involves both a temporal and a spatial axis. The differences between the different sub-types of apocalypses may be assessed in accordance with the varying emphasis which is placed on either axis. While the heavenly journeys seldom contain *ex eventu* prophecies, many recall primordial history which is also discussed in some historical apocalypses (4 Ezra and 2 Baruch). Both primordial history and *ex eventu* prophecies are ultimately directed to understanding the present. The primordial history shows the ultimate origins of the human situation and clarifies the forces at work in the present. The *ex eventu* prophecies show where the present is located in the duration of time and that the eschaton is already near (see Collins, 1977a). However, the apocalypses which include *ex eventu* prophecies obviously attach an importance to temporal duration which is not conveyed by primordial history, and which is lacking in the majority of the heavenly journeys. The only temporal feature which is common to all apocalypses is the expectation of a future judgment in which the wicked are punished and the good rewarded.

The rewards and punishments characteristically involve some form of afterlife for the individual (see Collins, 1974a). Only two Jewish apocalypses fail to refer to personal afterlife explicitly and it is quite probably implied in both. In the Apocalypse of Weeks the "elect righteous of the eternal plant of righteousness" are "elected" at the close of the seventh week. In the ninth week the world is written down for destruction and in the tenth the first heaven passes away. While the "elect righteous" are not explicitly said to survive this cosmic transformation, they are also not explicitly said to perish, and their survival is surely implied. Test Levi 2-5 refers to the heavenly location of the angels who minister to God for the sins of the righteous. By analogy with other apocalypses, we might infer that the righteous are destined to share the heavenly abode, but this is not explicit in the text. Test Levi 18 refers explicitly to personal afterlife when the gates of Paradise will be opened and the righteous will eat of the tree of life. (The Apocalypse of Weeks is also incorporated in a longer work which places great emphasis on personal afterlife, in 1 Enoch 91-104.) In one other case, the Animal Apocalypse, the reference to afterlife might be disputed because of the allegorical language, but there is at least a definitive eschatological transformation of the righteous ("all their generations were transformed and they all became white bulls" [1 Enoch 90:38] like Adam in 1 Enoch 85:3).

The prominence of personal afterlife emphasizes the definitive transcendent character of the eschatology of the apocalypses. The actual importance attached to personal afterlife is modified to some extent by the relative prominence of cosmic and/or political eschatology. In such works as the Apocalypse of Weeks and the Animal Apocalypse, the destiny of the individual is only one aspect of the wider eschatological transformation. Cosmic transformation is always a major factor in the "historical" apocalypses but also plays some part in all but a few late otherworldly journeys (Type IIc).

In all the apocalypses, otherworldly beings, especially angels, play an important part and indicate that human affairs are shaped in some part by superhuman forces. Descriptions of the heavenly or infernal regions play an important role in the otherworldly journeys, but much less so in the historical apocalypses. The importance of the heavenly geography is in roughly inverse proportion to the importance of past history. It is of significance that the heavens, like the periods of history, are often presented in an orderly number, which serves to reaffirm that there is ultimately a fixed order in the universe.

Some interest in heavenly realities is essential to all the apocalypses. Accordingly, the sense of communication with the heavenly world is a constant ingredient, and is explicitly involved in the manner of revelation by a heavenly mediator. Interest in political and historical realities is prominent in the "historical" apocalypses, and also in some heavenly journeys such as the Similitudes of Enoch and the Apocalypse of Abraham, but recedes in the purely "personal" apocalypses. All apocalypses, however, are concerned with human conduct on earth since this conduct becomes the basis for rewards and punishments in the next life. The communication with the heavenly world is never an end in itself. Both the temporal eschatology and the otherworldly revelation provide a framework which sets the present time and place of humanity in urgent relief. All the apocalypses are therefore hortatory in purpose, whether this purpose is expressed explicitly or not. In many cases the hortatory purpose is expressed in concluding instructions to the visionary and his subsequent actions, but the concluding elements are not found consistently throughout. However, the hortatory nature of these works is always implied by the expectation of judgment on human actions in the afterlife.

The transcendent character of the eschatology points to the underlying problem of all the apocalypses--this world is out of joint, one must look beyond it for a solution. The disorder of this world is explicit in the apocalypses which speak of persecution and other eschatological upheavals. It is implied, however, in all the apocalypses, both by the manner of revelation and by the eschatology. Since the order of this world is not apparent, revelation must come from outside, mediated by an otherworldly angelic figure to a pseudonymous figure from a time long past. Again, the eschatological solution involves either a cosmic transformation which fundamentally alters this world, or an otherworldly afterlife. In either case the realm of salvation lies beyond, or transcends, the present world and stands in sharp discontinuity with it (Collins, 1975a:33, 1977b: chaps. 3 and 6). In the "historical" apocalypses and some of the otherworldly journeys, the loss of order is due to historical and political factors. In the purely "personal" apocalypses, the causes are less explicit, but the persistent emphasis on judgment suggests sinfulness and injustice. The manner of revelation and the content of the apocalypses combine to suggest that such vindication can only be found beyond this world.

The common features of these writings in both manner of revelation and content justify their classification in the one genre "apocalypse." This generic classification does not at all diminish the significance of the differences between the sub-divisions we have noted. The "historical" apocalypses constitute a much more compact group of writings which might well be classified as a genre in itself. However, in view of the common usage of the term "apocalypse" for the otherworldly journeys, and the real and extensive similarities in manner of revelation and content, it seems preferable to regard the "historical" apocalypses simply as a sub-division of the broader genre.

THE JEWISH APOCALYPSES

Asterisks indicate either (1) that an element is possibly, but not certainly, present, or (2) is implicit, or (3) is present in a very minor way.

	Apoc Zephaniah	Test Abraham 10-15	3 Baruch	Test Levi 2-5	2 Enoch	Similitudes of Enoch	Heavenly Luminaries	1 Enoch 1-36	Apoc Abraham	2 Baruch	4 Ezra	Jubilees 23	Apoc of Weeks	Animal Apocalypse	Daniel 7-12
Manner of Revelation															
1.1.1 Visions	x	x	x	x	x	x	x	x	x	x	x		x	x	x
1.1.2 Epiphanies															x
1.2.1 Discourse					x		x						x	x	x
1.2.2 Dialogue	x	x	x	x	x	x		x	x	x	x				x
1.3 Otherworldly journey	x	x	x	x	x	x	x	x	x						
1.4 Writing							x				x	x			x
2. Otherworldly mediator	x	x	x	x	x	x	x	x	x	x	x	x	x	x	x
3.1 Pseudonymity	x	x	x	x	x	x	x	x	x	x	x	x	x	x	x
3.2 Disposition of recipient		x	x	x					x	x	x				x
3.3 Reaction of recipient			x	x	x	x	x	x	x	x	x			x	x
Temporal Axis															
4.1 Cosmogony						x				x	x				
4.2 Primordial events		x				x		x	x	x					
5.1 Recollection of past									x	x	x				
5.2 Ex eventu prophecy									x	x	x	x	x	x	x
6. Present salvation															
7.1 Persecution						x			x		x	x		x	x
7.2 Other eschat. upheavals			x			x	x		x	x	x	x	x	x	x
8.1 Judgment/destruction of wicked	x	x	x	x	x	x	x	x	x	x	x	x	x	x	x
8.2 of world	x*				x			x				x			
8.3 of otherworldly beings					x	x	x*	x				x	x	x	x
9.1 Cosmic transformation			x		x	x	x	x	x	x	x	x*	x	x*	x
9.2.1 Resurrection						x				x	x			x*	x
9.2.2 Other forms of afterlife	x	x	x	x*	x	x	x	x	x			x	x*	x	
Spatial Axis															
10.1 Otherworldly regions	x	x	x	x	x	x	x	x	x	x				x	x
10.2 Otherworldly beings	x	x	x	x	x	x	x	x	x	x	x	x	x	x	x
Paraenesis by Revealer															
11.										x					
Concluding Elements															
12. Instructions to recipient				x	x		x			x	x	x			x
13. Narrative Conclusion		x	x	x	x		x			x	x			x	x

SURVEY

Antecedents in Post-Exilic Prophecy

A convenient point of approach to the study of the Jewish apocalypses is provided by the ongoing debate about the OT precedents or origins of "apocalyptic" in the prophetic corpus. Some scholars find the link between prophecy and apocalyptic in the oracles of Proto-Zechariah, written shortly after the Babylonian exile (North, Gese). In Zechariah 1-6 we find a series of seven allegorical visions with interpretations by an angel. The interpretations refer on occasion to future events (2:4-5; 5:3-11) which might be termed eschatological, but this eschatology is not transcendent: it requires neither cosmic transformation nor individual transcendence of death but only the transformation of the land of Israel. Most often the interpretations refer to otherworldly realities, such as the angels who patrol the world (1:8-12; 6:1-4) or the eyes of the Lord (4:5). Proto-Zechariah anticipates the later apocalypses in manner of revelation and the disclosure of otherworldly realities, but lacks a distinctively apocalyptic eschatology (Hanson, 1975:251).

The second view of the prophetic antecedents of apocalyptic looks rather to Trito-Isaiah, Deutero- and Trito-Zechariah and the so-called Isaianic apocalypse (Isaiah 24-27) (Ploeger, Hanson). While the date of these writings is much disputed, Hanson has argued very persuasively that they derive from the aftermath of the Babylonian exile, contemporaneous with Proto-Zechariah. In form all these passages are prophetic oracles. They are presented as direct prophecies, not as visions with interpretations. The point of continuity between these writings and the later apocalypses lies in their eschatology. In the Isaianic passages the oracles speak of cosmic disruption and destruction, followed by a transcendent salvation, a new heaven and new earth in Isaiah 65-66, the destruction of death and a mythical banquet on the holy mountain in Isaiah 25. This salvation is certainly cosmic; it is less clear whether it also involves individual afterlife. The language of resurrection is used in Isa 26:19, but should probably be understood as the resurrection of the nation (as in Ezekiel 37). The heavenly world plays a limited part in these oracles insofar as God is asked to "rend the heavens and come down" (Isa 64:1) and will "punish the host of heaven in heaven" (Isa 24:21).

In Trito-Isaiah, and the Isaianic "apocalypse" and less clearly in Zechariah 9-14, Joel and Ezekiel 38-39, we may recognize some of the major characteristics of apocalyptic eschatology and the reflection of an early form of Jewish apocalypticism. However, all these writings must still be categorized formally as prophetic oracles, not as apocalypses, since they lack the apocalyptic manner of revelation, with an otherworldly mediator.

Both Proto-Zechariah and the post-exilic material in Isaiah have been related to apocalyptic because of real points of continuity with the later apocalypses. In Proto-Zechariah this continuity lies in the manner of revelation and in its emphasis on otherworldly, heavenly, realities. In the Isaianic material the continuity lies in the transcendent character of the eschatology. The Jewish writings which we will designate as apocalypses are precisely those which combine these elements: a mediated revelation, otherworldly realities and transcendent eschatology.

The only full-blown apocalypse in the Hebrew Bible is, then, found in Daniel 7-12. Daniel is not, however, the oldest apocalypse, since it is very probably antedated by some sections of 1 Enoch (1-36, the "Apocalypse of Weeks" and the "book of the Heavenly Luminaries." The "Animal Apocalypse" is roughly contemporary with Daniel). There is little to indicate that Daniel was dependent on Enochic tradition (Glasson's argument, that the "Son of Man" imagery in Daniel 7 is derived from 1 Enoch 14, is not convincing). However, both Daniel and 1 Enoch 1-36 undoubtedly influenced later apocalypses to varying degrees. These two early apocalypses also represent two distinct types of apocalyptic revelation: Daniel sees visions which are interpreted by an angel, after the precedent of Zechariah; Enoch goes on an otherworldly journey (1 Enoch 17-36). These two types of revelation reflect the main distinction we will find within the Jewish apocalypses. We will proceed by first examining the apocalypses which do not contain an otherworldly journey and then return to those that do.

Type Ia: "Historical" Apocalypses with No Otherworldly Journey

Daniel

The book of Daniel can be dated with relative precision between the second campaign of Antiochus Epiphanes against Egypt in 167 BCE and his death in 164. It is probable that the court-tales in Daniel 1-6 are older than the rest of the book and are incorporated here to provide a fictional background for the visions of chapters 7-12 (Collins, 1977b:27-65). The apocalyptic element in the book is confined to the later chapters. It is true that there are points of formal continuity between the court-tales and the visions. Most significantly Daniel 2 includes a dream-vision and allegorical interpretation with an eschatological conclusion in which "the God of heaven will establish a kingdom which will never be destroyed." Formally this dream-vision in Daniel 2 is very similar to both the visions of Zechariah and those of Daniel 7-12. It is significant, however, that the interpreter is a human wise-man, not an angel. Similar examples of the interpretation of mysterious signs by the wise Daniel are found in chapter 4 (again an allegorical vision) and chapter 5 (the writing on the wall). Each of these chapters contains a prophecy of a transformation of the political order, but only chapter 2 can be described as eschatological, insofar as the transformation will be definitive and permanent. The nature of the eschatological kingdom set up by the God of heaven in Daniel 2 is not clarified. It will make an end of all other kingdoms and will itself never be destroyed. It will be a transcendent kingdom in the sense that it will be set up by God. It is not clear, however, whether it will involve cosmic transformation--changes in the nature of the world or of human beings. There is no suggestion of a personal afterlife.

Daniel 7-12 consists of three visions (chaps. 7, 8 and 10-12) and a prophecy (chap. 9). (The prayer in chap. 9 may well be a later addition, but it does not modify the apocalyptic character of the book.) These four units are clearly parallel in the sense that they cover the same material and use similar imagery to describe it. They should not be regarded as distinct independent apocalypses but as complementary formulations which form a composite whole. In each case the revelation is mediated by an angel. Each unit involves a treatment of history, eschatological crisis, judgment/destruction and salvation. In Daniel 7 the salvation is in the form of a universal and everlasting kingdom. In Daniel 12 it is expressed as a resurrection from the dead and a transformation of the wise leaders to "shine like stars" (12:2-3). While the temporal, historical axis is the more immediately obvious, the vertical axis which contrasts the heavenly world with the earthly is no less important. The revelation is mediated by angels. The archangel Michael plays a decisive role in chapters 10-12. The "one like a son of man" in Daniel 7 comes on the clouds of heaven and it is most probable that both he and the "holy ones of the Most High" are angelic beings. The wise leaders become "like the stars" (12:3) which were often identified with the heavenly, angelic host. The judgment scene in Daniel 7 includes a vision of the divine throne. While Daniel lacks the interest in otherworldly geography characteristic of much of the Enoch tradition, the vertical, heavenly imagery is still an essential part of the work (see further, Collins, 1977b).

The "Animal Apocalypse"

The "Dream Visions" of Enoch (1 Enoch 83-90) are dated to the Maccabean revolt and so are virtually contemporary with the book of Daniel. This section of 1 Enoch consists of two visions. The first, in 1 Enoch 83-84, is a simple vision of cosmic destruction which is then summarized rather than interpreted by Mahalalel. The content of the vision is the destruction of the earth. There is no antecedent history or crisis, although the destruction is understood as a punishment for sin. Enoch responds by praying that a righteous remnant might be preserved. Otherwise there is no reference to any form of salvation. It is not clear whether the destruction in question is eschatological or refers to the Flood. This vision is too elliptic to be classified as an apocalypse. It can be more properly associated with such OT prophecies of destruction as Amos 7:4 and Jer 4:23-28. This first vision is not found in the Aramaic fragments from Qumran (Milik, 1976:41).

The second dream-vision, the so-called Animal Apocalypse, is an allegorical history of the world from creation to the messianic kingdom. There is no explicit interpretation although the allegory clearly demands one. However, Enoch is guided by the archangels (87:3-4) so we may say that the visions are mediated by angels though not interpreted. These angels lift Enoch up "to a lofty place" (87:3) which Milik (1976:46) equates with "the first paradisiac abode of Enoch" but he does not undertake a heavenly journey. The revelation continues in the form of allegorical visions of human history, culminating in a judgment on human oppressors and angelic beings (the stars, 90:24). The eschatological renewal is focused mainly on the new temple (90:29). There is a restoration of "all that had been dispersed" (90:33) and "all their generations were transformed and they became white bulls," like Adam in 85:3. Angelic beings play an extensive part throughout. The guilty "stars" and "shepherds" are punished in a fiery abyss (chap. 90).

The two visions in 1 Enoch 83-90 are not intrinsically related. They are not parallel and complementary like the visions of Daniel. While they may well come from the same author, they must be regarded as two distinct compositions.

The "Apocalypse of Weeks"

The so-called "Apocalypse of Weeks" (1 Enoch 93; 91:12-17) is usually dated shortly before the Maccabean revolt since it fails to refer to these events. If this dating is correct, it antedates both Daniel and the "Animal Apocalypse." Milik (1976: 255) denies that "serious evidence" exists that it is older than the rest of 1 Enoch 91-104, but it does seem to constitute a formally independent unit. However, its literary form is problematic for two reasons. First, while Enoch claims to have received his revelation "through the word of the holy angels" (93:2) the content of the revelation is not put in the mouth of an angel but is recited by Enoch himself. Thus we have the re-telling rather than a direct presentation of an apocalypse. Second, the "Apocalypse of Weeks" is now embodied in the larger literary unit of 1 Enoch 91-104, the so-called "Letter of Enoch" or "Book of Exhortation." The larger composition is informed by an apocalyptic eschatology (especially in chaps. 103-104) and claims revelation based on heavenly tablets and books (103:2) but the revelatory elements are subordinated to the direct exhortation which makes up the great bulk of the work. The larger unit is usually dated in the first quarter of the first century BCE (Charles, Ruppert). Despite these problems, the "Apocalypse of Weeks" is sufficiently similar to the other apocalypses to merit inclusion here as an independent apocalypse.

It may be that this apocalypse presupposes a heavenly journey of Enoch, in which he encountered the angels and saw the heavenly tablets. However, no such journey is recounted within this apocalypse. The emphasis is on the horizontal review of history which is divided into "weeks." The eschatological crisis comes in the seventh week with the rise of "an apostate generation" and "the eternal plant of righteousness." There is a judgment on oppressors in the eighth week. In the ninth the world is written down for destruction. In the tenth is "the great eternal judgment" with vengeance among the angels. The first heaven is replaced by a new one. Since the godless are explicitly destroyed in 91:14, the survival of the righteous seems clearly implied. Angelic beings figure in the process of revelation and in the judgment.

Jubilees 23

Jubilees, another revelatory writing of the second century BCE, is even more problematic in its relation to the genre apocalypse. This work is variously dated to the end of the second century (Charles) or to a time shortly after the Maccabean revolt, before the establishment of the Qumran community (Jaubert, Vander Kam). It consists of "the divisions of the days of the law and of the testimony, of the events of the years, of their (year) weeks, of their Jubilees throughout all the years of the world, as the Lord spake to Moses on Mt. Sinai." In fact, it is an expansionistic paraphrase of Genesis. The manner of revelation in chapters 1 and 2 is similar to the apocalypses but the content of the angelic revelation has little apocalyptic or eschatological material. Chapter 23 is an exception. There we find an *ex eventu* prophecy of history between the time of Abraham and the Maccabean revolt, followed by an eschatological crisis. Then, "there shall be no Satan nor any evil destroyer." In addition to the cosmic transformation, the righteous will enjoy an afterlife: "Their bones shall rest in the earth and their spirits shall have much joy" (23:31). Angels are prominent throughout Jubilees, though not especially in chapter 23.

There is also an eschatological passage in Jubilees 1 which includes an *ex eventu* prophecy (1:5-19) and cosmic transformation (1:23-29). This passage, however, is not included in the angelic revelation, but is spoken directly by God to Moses. Since Jubilees 23 is included in the angelic revelation and is typically apocalyptic in content, it must be included in the list of apocalypses despite the fact that it is not an independent composition. The apocalyptic eschatology and worldview are presupposed throughout Jubilees, but the book as a whole is clearly not an apocalypse.

4 Ezra

There are two further major apocalypses which do not refer to heavenly journeys but, like Daniel, the "Apocalypse of Weeks" and the "Animal Apocalypse," make extensive use of historical reviews. These works are 4 Ezra and 2 Baruch, both of which were written in the late first century CE, in the aftermath of the fall of Jerusalem. Both of these books are composite in the same sense as Daniel 7-12: they can each be divided into seven sections, each of which is formally complete in itself. Because of this and more particularly because of alleged inconsistencies in traditions and theological content, the scholars of a previous generation (e.g. Box and Charles, but also more recently Klijn) tended to see these books as compilations of multiple literary sources. More recent scholarship (Stone, 1966; Breech; Bogaert) has reacted against this position. In each work the sevenfold division argues for at least editorial unity. The alleged discrepancies and inconsistencies have been shown to be less substantial than Box and Charles had argued. Such inconsistencies as are found can be most easily explained by the use of traditional material or by the technique of recapitulation, by which the apocalyptist juxtaposes parallel complementary formulations of the same material (cf. Yarbro Collins on the NT book of Revelation).

4 Ezra is composed of three dialogues between the visionary and an angel (3:4-5:19; 5:20-6:34; 6:35-9:22) and three allegorical visions (9:23-10:57; 10:58-12:35; 12:51-58). The book ends in chapter 14 with a dialogue between God and Ezra which climaxes with the inspired writing of ninety-four books.

The continuity of 4 Ezra with Daniel and the apocalypses in 1 Enoch is most clearly shown in the three allegorical visions which contain the usual schema of a review of history, eschatological crisis, judgment/destruction of adversaries and both cosmic and personal transformation. The visions pay minimal attention to the heavenly regions but the vision of Zion in chapter 10 could be interpreted as the heavenly Jerusalem. Otherworldly beings are less prominent here than in other apocalypses, but the angelic interpreter persists in chapter 10. The "Man from the Sea" in chapter 13, while not distinctly angelic, is definitely otherworldly.

The dialogues of chapters 3-9 are formally different from the visions of chapters 10-14 insofar as they contain no allegorical visions. Instead the revelation is given in the course of dialogues between the visionary and an angel. These dialogues provide the occasion for an extensive expression of the problems besetting the seer, which is seldom possible in the visions. The dialogues deal at length with creation and the primordial history of Adam. They contain no *ex eventu* prophecies of history, but the eschatological upheavals receive great prominence. The third dialogue has a lengthy account of the judgment which involves two stages: the first culminating in the 400-year reign of the Messiah, and then, after seven days of primeval silence, the resurrection and general judgment.

In general the dialogues are marked by a strong denial that the visionary has any knowledge of otherworldly regions: "Into the deep I have not descended, nor as yet gone down into Hades. Neither to heaven have I ever ascended, nor entered Paradise" (4:8). In fact the dialogues further insist on Ezra's ignorance of the earthly world. Despite this strong anti-mystical tendency, which contrasts sharply with other apocalypses, the otherworldly regions still play a part, for: "The underworld and the chambers of souls...hasten to deliver what has been entrusted to them" (4:41-42) and the righteous after death are "gathered in their chambers...guarded by angels" (7:95). The role of angelic beings is limited to the angelic interpreter and the angels who guard the chambers of the dead in 7:95. The Messiah, who will be "revealed" (7:28) may be otherworldly, but his humanity is shown by his death.

4 Ezra taken as a whole contains the fullest spectrum of apocalyptic elements of the works examined so far, since it includes reflection on creation and primeval history. The emphasis is somewhat different from the earlier apocalypses since it shows less interest in otherworldly elements and more in the national hopes of Israel. The use of the dialogue form leads to a more extensive articulation of the problems of theodicy which create the need for revelation.

2 Baruch

All commentators have recognized that 2 Baruch and 4 Ezra are closely related in both provenance and theology (Charles, 1913: 553-554). The composition of the book has been summarized by Charles as follows (474): "If we disregard the letter to the tribes in captivity (lxxviii-lxxxvi) the book falls naturally into seven sections separated by fasts save in one case (after xxxv).... These sections, which are of unequal length are (1) i-v.6; (2) v.7-viii; (3) ix-xii.4; (4) xii.5-xx; (5) xxi-xxxv; (6) xxxvi-xlvi; (7) xlvii-lxxvii." However, the fast at 5:7 does not indicate a new section. This is only a fast "until evening" whereas the other fasts last seven days. Chapters 1-8 constitute one opening section which provides the (fictional) narrative context for the rest of the book by describing the fall of Jerusalem to the Babylonians. Such narrative introductions are not uncommon in apocalypses. We might compare the tales in Daniel 1-6 and the legends in the Apocalypse of Abraham. This passage is not eschatological but it is noteworthy for its attention to heavenly realities--the "other" Jerusalem in 4:2-7 which was created with Paradise and revealed to Abraham and Moses, and the angels who carry out the destruction of Jerusalem. The second section (9:1-12:4) is merely a lament for Jerusalem with a minimal reference to eschatological expectation in 12:4. In fact, this section serves as an introduction to a dialogue between the seer and "a voice from the height" which proclaims "the word of the mighty God" (13:1-2). This dialogue (12:5-20) deals with the problem of theodicy and concludes with an adumbration of eschatology--"Therefore I have now taken away Zion that I may more speedily visit the world in its season." By this allusion, this section also points forward to the fuller eschatology of the following sections.

The heart of the book, then, lies in Charles' sections 5, 6 and 7. (The letter in chaps. 78-86 forms a hortatory conclusion which is actually the seventh section of the book. It draws on the eschatological revelations of the rest of the book, but is not itself a revelation.)

The three main eschatological sections of the work constitute parallel complementary revelations. Each involves visions and dialogue. God himself interprets the vision in chapter 39. In chapters 55-74 the interpretation is provided by the angel Ramiel. The content includes reference to the work of creation in chapters 21 and 48 and repeatedly to the sin of Adam. *Ex eventu* prophecies play a major role in the allegorical visions: the four kingdoms (39:2-5) and the cloud and water vision (chap. 68). Eschatological upheavals are described at length. Cosmic transformation is described in chapters 29; 44:8-12; 73-74. It should be noted that the transformation in chapter 29 precedes the resurrection. The statement in 30:1 that the Messiah will "return in glory" corresponds to the death of the Messiah in 4 Ezra 7:29. In short, salvation comes in two stages, first a period of national exaltation and then the resurrection. Again in 40:3 the reign of the Messiah will last until "the world of corruption is at an end and until the times aforesaid are fulfilled": i.e., it is not the ultimate state of salvation which follows the resurrection. In chapters 72-74 a period of national exaltation also precedes the advent of the incorruptible world.

Resurrection is explicit in 30:2, 42:8 and chapters 49-52. In chapters 49-52 there is a detailed discussion of the nature of the resurrection which is said to involve becoming like the angels and equal to the stars.

As in 4 Ezra, relatively little attention is paid to otherworldly regions, but we find reference to the treasuries where the souls of the righteous are preserved (30:2). When Baruch is told that he will pass from the regions which are now seen (43:2) we may assume that he goes to otherworldly regions. According to 51:8, the righteous, at the resurrection, "shall behold the world which is now invisible to them...for in the heights of that world shall they dwell." Otherworldly beings are not prominent in 2 Baruch, but we still find an angelic mediator, and the righteous dead are said to become like the angels. Angels play an active role in the destruction of Jerusalem in chapters 7-8 and 80.

2 Baruch and 4 Ezra share the same outline as the earlier apocalypses but expand it by their interest in protology. However, they show some distinct emphases, both in form of revelation and in content. In form they make extensive use of dialogues and often receive their revelations from God without an interpreting angel (although the angelic mediator still plays a significant role in both). In content these apocalypses are distinguished by the provision for a temporal fulfillment of national eschatology before the resurrection and final judgment and the decreased interest in the heavenly world. The use of the dialogue form also leads to a more extensive discussion of theodicy than is found in the earlier apocalypses. These differences in emphasis do not constitute a new genre, but show that apocalypses admit of various nuances in theological viewpoint.

Summary

Each of the apocalypses considered so far is built on two axes: the temporal contrast of past/present and future, and the spatial axis of this world and the heavenly. Both these elements are essential to all apocalypses. Even in 4 Ezra, where we find some polemic against otherworldly mysticism, heavenly regions and beings play an important part. Yet the emphasis in each of the works discussed above falls on the temporal axis. Each contains an *ex eventu* prophecy of history. Daniel, the Animal Apocalypse, 4 Ezra and 2 Baruch are clearly related to historical crises of the Jewish people--the persecution of Antiochus Epiphanes and the destruction of Jerusalem and the temple by the Romans. Jubilees 23 is also very probably influenced by the upheavals in the time of Antiochus. The Apocalypse of Weeks is set against the broader "apostate generation" of the post-exilic period. All these apocalypses arise directly out of the historical experience of the Jewish people. The individual mysticism of the visionary is used to disclose the fate of the people, and even of the cosmos. The judgment has a public character. The individual soul is not judged in isolation. The judgment is part of the resolution of the political crisis and of the transformation of the world. These apocalypses, then, may be referred to as the "historical" apocalypses.

Type II: Otherworldly Journeys

Another group of Jewish apocalypses, which also extends chronologically from the second century BCE to the end of the first century CE, places greater emphasis on the spatial symbolism of transcendence and less on the temporal and historical. These apocalypses are distinguished by their use of otherworldly journeys as the medium of revelation. Within Type II it is possible to distinguish three sub-groups by their varying attention to history and cosmic eschatology.

Type IIa: Apocalypses with An Otherworldly Journey and a Review of History

The Apocalypse of Abraham

The Apocalypse of Abraham is the only work in this type. It may be dated "within narrow limits, with some probability" (Box, 1919:xv) fairly shortly after the fall of Jerusalem, since that catastrophe "forms the central part of the picture and the revelation leads up to it as a sort of climax." It is therefore roughly contemporary with 4 Ezra and 2 Baruch. The book falls into two quite different sections. Chapters 1-8 consist of the tale of Abraham's conversion from idolatry. This section is not apocalyptic in form but provides the context for the second part of the book. The second section, chapters 9-32, is associated with the sacrifice of Abraham in Genesis 15. Abraham is told that "in this sacrifice I will lay before thee the ages (to come), and make known to thee what is reserved" (chap. 9). The angel Jaoel is sent to assist him and enable him to ward off Azazel. This part of the narrative (chaps. 9-14) is still introductory. In chapter 15, however, the heavenly vision begins when God takes Abraham up to heaven on the wing of a pigeon.

God himself explains to Abraham what he sees on his journey (chaps. 19-31) but he is accompanied on the journey by an angel. The content of the revelation is primarily the heavenly regions, but temporal elements also play an important part. In chapter 21 the panorama which Abraham sees below him is said to include the Garden of Eden, and in chapter 24 he sees Adam and Eve and the Adversary and Cain and "the slaughtered Abel." The synopsis of history from creation to judgment in chapters 24-27 includes a résumé of the history prior to Abraham (which is, in effect, the primordial history). The history of Israel from Abraham to the judgment is telescoped in a vision of the temple in chapter 25, the destruction of the temple in chapter 27 and an enigmatic periodization of history into four "issues" of which the fourth is a hundred years, in chapter 28. The eschatological upheavals, including ten plagues, are described in chapter 29 and again in chapter 30. Since the era of salvation is a new Age, cosmic transformation would seem to be implied. Explicit reference is made to the ingathering of the exiles in chapter 31.

The wicked are abandoned to the fires of Hades, but we are given little description of the fate of the righteous. In chapter 29 "they shall live and be established through sacrifices and gifts of righteousness and truth" and "shall rejoice in Me continually." Box (xxvii) is probably right in recognizing the description of the Garden of Eden in chapter 21 as a proleptic vision of the rewards of the righteous.

The eschatological material is interrupted in chapter 29 by an enigmatic passage about "a man going out from the left side of the heathen" who is insulted and beaten, who is "worshipped by the heathen with Azazel." While the references to the left side of the heathen and to Azazel are problematic, the passage should most probably be read as a Christian insertion referring to Christ.

Type IIb: Otherworldly Journeys with Cosmic and/or Political Eschatology

1 Enoch 1-36

The opening section of 1 Enoch (The Heavenly Journeys of Enoch or the Book of the Watchers) is quite probably the oldest of all the Jewish apocalypses. The Aramaic fragments from Qumran show "that from the first half of the second century B.C. onwards the Book of the Watchers had essentially the same form as that in which it is known through the Greek and Ethiopic versions" (Milik, 1976:25), although older sources may have been incorporated (e.g. in the story of the Watchers). The entire work (chaps. 1-36) was dated by Charles (1913:349) to the first third of the second century BCE, since it seems to be presupposed by the author of the Animal Apocalypse. The date of the Qumran fragments makes a third century date more likely and Nickelsburg has suggested a date at the end of the fourth century for chapters 6-11 (Nickelsburg, 1977b). Milik (1976:31) has tried to push the date of chapters 6-19 back several centuries by arguing that they are presupposed in Genesis 6, but this suggestion is highly implausible. The dependence of 1 Enoch 6-11 on Genesis has been satisfactorily shown by Hanson (1977) and Nickelsburg (1977b).

The work may be divided into three sections. Chapters 1-5 constitute an introduction and framework for the following chapters. The manner of revelation is similar to that of Daniel and the other apocalypses hitherto reviewed.

The immediate content of chapter 1 is the judgment of God on "all flesh," the world and the Watchers. The remainder of the opening section (chaps. 2-5) appeals to the fixed order of heavenly bodies and earthly creation. Humanity is reproached for its lack of steadfastness and threatened with judgment. The allusions to salvation are minimal and vague, but the opening chapter clearly sets the remainder of 1 Enoch in the context of cosmic judgment.

The second section, 1 Enoch 6-16, tells the story of the fall of the angels (as in Genesis 6). The relevance of this section for the subsequent apocalypse would appear to be threefold:

1. It provides a paradigm of judgment, which includes cosmic judgment in the flood and the confinement of the fallen angels in the netherworld.
2. This judgment is proclaimed to Enoch in a vision when he is lifted up to heaven in chapters 14-16.
3. It illustrates the interpenetration of the heavenly angelic world with the human.

The apocalyptic core of 1 Enoch 1-36 lies in the journeys of Enoch in chapters 17-36. Enoch had already been elevated to heaven in chapter 14. Enoch's vision consists of his view of the supernatural terrain. Interpretative comments are provided by various angels. The journeys do not involve ascent or descent but are "horizontal." They are, however, otherworldly since they take Enoch to the mythical regions at the extremities of the earth (Milik, 1976:35-41). There he sees the storehouses of the stars, winds, etc., but also the places where "the spirits of the souls of the dead" are kept until the day of judgment and which are also places of intermediate reward or punishment (chap. 22), the fire which persecutes the luminaries of heaven (chap. 23) and the valley of judgment (chap. 27). The entire vision leads to the praise of God for all his wondrous works. It is clear that such praise is demanded by the order of nature, and that human rebellion leads to judgment--as is adumbrated in chapters 2-5. Much of the journeys is concerned with the apparatus of reward, punishment and judgment.

The Book of the Heavenly Luminaries

Another very old apocalypse is found in 1 Enoch 72-82. There is no description of Enoch's ascent to the heavens but the visions range all over the heavens, to the ends of the earth (76:1) so a journey is implied. This book is presupposed in Jubilees 4: 17,21 and so must be dated no later than the first quarter of the second century BCE. Milik (1976:7-22) has shown that the Aramaic fragments from Qumran reflect a longer text than the Ethiopic and claims one fragment, 4Q Henastr[a], must be dated to the end of the third century BCE. Milik also suggests that this section of 1 Enoch is presupposed in Gen 5:23, and indeed by the entire biblical chronology, but this suggestion is not compelling.

The Book of the Heavenly Luminaries places its predominant emphasis on heavenly, specifically astronomical, data. This data is considered important because it determines human lives, but in a very special way--it determines the true calendar. This highly specific emphasis on a particular regulation marks this section of 1 Enoch as a rather peculiar adaptation of apocalyptic writing. Nevertheless, it shares the major characteristics of the other apocalypses, both in manner of revelation and in content. The temporal references are minimal but eschatological expectations determine the horizon of the work. Chapter 80 refers to an eschatological crisis: "in the days of the sinners the years shall be shortened..." (80:2-8). In 80:8, "punishment shall come upon them so as to destroy all." The most obvious antecedent of "them" is "the sinners" (80:7) but the reference may also extend to the "chiefs of the stars" (80:6). Cosmic transformation is implied in 72:2: "till the new creation which dureth till eternity." Some form of afterlife is envisaged in 81:4-10. Milik (1971:341) has questioned whether this chapter originally belonged to the Book of Heavenly Luminaries, and dates it after the Animal Apocalypse, but before Jubilees. The interest in individual salvation in this section of 1 Enoch is certainly less than in other apocalypses, but chapter 81 is not incongruous with the rest of the work.

The Similitudes of Enoch

The two early Enochic apocalypses which use the medium of otherworldly journey pay virtually no attention to historical and political events, in sharp contrast to such apocalypses as Daniel. The Similitudes of Enoch (1 Enoch 37-71) however are conspicuously influenced both by the tradition of Enoch's heavenly journey and by Daniel, and show that the heavenly journey can also serve as a medium of revelation with political import.

Despite the recent attempt of Milik (1971, 1976) to attribute the Similitudes (1 Enoch 37-71) to a Christian of the second or third century CE, there can be little doubt that they are Jewish and early (Greenfield: xvii). It is very highly improbable that a Christian author would have identified Enoch with the Son of Man (71:14). The most reliable indications of date are still the references to the invasion of Palestine by the Parthians in 40 BCE (56:5-7) and to Herod's attempt to heal himself in the waters of Callirhoe (67:7-9). Since there is no reference to any event later than Herod, the Similitudes should be dated some time about the turn of the era.

The work is divided into three "Parables": chapters 38-44, 45-57 and 58-71. Each is prefaced by an oracle (38, 45, 58) which proclaims a coming judgment and discusses the fate of the righteous and the wicked. These oracles provide the focus for the application of the visions which follow.

The medium of revelation is a combination of otherworldly journey and visions. The otherworldly journey is explicitly mentioned in 39:3 in the first Similitude and 52:1 in the second, but is implied throughout. The visions which follow are not treated as allegories and there is no sustained interpretation, but Enoch is accompanied by an angel who occasionally identifies figures and objects.

The content of the visions is primarily concerned with heavenly realities—stars and angels (also the "Son of Man" figure, who is at least like an angel)—but also "the resting places of the righeous...their dwellings with his righteous angels" (39:4-5). Yet all the visions are dominated by the expectation of a coming judgment envisaged in a heavenly court. The temporal axis remains important.

Primordial events are recalled in the "Noachic" fragments in chapters 54-55 (2nd Similitude), chapters 65-67 (third) and in chapters 68-69 which deal with the transgression and judgment of the angels. These fragments seem out of context, but they serve to provide paradigms for the coming judgment. Scenes of judgment dominate the entire work. The wicked, especially the kings and the mighty, are condemned. The judgment on angelic beings is found chiefly in the passages which relate the primordial history of the Watchers (especially chap. 68). Cosmic transformation of heaven and earth is explicitly promised in 45:4-5. In chapter 57 the pillars of the earth are moved in a transformation which follows the eschatological struggle. In 51:1 the earth will "give back that which has been entrusted to it" (also 62:15). The righteous enjoy a heavenly afterlife—their dwellings are with the angels (39:5) or in the "garden of life" (61:12).

There are no concluding narratives at the end of the Similitudes but two further visions are added in chapters 70 and 71. The first tells how the seer was "raised aloft on the chariots of the spirit" and saw the dwelling places of the righteous. Chapter 71 repeats this in a more elaborate form with greater detail on Enoch's vision of the angels and the throne. At the end, Enoch is identified as the Son of Man (v. 14). The fact that chapter 71 simply repeats and expands what is told in chapter 70 raises some doubt whether it was originally part of the Similitudes. It is also not clear whether the identification of Enoch with the "Son of Man" should be presumed throughout the Similitudes. Despite the arguments of Casey (1976), such an identification remains problematic since it requires the pre-existence of Enoch and assumes that Enoch is seeing himself throughout the visions. As they now stand, chapters 70 and 71 constitute a conclusion to the Similitudes which narrate the subsequent experience of the visionary. Like the Similitudes, they contain heavenly journeys and visions of heavenly secrets and the eternal dwellings of the righteous, but they omit the scenes of judgment.

2 Enoch, or the Slavonic Book of Enoch

The Slavonic Book of Enoch (the Book of the Secrets of Enoch) has survived in two recensions, one long and one short. The most recent editor (Vaillant) has argued convincingly that the longer of these is redactional. The shorter text is clearly Jewish and has no Christian elements. The attempt of Milik (1971: 373, 1976:107-116) to date the book as late as the ninth century CE has been rejected by Greenfield (xviii) and Stone (forthcoming). The book can most plausibly be dated with Charles to the first century CE, prior to the fall of the Temple, in view of the author's preoccupation with sacrifices. Charles (1913:426) ascribed the book to Egyptian Judaism and this view has been generally accepted.

This work begins with an ascent of Enoch through seven heavens. Two themes are emphasized: the order of creation and the eschatological judgment. The third heaven is occupied by the places of reward and punishment prepared for humanity. Then an angel dictates to Enoch "all the works of heaven and earth" and God tells him how he created the world (with some unusual mythological details). Enoch is then granted thirty days to return to earth and instruct his children. The apocalypse concludes with lengthy exhortations, after which Enoch is taken back to heaven. (The legend of the birth of Melchizedek, which is appended, does not pertain to the revelation of Enoch and so not to the apocalypse as such.)

Both the cosmology and the eschatology of the book are clearly in the service of exhortation. While the main emphasis falls on the vertical, spatial aspects, the temporal expectation of a judgment is also important. This involves not only a judgment of individuals but a general judgment which will mark the end of created time. Those who escape will enjoy eternity in the "grand siècle" where there is no time.

Testament of Levi, 2-5

A brief apocalypse involving a journey through the heavens is embedded in the Testament of Levi in chapters 2-5. Because of the complicated history of the Testaments (see the discussion of the Testaments of the 12 Patriarchs in the section on related categories of literature below), it is impossible to fix the date of this passage with any confidence. The apocalypse is substantially Jewish, despite the presence of Christian redactional elements.

The content of the vision is dominated by the heavenly regions and the angelic beings, but the heavenly secrets have eschatological implications--e.g. the armies in the second heaven are "ordained for the day of judgment to work vengeance on the spirits of deceit and of Beliar" (3:3). The entire vision leads to an eschatological prophecy in chapter 4.

In Test Levi 8 there is another heavenly vision but this passage does not involve transcendent eschatology.

Summary

The apocalypses with heavenly journeys, like the historical apocalypses, are constructed on two axes, the temporal contrast of present and future and the spatial contrast of heaven (and infernal regions) and earth. In these apocalypses the spatial elements predominate. References to historical events are rare, but the primordial history is more frequently recalled. These apocalypses show less concern with historical crises and more with the transcendence of the individual.

Yet the line between these works and the "historical" apocalypses cannot be drawn too sharply. The Similitudes of Enoch, despite their lack of historical reviews, are evidently concerned with historical and political affairs. The other works are less obviously concerned with historical affairs but all find some place for cosmic transformation. While there is a clear shift in emphasis from the historical and communal to the spatial and individual, both axes remain essential to the apocalypses. All the visions culminate in the expectation of a coming eschatological judgment.

Type IIc: Otherworldly Journeys with Only Personal Eschatology

3 Baruch

The Greek Apocalypse of Baruch is possibly (but not certainly) cited by Origen (Denis: 79). Otherwise the only indication of date is the fictive setting after the Fall of Jerusalem. The work does not show anything like the intense obsession with the fall of the Temple which we find in 2 Baruch or 4 Ezra, and is not apparently interested in national restoration. The pseudonym and its implied setting do not of themselves require a date near the Fall of Jerusalem. The central feature of 3 Baruch, the journey through a numbered series of heavens (here five) finds its closest parallels in 2 Enoch or in early Christian apocalypses such as the Ascension of Isaiah. 3 Baruch contains some Christian redactional elements in 4:8-17 and in chapters 11-16.

Temporal considerations play very little role in 3 Baruch. There is no reference to historical events and no eschatological crisis. There are eschatological rewards and punishments but they are purely individual and involve no public scene of judgment. Those who gave counsel to build the tower are punished in the second heaven. In the third heaven Baruch sees a dragon who eats the bodies of those who spend their life wickedly, and reference is made to Hades and the eternal fire where the wicked are punished. The elaborate description of the intercession of the angels in chapters 12-16 clarifies the process of judgment, although it culminates in rewards and punishments of an earthly character. Reference is made to the "place where the souls of the righteous come" in the fourth heaven in chapter 10.

In part, the revelation is designed to satisfy Baruch's cosmological curiosity--e.g. on the thickness of the first heaven in chapter 2--but some of the curiosities, such as the Phoenix in chapter 6, are directly related to human affairs. Angels play an immediate role in human affairs, as is shown emphatically by the intercession of the angels in chapters 12-16.

The Testament of Abraham

As is well known, the Testament of Abraham is not a testament but rather the story of Abraham's death and the events leading up to it, and notably his failure to make a testament (Denis: 31). The text survives in two Greek recensions (A, the longer, and B) and also in Slavonic, Arabic, Coptic and Ethiopic. There is no scholarly consensus as to which recension is older. James (1892) and Box (1927) regarded A as the older form and B as a later abridgement. Recently Nickelsburg (1976) has also argued in favor of the priority of A. On the other hand, Turner's thesis of the priority of B has been recently defended by Schmidt. Delcor regards the two recensions as independent adaptations of an original story. The question is further complicated by disagreements between the versions. The date is also a subject of controversy. Delcor attributes the work to the late first century BCE or the early first century CE, because of a supposed polemic against the Testament of Job. Unfortunately, the date of the Testament of Job is equally uncertain. Others locate it somewhere in the first or second centuries CE. There is general agreement that the work was composed in Egypt, but Schmidt argues that the short recension (B)--which he regards as the original--was composed in Palestine. Finally, James' thesis that the work is Christian has been universally rejected.

Despite the uncertainty of the exact provenance, there is an adequate consensus that the Testament of Abraham derives from Egyptian Judaism about the first Christian century. Further, despite many significant differences in detail, there is sufficient similarity between the two recensions to yield a common outline.

The Testament of Abraham falls naturally into two sections. The dominant form is a legend about the death of Abraham. The Lord sends the Archangel Michael to announce to Abraham his imminent death. In the long recension, Abraham refuses to die until he has seen "all the inhabited world" (chap. 9). In the short recension, Abraham does not actually refuse to die, but asks to be shown all creation in heaven and on earth. There follows a heavenly journey in both recensions. Subsequently, Abraham is returned to earth. In the long recension, Abraham again refuses to die and has a long dialogue with Death before he is finally tricked and carried off to Paradise. In the short recension, Abraham also converses with Death but does not actually refuse to die. Finally God draws forth Abraham's soul as by a dream.

The heavenly journey in each recension (chaps. 10-15 in Rec. A; chaps. 8-12 in B) is integrated in the larger narrative, but may nevertheless be regarded as an apocalypse in itself.

At first, Abraham is shown everything that is happening in the world, but then he is taken to view the judgment and punishment of souls. Emphasis is laid, especially in Rec. A, on the need for mercy (which Abraham lacks at first) and the power of intercession.

The Apocalypse of Zephaniah

This work is known from a quotation by Clement (Strom 5.11.77) which says the prophet was lifted up by the spirit into the fifth heaven and "beheld angels that are called Lords." We also have two fragments, one in Achmimic and one in Sahidic, published by Steindorff in 1899. Steindorff called the Achmimic an "anonymous apocalypse" but the two fragments are generally thought to belong together (James: 73) and are combined in Riessler's translation. The identity of the Achmimic fragment is, however, open to question. The quotation from Clement is not found in either passage but it is quite compatible with them. We have no clear indication of date and provenance. The fact that it has been preserved in Egyptian dialects might be thought to favor an Egyptian origin but this is by no means necessary. The date must be earlier than Clement, so the possible time-span within which it could have been written coincides roughly with that of the Testament of Abraham.

Despite the fragmentary state of this apocalypse, the basic features can be discerned. *Manner of revelation*: Visions and dialogue are contained within the heavenly journey. An interpreting angel accompanies the pseudonymous seer. *Content*: All the revelation is otherworldly in character but the primary focus is on the judgment and punishment of the individual dead. The description of otherworldly regions (both infernal and heavenly) and of angelic beings predominates.

Summary

3 Baruch, Testament of Abraham and Apocalypse of Zephaniah differ from the other apocalypses by their lack of any interest in cosmic transformation. Here the eschatology is on a purely individual basis. Even 3 Baruch, which has its fictive setting after the Fall of Jerusalem, shows no interest in the history of the Jewish people, or in communal restoration. It is significant that none of these three works can be dated with any confidence before the first century CE.

Yet these works cannot be sharply distinguished from the other apocalypses since they are evidently very similar to such works as 1 Enoch 1-36 and 2 Enoch. Rather, they represent one extremity of a spectrum. Even here, while the emphasis has shifted decisively to the spatial axis, the temporal axis remains essential since the judgment, rewards and punishment are deferred to the afterlife. These works, then, may be classified as a sub-type of the genre "apocalypse."

Other Jewish Apocalypses

With the possible exception of some fragmentary works from Qumran, the preceding list exhausts the corpus of extant Jewish apocalypses which can be dated with any plausibility before the Bar Kockba revolt. In the other works which we shall review, the divergence from the characteristics of the apocalypses reviewed above is too significant to admit classification in the same genre.

There is no doubt that the original corpus of Jewish apocalypses was more extensive than this. It is possible that other Jewish apocalypses can be extracted from Christian writings. So, for example, it is widely believed that the Apocalypse of Elijah, the Apocalypse of Sedrach and the Ascension of Isaiah are

Jewish apocalypses reworked by Christians. However, the Christian redactional activity in these works is so extensive that it is impossible to reconstruct the Jewish originals with any confidence, and they are better treated as Christian works. The recent attempt of Rosenstiehl to maximize the Jewish element in the Apocalypse of Elijah must be treated with caution.

The so-called "Apocalypse of Moses" in the Adam literature is not an "apocalypse" in the same sense as the works described above. It contains elements of apocalyptic eschatology (e.g. 13:2-5, which speaks of "the end of times" when the "delights of paradise will be restored") but it is a narrative paraphrase of the story of the Fall, not a revelation.

The largely parallel Life of Adam and Eve does contain a revelation in chapter 29 which was revealed to Adam "when he had eaten of the tree of knowledge, and knew and perceived what will come to pass in this age." The eschatological section of this passage is very probably Christian--"And thereafter God will dwell with men on earth (in visible form)" (29:7). If this verse is removed, there remains an *ex eventu* prophecy of the history of Israel, culminating in national restoration. It is not clear how far a cosmic transformation is involved. There is no reference to personal afterlife. This passage has definite affinities with apocalyptic eschatology but it is presented as an instruction of Adam to Seth, not as a revelation to Adam mediated by a heavenly being. This revelation in the Life of Adam and Eve is preceded by a passage in chapters 25-28 in which Adam is "caught up into the Paradise of righteousness" on a chariot. However, that passage deals with the divine sentence on Adam and the promise of mercy to his progeny. It is not explicitly related to the revelation in chapter 29. Heavenly visions such as this occur in several other Jewish writings of the period. We do not consider them to constitute "apocalypses" unless they have eschatological content.

Related Types

A number of other writings have much in common with apocalypses and share a common worldview with them, but differ in some essential respect: they either lack the mediation by an otherworldly figure or the transcendent eschatology of the apocalypses or both. We append here a brief review of the main types of related writing which are often loosely categorized as apocalyptic, but should be distinguished from the apocalypses.

Testaments

A testament is a farewell address of a father to his sons or a leader to his successors. One of the time-honored components of such farewell speeches was prediction of the future. In Jewish writings of the Hellenistic age, these predictions were naturally influenced by contemporary eschatology. Consequently the genre "testament" could be used as vehicle for apocalyptic eschatology. However, in all the works which we have designated as "apocalypses" the claim that the content is "revealed" and therefore authoritative is based on the vision or heavenly experience of the fictional author. In testaments, even eschatological testaments, the authority of the prediction is based on the prestige of the patriarch and the fact that it is his farewell address.

One point of similarity between the manner of revelation in apocalypses and testaments should be noted, however. That is the common use of pseudepigraphy, which reflects a common sense that revelation is not given directly and must be bolstered by the authority of a figure from the ancient past. While revelation in the testaments is not mediated by an otherworldly being, it is mediated by a figure whose antiquity and status distinguishes him from common humanity.

Two testaments are especially closely related to the apocalypses: the "Letter of Enoch" or "Book of Exhortations" in 1 Enoch 91-104 and the Testament (or Assumption) of Moses.

1 Enoch 91-104

1 Enoch 91-104 is usually dated to the first quarter of the first century BCE (Charles, Ruppert). It is presented as an instruction of Enoch to his sons and consists largely of admonitions to the righteous and woes for the sinners, but the exhortation is set in the context of an apocalyptic eschatology. Enoch claims to derive his revelation from heavenly tablets and holy books (103:2) but the dominant form of the work is the exhortation of Enoch to his sons. The claim to revelation and the revealed eschatology, while basic to the thought-structure of the work (Nickelsburg, 1977a), do not determine the literary structure, but are adduced intermittently to support the hortatory argument. The eschatological perspective is provided in part by the Apocalypse of Weeks which is integrated into this work in chapters 93 and 91:12-17. We also find eschatological allusions throughout, e.g. in 92:10 the righteous are raised from their sleep. In chapter 104 the righteous share the life of the angels. The eschatological rewards and punishments are located in heaven and the netherworld. Angelic beings play a prominent role throughout.

1 Enoch 91-104 is therefore an important document for Jewish apocalypticism and apocalyptic eschatology, but it is not in the literary form of an apocalypse.

The Testament of Moses

The same is true of the Testament of Moses. The work is presented as Moses' farewell address to Joshua and is partly modelled on Deuteronomy 31-34 (D. Harrington in Nickelsburg, 1974: 59-68). The basic document dates to the time of Antiochus Epiphanes, but it was updated by the insertion of chapter 6 after the death of Herod.

The content of the Testament of Moses is organized in terms of an eschatological pattern, which may be correlated with the paradigm given in the Introduction to this volume.

5.2	*Ex eventu* prophecy of history occupies chaps. 2-7
7.1	The eschatological crisis in chaps. 8-9 takes the form of persecution.
8.1/8.2	Judgment and destruction on sinners and the world follows in chap. 10:1-7.
9.1	Cosmic transformation is probably implied by the cosmic destruction in chap. 10.
9.2.2	The exaltation of Israel to the heaven of the stars in 10:8-9 presumably involves the exaltation of the individual Israelites as a counterpart to the punishment of their enemies in Gehenna.

10.1 The otherworldly regions of heaven and Gehenna are the scene of the eschatological rewards and punishments.
10.2 An angel of God and Satan appear in the eschatological denouement in chap. 10.

This eschatological pattern is encased in a narrative framework which includes the exhortation of Moses to Joshua. The Testament of Moses, then, is especially similar to those "historical" apocalypses which include an *ex eventu* prophecy of history. In form of presentation, however, it is a testament and not an apocalypse.

The Testaments of the 12 Patriarchs

The Testaments of the 12 Patriarchs contain some Christian and diverse Jewish material and their provenance is a matter of intense controversy. M. de Jonge (1953, 1975) holds that the Testaments are essentially Christian, composed about 200 CE, but incorporating Jewish traditional material. J. Becker (1970, 1974), on the other hand, distinguishes two Jewish editions of the work (one from the early second century BCE and the other some time later, both probably from Egyptian Judaism), and a final Christian redaction. The complicated source critical questions are further complicated by text-critical problems. The evidence including the new data from Qumran is reviewed by Becker (1974:17-31).

The Testaments of the 12 Patriarchs place far greater emphasis on exhortation than the Testament of Moses. They typically conclude with predictions, but these do not necessarily involve apocalyptic eschatology. The clearest affinities with the apocalypses are found in Test Levi 14-18, which conforms to the eschatological pattern of the "historical" apocalypses. Test Levi also includes an apocalypse in chapters 2-5 which has already been discussed. Test Judah 21-24 also consists of an eschatological prophecy and a similar example of apocalyptic eschatology is found in Test Dan 5:7-13. However, the eschatology of the Testaments of the 12 Patriarchs is not consistently apocalyptic.

The Testament of Job

One other Jewish testament must be mentioned briefly. The Testament of Job carries no clear indication of its date, but is usually located in Egyptian Judaism about the turn of the era. Unlike the Testaments of the 12 Patriarchs, it shows no concern for the eschatology of the Jewish people. Instead, it is informed by an apocalyptic eschatology similar to what we find in 3 Baruch. Job has heavenly visions in which he gains insight into heavenly realities (Collins, 1974b). These insights enable him to endure in his earthly trials. At the end of the book he is transferred to heaven in a chariot. Test Job is a testament in form, and not an apocalypse, but it attests one type of apocalyptic eschatology (that of the purely "personal" apocalypses) just as some of the Testaments of the 12 Patriarchs and the Testament of Moses attest another (that of the "historical" apocalypses).

Oracles

The Sibylline Oracles

There are obvious similarities between the "historical" apocalypses and the Jewish Sibylline Oracles. Like the eschatological testaments, these oracles share with apocalypses the use of pseudonymity. However, they are oracles and not apocalypses because they claim direct inspiration of the Sibyl. There is no mediation by an angel, interpretation of scripture, or dialogue.

The Sibylline Oracle which most closely resembles the eschatology of the apocalypses is Sib Or 4. This oracle consists of an old, anti-Macedonian oracle, which was not necessarily Jewish, updated by a Jew towards the end of the first century CE (Flusser, 1972; Collins, 1974c). It contains an *ex eventu* prophecy, schematized by four kingdoms and ten generations and culminating in confusion and disasters (49-161) with destruction of the world by fire, as a punishment for sinners (173-177). The restoration of the world is implied and the righteous are resurrected on earth. The interest in the heavenly, angelic world common to the apocalypses is lacking here, but the wicked are punished in the netherworld. The threat of eschatological destruction is used by the Jewish redactor to frame an exhortation in verses 162-170. The destruction is conditional upon the reaction to this exhortation. Such a conditional element is foreign to the apocalypses.

The first and second books of the present Sibylline collection are in reality one oracle, originally Jewish but updated by a Christian who disrupted the original order considerably (Geffcken, 1902b). The original Jewish oracle should probably be dated to the first century CE (Kurfess). Here again we find history divided into ten periods. The eschatology of the Jewish oracle is difficult to determine because of the extensive Christian interpolations in Sib Or 2. If the passage 154-176, which is evidently Jewish, can be taken as the original conclusion, then the expectation of the author was directed towards a universal Jewish kingdom. The Jewish stratum of these books appears to come from Phrygia (Geffcken, 1902b:50).

The oldest stratum of the Jewish Sibylline oracles is found in the third book, of which verses 97-155 and 489-829 date from the mid-second century BCE and derive from Egyptian Judaism (Collins, 1974d). The eschatology of Sib Or 3 differs from that of the apocalypses (Type Ia) primarily in the nature of salvation. There is no suggestion here of personal afterlife or of a new creation. The era of salvation will be ushered in by the "seventh king" (193, 318, 608) or the "king from the sun" (652) who must be understood as a Ptolemaic king, probably an ideal one whose arrival was still awaited (Collins, 1974d:43). This conception finds its closest parallels, not in the apocalypses, but in the royal eschatology of Isaiah (e.g. chaps. 9 and 11). A measure of cosmic transformation is certainly implied, even in Isaiah, but the radical break between the present order and the age to come, which is characteristic of the apocalypses, is lacking.

Later stages of the Egyptian Sibylline tradition are represented by some of the additions to Sib Or 3 and by Sib Or 5. Sib Or 3:75-92 was written shortly after the defeat of Cleopatra (Collins, 1974d:69-70). Sib Or 3:63-74 and all of Sib Or 5 date from the end of the first or early second century CE. These oracles resemble the apocalypses in their emphasis on cosmic destruction. The intensity of this conception is most graphically expressed in the elaborate battle of the stars with which book 5 concludes (512-530). However, they lack the apocalyptic portrayal of transcendent salvation. There is no suggestion of personal afterlife. Even the restoration of the Jews is only briefly mentioned in 5:281 and 420-428, and it is not clear how far their restored state transcends the normal human condition. The persistent conclusion of these oracles is destruction rather than salvation. It is striking that even the "savior-king" is identified chiefly by destructive action (e.g. 5:108-110).

The Qumran Scrolls

The distinction between apocalypticism and apocalyptic eschatology on the one hand and the literary genre "apocalypse" on the other has its greatest significance in the case of the Qumran scrolls. Several of these writings display a worldview very similar to the apocalypses but they belong to distinct genres: *serek* (1QM, 1QS), *pesharim* and related works such as 11QMelch, *hodayot*. Only a few fragmentary works from Qumran can be classified as apocalypses with any justification, and even these are open to question. The work which is closest to the form of an apocalypse is "4Q Visions de 'Amram" published by Milik (1972). Amram recounts a vision in which two angelic beings are engaged in a dispute on his account. One of these is the angel of darkness, Malkî-reša', and the other is the angel of light, probably Melkizedek (Malkî-sedeq). Amram engages in a dialogue with these angelic figures. 4Q Visions de 'Amram then utilizes the same manner of revelation as the apocalypses: vision, dialogue with angels, pseudonymous seer. It is quite probable that the visions also have eschatological import. Milik (1972:90) adduces a fragment which he ascribes to a "Testament of 'Amram" where the eschatological destiny of the Sons of Light and of Darkness is explicitly noted. It is not clear, however, whether this is part of the same text. 4Q Visions de 'Amram, insofar as it is now known, is probably a fragment of an apocalypse, but is incomplete.

Another fragmentary work, 4Q Ps Daniel, contains the typical eschatological pattern of the apocalypses. There are three Aramaic fragments, two of which are copies of the same work. It is not certain that the third fragment belongs to the same composition. If Milik (1956) is correct that the three fragments belong together, then the eschatological pattern is quite elaborate. There is a lengthy review of world history. Milik (1956) argues that the period after the Flood is divided between four kingdoms, but the only evidence for this is a fragmentary reference to the "first kingdom" (vs. 20). The third fragment contains fragmentary allusions to an eschatological crisis, the destruction of evil, and the resurrection of the dead. The main difference between this work and the apocalypses lies in the manner of revelation. There is no reference to an angelic mediator nor to the manner by which Daniel received the revelation at all. We are simply told that he spoke "in the presence of the king." Because of the fragmentary nature of the text we cannot be sure that the revelation was not mediated. Insofar as it is known, however, 4Q Ps Daniel is a prophecy with apocalyptic eschatology, not an apocalypse.

Two other fragmentary works require a brief reference. The "Vision of the New Jerusalem" is attested in a number of fragments: 1Q32, 2Q24, 5Q15. Clearly based on Ezekiel 40-48, this work tells how the seer is shown the measurements of the New Jerusalem by an angelic guide. We are reminded of the heavenly journeys of the apocalypses. The New Jerusalem also presumably implies a temporal eschatology when it will be revealed. However, the work is simply too fragmentary to permit any conclusions as to its genre.

The same is true of the "Angelic Liturgy" published by Strugnell. The work is important for apocalypticism as it shows an interest in the angelic world reminiscent of the more mystical apocalypses such as 3 Baruch or 2 Enoch. It must also be regarded as an antecedent of Merkabah mysticism. However, insofar as the work is now known, it lacks both the manner of revelation and the eschatology which distinguish the apocalypses.

The Enochic "Book of Giants" (Milik, 1976:298-317) is also too fragmentary to permit definitive classification. It appears to be similar to 1 Enoch 6-16 and to be concerned with the primeval history of the Watchers, rather than human history. While the judgment on the Watchers may have cosmic proportions, it is primeval rather than eschatological.

Finally, Milik (1976:254) refers to "an Apocalypse of Ten Jubilees" which will be edited by J. Strugnell under the sigla 4Q384-389. This work is attributed to Ezekiel, and evidently bears some resemblance to 11Q Melchizedek, but is extremely fragmentary. Any discussion of this work will have to await the official publication.

SELECT BIBLIOGRAPHY

GENERAL

Bousset, W.
1926
Die Religion des Judentums im späthellenistischen Zeitalter. 3rd ed. Ed. H. Gressmann. Tübingen: Mohr.

Betz, H. D.
1969
"On the Problem of the Religio-Historical Understanding of Apocalypticism." *JTC* 6: 134-156.

Charles, R. H.
1913
Apocrypha and Pseudepigrapha of the Old Testament. Vol. 2. Oxford: Clarendon.

Collins, J. J.
1974a
"Apocalyptic Eschatology as the Transcendence of Death." *CBQ* 36: 21-43.

1975a
"Jewish Apocalyptic against its Hellenistic Near Eastern Environment." *BASOR* 220: 27-36.

1977a
"Pseudonymity, Historical Reviews and the Genre of the Apocalypse of John." *CBQ* 39: 329-343.

1977c
"Cosmos and History: Jewish Wisdom and Apocalyptic in the Hellenistic Age." *HR* 17: 121-142.

Denis, A.-M.
1970
Introduction aux Pseudépigraphes Grecs d'Ancien Testament. SVTP 1. Leiden: Brill.

Hanson, P. D.
1976a
"Apocalypse, Genre." "Apocalypticism." IDBSup 27-34.

1976b
"Prolegomena to the Study of Jewish Apocalyptic." Pp. 389-413 in *Magnalia Dei. The Mighty Acts of God.* Eds. F. M. Cross, W. E. Lemke and P. D. Miller, Jr. Garden City, NY: Doubleday.

James, M. R.
1920
The Lost Apocrypha of the Old Testament. London: SPCK.

Koch, K.
1972
The Rediscovery of Apocalyptic. SBT 2/22. Naperville, IL: Allenson.

Rad, G. von
1965
Theologie des Alten Testaments. 4th ed. Vol. 2. Munich: Kaiser.

Riessler, P.
1928
Altjüdisches Schrifttum Ausserhalb der Bibel. Darmstadt: Wissenschaftliche Buchgesellschaft (reprinted, 1966).

Rowley, H. H.
1964
The Relevance of Apocalyptic. New York: Association.

Russell, D. S.
1964
The Method and Message of Jewish Apocalyptic. Philadelphia: Westminster.

Schmidt, J. M.
1969   *Die jüdische Apokalyptik.* Neukirchen-Vluyn: Verlag des Erziehungsvereins.

Schmithals, W.
1975   *The Apocalyptic Movement.* Nashville: Abingdon.

Stone, M. E.
forthcoming   "Apocalyptic Literature." *Compendia Rerum Iudaicarum ad Novum Testamentum.* Philadelphia: Fortress.

Weinel, H.
1923   "Die spätere christliche Apokalyptik." Pp. 141-173 in *Eucharisterion. Festschrift für Hermann Gunkel.* Ed. H. Schmidt. Göttingen: Vandenhoeck & Ruprecht.

PROPHETIC PRECEDENTS OF APOCALYPTIC

Erling, B.
1972   "Ezekiel 38-39 and the Origins of Jewish Apocalyptic." *Ex Orbe Religionum: Studia Geo Widengren Oblata* I: 104-114. Leiden: Brill.

Gese, H.
1973   "Anfang und Ende der Apokalyptik, dargestellt am Sacharjabuch." *Theologie und Kirche* 70: 20-49.

Hanson, P. D.
1975   *The Dawn of Apocalyptic.* Philadelphia: Fortress.

Millar, W. R.
1976   *Isaiah 24-27 and the Origin of Apocalyptic.* HSM 11. Missoula: Scholars Press.

North, R.
1972   "Prophecy to Apocalyptic via Zechariah." VTSup 22: 47-71.

Ploeger, O.
1968   *Theocracy and Eschatology.* Richmond, VA: Knox.

Daniel

Collins, J. J.
1977b   *The Apocalyptic Vision of the Book of Daniel.* HSM 16. Missoula: Scholars Press.

Glasson, T. F.
1976   "The Son of Man Imagery: Enoch xiv and Daniel vii." *NTS* 23: 82-90.

Hartman, L. F. and Di Lella, A. A.
1978   *The Book of Daniel.* AB 23. Garden City: Doubleday.

1 Enoch

Ethiopic Text

Charles, R. H.
1906   *The Ethiopic Version of the Book of Enoch.* Anecdota Oxoniensia, Semitic Series 11. Oxford: Clarendon.

Greek Fragments

Black, M.
1970   *Apocalypsis Henochi Graece. Fragmenta Pseudepigraphorum quae supersunt Graeca.* PVTG 3. Leiden: Brill.

Aramaic Fragments

Milik, J. T.
   1976   *The Books of Enoch.* Oxford: Clarendon.

Translation and Commentary

Charles, R. H.
   1893   *The Book of Enoch.* Oxford: Clarendon.

   1913   "1 Enoch." *APOT* 2: 163-281.

Studies

Casey, M.
   1976   "The Use of Term 'Son of Man' in the Similitudes of Enoch." *JSJ* 7: 11-29.

Dexinger, F.
   1977   *Henochs Zehnwochenapokalypse und Offene Probleme der Apokalyptikforschung.* Leiden: Brill.

Greenfield, J. C.
   1973   "Prolegomenon." Pp. xi-xlvii in Hugo Odeberg, *3 Enoch or the Hebrew Book of Enoch.* New York: Ktav.

Hanson, P. D.
   1977   "Rebellion in Heaven, Azazel, and Euhemeristic Heroes in 1 Enoch 6-11." *JBL* 96: 195-233.

Milik, J. T.
   1971   "Problèmes de la Littérature Hénochique à la Lumière des Fragments Araméens de Qumrân." *HTR* 64: 233-278.

Nickelsburg, G. W.
   1972   *Resurrection, Immortality and Eternal Life in Intertestamental Judaism.* HTS 26. Pp. 70-78 (Similitudes), 112-129 (chaps. 102-104). Cambridge, MA: Harvard.

   1977a   "The Apocalyptic Message of 1 Enoch 92-105." *CBQ* 39: 309-328.

   1977b   "Apocalyptic and Myth in 1 Enoch 6-11." *JBL* 96: 383-405.

Ruppert, L.
   1972   *Der leidende Gerechte.* (Similitudes and chaps. 91-104). Würzburg: Echter.

Suter, D. W.
   1977   "Tradition and Composition in the Parables of Enoch." Unpublished Dissertation. Chicago: University of Chicago.

Theisohn, J.
   1975   *Der auserwählte Richter.* SUNT 12. Göttingen: Vandenhoeck & Ruprecht.

Jubilees

Ethiopic Text

Charles, R. H.
   1895   *The Ethiopic Version of the Hebrew Book of Jubilees.* Oxford: Clarendon.

Translation and Commentary

Charles, R. H.
1902   *The Book of Jubilees.* London: Black.

1913   "The Book of Jubilees." *APOT* 2: 1-82.

Studies

Davenport, G. L.
1971   *The Eschatology of the Book of Jubilees.* Studia Post-Biblica 20. Leiden: Brill.

Jaubert, A.
1963   *La notion d'alliance dans le judaïsme aux bords de l'ère chrétienne,* 89-115. Paris: Seuil.

Testuz, M.
1960   *Les idées religieuses du Livre des Jubilés.* Paris: Menard.

VanderKam, J. C.
1977   *Textual and Historical Studies in the Book of Jubilees.* HSM 14. Missoula: Scholars Press.

4 Ezra

Latin Text

Violet, B.
1910   *Die Esra-Apokalypse I: Die Überlieferung.* GCS 18. Leipzig: Hinrichs.

Translation and Commentary

Box, G. H.
1912   *The Ezra Apocalypse.* London: Pitman.

1913   "4 Ezra." *APOT* 2: 542-624.

Myers, J. M.
1974   *I and II Esdras.* AB 42. Garden City, NY: Doubleday.

Studies

Breech, E.
1973   "These Fragments I Have Shored against My Ruins: The Form and Function of 4 Ezra." *JBL* 92: 267-274.

Harnisch, W.
1969   *Verhängnis und Verheissung der Geschichte: Untersuchungen zum Zeit- und Geschichtesverständnis im 4 Buch Esra und in der Baruch-Apokalypse.* Göttingen: Vandenhoeck & Ruprecht.

Stone, M. E.
1965   "Features of the Eschatology of IV Ezra." Unpublished Dissertation. Cambridge, MA: Harvard.

1966   "The Concept of the Messiah in IV Ezra." Pp. 295-312 in *Religions in Antiquity.* Studies in Memory of E. R. Goodenough. Ed. J. Neusner. Leiden: Brill.

Thompson, A. L.
1977   *Responsibility for Evil in the Theodicy of IV Ezra.* SBLDS 29. Missoula: Scholars Press.

2 Baruch

Dedering, S.
    1973   *Apocalypse of Baruch.* The Old Testament in Syriac According to the Peshitta Version. Leiden: Brill.

Kmosko, M,
    1907   *Patrologia Syriaca* 1/2. Ed. R. Graffin. Paris: Firmin Didot.

Translation and Commentary

English
Charles, R. H.
    1896   *The Apocalypse of Baruch.* London: Black.

    1913   "2 Baruch or the Syriac Apocalypse of Baruch." *APOT* 2: 470-526.

German
Klijn, A. F. J.
    1976   *Die syrische Baruchapokalypse.* Jüdische Schriften aus hellenistisch-römischer Zeit 5/2. Gütersloh: Mohn.

Violet, B.
    1924   *Die Apokalypsen des Esra und des Baruch in deutscher Gestalt.* GCS 32. Leipzig: Hinrichs.

French
Bogaert, P.
    1969   *L'Apocalypse syriaque de Baruch.* 2 vols. Paris: Cerf.

Studies

Harnisch, W.
    1969   [Above under 4 Ezra]

Klijn, A. F. J.
    1970   "The Sources and the redaction of the Syriac Apocalypse of Baruch." *JSJ* 1: 65-76.

Apocalypse of Abraham

Slavonic Text (Codex Sylvester)

Tikhonravov, N.
    1863   *Memorials of Russian Apocryphal Literature* 1: 32-53. Moscow.

    [On other mss., see Box (1919) x-xv (below)]

Translation and Commentary

German
Bonwetsch, G. N.
    1897   *Die Apokalypse Abrahams.* Leipzig: Deichert.

English
Box, G. H.
    1919   *The Apocalypse of Abraham.* London: SPCK.

Studies

Meyer, R.
    1952   "Abraham-Apokalypse." RGG^3 1: 72.

Rubinstein, A.
    1953   "Hebraisms in the Slavonic 'Apocalypse of Abraham.'" *JJS* 4: 108-115.

Stone, M. E.
    forthcoming   [Above under General]

2 Enoch

Slavonic Text and French Translation

Vaillant, A.
    1952   *Le Livre des Secrets d'Hénoch*. Paris: Institut des Études Slaves.

English Translation and Commentary

Morfill, W. R. and Charles, R. H.
    1896   *The Book of the Secrets of Enoch*. Oxford: Clarendon.

Forbes, N. and Charles, R. H.
    1913   "2 Enoch, or the Book of the Secrets of Enoch." *APOT* 2: 425-469.

Studies

Greenfield, J. C.
    1973   [See above under 1 Enoch: xviii-xx]

Pines, S.
    1970   "Eschatology and the concept of time in the Slavonic Book of Enoch." Pp. 72-87 in *Types of Redemption*. Studies in the History of Religions 18. Eds. R. J. Z. Werblowski and C. J. Bleeker. Leiden: Brill.

Rubinstein, A.
    1962   "Observations on the Slavonic Book of Enoch." *JJS* 13: 1-21.

3 Baruch

Greek Text

Picard, J.-C.
    1967   "Apocalypsis Baruchi Graece." Pp. 63-96 in *Testamentum Jobi. Edidit S. P. Brock. Apocalypsis Baruchi Graece. Edidit J.-C. Picard*. Leiden: Brill.

Translation and Commentary

Hughes, H. M.
    1913   "3 Baruch or the Greek Apocalypse of Baruch." *APOT* 2: 527-541.

Hage, W.
    1974   *Die griechische Baruch-Apokalypse*. Jüdische Schriften aus hellenistisch-römischer Zeit 5/1. Gütersloh: Mohn.

Studies

Denis, A.-M.
    1970   [See above under General: 79-84]

Picard, J.-C.
    1970   "Observations sur l'Apocalypse Grecque de Baruch." *Semitica* 20: 77-103.

Testament of Abraham

Greek Text and Translation

Stone, M. E.
1972   *The Testament of Abraham.* Missoula: Scholars Press.

Studies

Box, G. H.
1927   *The Testament of Abraham.* London: SPCK.

Delcor, M.
1973   *Le Testament d'Abraham.* SVTP 2. Leiden: Brill.

James, M. R.
1892   *The Testament of Abraham.* Texts and Studies 2/2. Cambridge: Cambridge University.

Nickelsburg, G. W. (ed.)
1976   *Studies on the Testament of Abraham.* SBLSCS 6. Missoula: Scholars Press.

Schmidt, F.
1971   "Le Testament d'Abraham. Introduction, édition de la recension courte, traduction et notes." Unpublished Dissertation. Strasbourg.

Turner, N.
1954-55   "The 'Testament of Abraham': Problems in Biblical Greek." *NTS* 1: 219-223.

Apocalypse of Zephaniah

Coptic Text and German Translation

Steindorff, G.
1899   *Die Apokalypse des Elias, eine unbekannte Apokalypse und Bruchstücke der Sophonias-Apokalypse.* Texte und Untersuchungen zur Geschichte der Altchristlichen Literatur. NF 2/3a. Leipzig: Hinrichs.

Translation (German)

Riessler, P.   [Above under General: 168-177]

Studies

Denis, A.-M.   [Above under General: 192-193]

Frey, J. B.
1928   "Apocryphes de l'Ancien Testament, 16. Quelques apocryphes plus tardifs ou fragmentaires, 4° Les Apocalypses d'Elie et de Sophonie." *Dictionnaire de la Bible.* Supplement 1: 456-458.

James, M. R.   [Above under General: 72-74]

Meyer, R.
1962   "Zephanja-Apokalypse." RGG^3 6: 1900-1901.

Weinel, H.   [Above under General: 141-173]

Other Jewish Apocalypses

Rosenstiehl, J.-M.
    1972   *L'Apocalypse d'Elie. Introduction, Traduction et Notes.* Paris: Guethner.

Wells, L. S. A.
    1913   "The Books of Adam and Eve." *APOT* 2: 123-154.

RELATED TYPES

Testament of Moses

Latin Text, Translation and Commentary

Charles, R. H.
    1897   *The Assumption of Moses.* London: Black.

Laperrousaz, E. M.
    1970   "Le Testament de Moïse." *Semitica* 19.

Translation and Commentary

Brandenburger, E.
    1976   *Himmelfahrt Moses.* Jüdische Schriften aus hellenistisch-römischer Zeit 5/2. Gütersloh: Mohn.

Charles, R. H.
    1913   "The Assumption of Moses." *APOT* 2: 407-424.

Studies

Licht, J.
    1961   "Taxo or the Apocalyptic Doctrine of Vengeance." *JJS* 12: 95-103.

Nickelsburg, G. W. (ed.)
    1973   *Studies on the Testament of Moses.* SBLSCS 4. Missoula: Scholars Press.

Yarbro Collins, A.
    1976   "Composition and Redaction of the Testament of Moses 10." *HTR* 69: 179-186.

Testaments of the 12 Patriarchs

Greek Text

Charles, R. H.
    1908   *The Greek Versions of the Testaments of the Twelve Patriarchs.* Oxford: Clarendon.

De Jonge, M.
    1964   *Testamenta XII Patriarcharum.* Leiden: Brill.

Aramaic Fragments

Milik, J. T.
    1955a   "Le Testament de Lévi en Araméen, Fragment de la grotte IV de Qumrân." *RB* 62: 398-406.

    1955b   DJD I: 88-89.

    1966   "Fragment d'une Source du Psautier (4QPs 89)." *RB* 72: 94-106.

Translations and Commentary

Charles, R. H.
    1908   *The Testaments of the Twelve Patriarchs.* Oxford: Clarendon.

    1913   "The Testaments of the Twelve Patriarchs." *APOT* 2: 282-367.

Becker, J.
    1974   *Die Testamente der zwölf Patriarchen.* Jüdische Schriften aus hellenistisch-römischer Zeit 3/1. Gütersloh: Mohn.

Studies

Becker, J.
    1970   *Untersuchungen zur Entstehungsgeschichte der Testamente der zwölf Patriarchen.* Leiden: Brill.

De Jonge, M.
    1953   *The Testaments of the Twelve Patriarchs.* Assen: van Gorcum.

    1975   *Studies in the Testaments of the Twelve Patriarchs.* Leiden: Brill.

Testament of Job

Text and Translation

Kraft, R. A.
    1974   *The Testament of Job.* Missoula: Scholars Press.

Studies

Collins, J. J.
    1974b   "Structure and Meaning in the Testament of Job." Pp. 35-52 in SBLASP 1. Ed. G. MacRae. Missoula: Scholars Press.

Philonenko, M.
    1968   "Le Testament de Job." *Semitica* 18.

Spittler, R.
    1971   "The Testament of Job." Unpublished Dissertation. Cambridge, MA: Harvard.

Sibylline Oracles

Greek Text

Geffcken, J.
    1902a   *Die Oracula Sibyllina.* GCS 8. Leipzig: Hinrichs.

Rzach, A.
    1891   *Oracula Sibyllina.* Leipzig: Freytag.

Translation and Commentary

Kurfess, A.
    1951   *Sibyllinische Weissagungen* (Books I-XI, German). Berlin: Heimeran.

Lanchester, H. C. O.
    1913   "The Sibylline Oracles" (Books III-V). *APOT* 2: 368-406.

Studies

Collins, J. J.
    1974c   "The Place of the Fourth Sibyl in the Development of the Jewish Sibyllina." *JJS* 25: 365-380.

Collins, J. J.
1974d   *The Sibylline Oracles of Egyptian Judaism.* SBLDS 13.
             Missoula: Scholars Press.

Geffcken, J.
1902b   *Komposition und Entstehungszeit der Oracula Sibyllina.*
             Texte und Untersuchungen zur Geschichte der Altchristlichen
             Literatur. NF VIII/1. Leipzig: Hinrichs.

Flusser, D.
1972   "The four empires in the Fourth Sibyl and in the Book of
             Daniel." *Israel Oriental Studies* 2: 148-175.

Nikiprowetzky, V.
1970   *La Troisième Sibylle.* Etudes Juives IX. Paris: Mouton.

Qumran

Details of publications and select bibliography on the scrolls can be found in:

Fitzmyer, J. A.
1975   *The Dead Sea Scrolls. Major Publications and Tools for
             Study.* SBLSBS 8. Missoula: Scholars Press.

The following works are of relevance here:

Collins, J. J.
1975b   "The Mythology of Holy War in Daniel and the Qumran War
             Scroll." *VT* 25: 596-612.

Cross, F. M.
1961   *The Ancient Library of Qumran and Modern Biblical Studies.*
             Rev. ed. Garden City, NY: Doubleday.

Kuhn, H.-W.
1966   *Enderwartung und gegenwärtiges Heil.* SUNT 4. Göttingen:
             Vandenhoeck & Ruprecht.

Milik, J. T.
1956   "Prière de Nabonide et autres écrits d'un cycle de Daniel."
             RB 63: 407-415.

1972   "4Q Visions de ʿAmram et une citation d'Origène." *RB* 79:
             77-97.

Strugnell, J.
1960   "The Angelic Liturgy at Qumran--4Q Serek Šîrôt ʿÔlat
             Haššabbāt." Pp. 318-345 in *Congress Volume, Oxford, 1959.*
             VTSup 7. Leiden: Brill.

Yadin, Y.
1962   *The Scroll of the War of the Sons of Light against the Sons
             of Darkness.* Oxford: Oxford University.

THE EARLY CHRISTIAN APOCALYPSES

Adela Yarbro Collins
McCormick Theological Seminary

SYNOPSIS

Not much systematic study of early Christian apocalyptic literature has been done. The starting points are still the introductory essays and studies of individual books in Hennecke-Schneemelcher, volume 2; the essay by Weinel on later apocalypses; and M. R. James' The Apocryphal New Testament. J. Lindblom (1968) has done some helpful phenomenological studies on revelatory aspects of the NT books and of early Christian literature up to the middle of the second century, but he did not address the question of genre.

The purpose of this essay is to define the genre "apocalypse" within the corpus of early Christian literature and to elucidate the subtypes of writings within this category. A number of works have been systematically excluded. The Coptic works from Nag Hammadi and those in the Askew, Berlin and Bruce Codices are not included here since they are treated by F. Fallon in a separate essay. Other works are excluded because of their dates. For the purposes of this essay, "early Christian" is understood as belonging to the first three centuries of the common era. Works containing clear historical references to events which occurred in the fourth century or later have been excluded. An exception has been made for works which have several literary stages if at least one of the earlier stages dates prior to the fourth century (for example, the Apocalypse of Paul). Works which have no clear indication of a post-third century date have been included. Passages in patristic works which treat eschatological matters have not been included because they are different in literary form from works usually referred to as "apocalypses."

Definition and Typology

The approach taken in this study has been primarily inductive. The works commonly regarded as "apocalyptic" in modern scholarly discussion and other similar works from the same period have been examined from the point of view of form and content and compared so that the significant recurring characteristics could be determined. The result of this study was the delineation of a group of texts which constitute a recognizable type of writing and whose major characteristics are included in the master-paradigm in the Introduction to this volume. Some of the writings examined differed from those in this group in significant ways. Yet, because they also have important similarities to the texts which constitute the coherent group, these other writings are treated at the end of this essay as "related types."

The significant recurring characteristics of the works which constitute the coherent group are, in part, the basis of the definition given in the Introduction to this volume. It is repeated here for convenience and clarity: *"Apocalypse" is a genre of revelatory literature with a narrative framework in which a revelation is mediated by an otherworldly being to a human recipient, disclosing a transcendent reality which is both temporal, insofar as it envisages eschatological salvation, and spatial, insofar as it involves another, supernatural world.* There are twenty-four early Christian texts which fit this definition. Of these, fourteen are entire works, each of which can be called an apocalypse as a whole. In one case we are dealing with fragments of a work which could probably be classified as an apocalypse (the Book of Elchasai). In the other nine cases the texts in question are parts of larger works which may or may not have once circulated independently, but which are understandable as units apart from their present literary context.

The early Christian apocalypses may be divided into two basic types according to the mode of revelation: those in which the primary mode of revelation is the vision or audition (Type I) and those in which the primary mode of revelation is the otherworldly journey (Type II). Each of these basic types may be subdivided according to variations in eschatological content. The results of the discussion in the main part of this essay of the individual texts is anticipated here to provide an overview of the material.

Type Ia: "Historical" Apocalypse with No Otherworldly Journey

The distinctive element in this type is the presence of a review of history in the form of an *ex eventu* prophecy. The only early Christian apocalypse which contains this element is Jacob's Ladder. The *ex eventu* prophecy is in two parts. In the first part (4-6) the experiences of the descendants of Jacob are foretold. In the second (7-8), the coming of a man from the Most High (apparently Christ) who will be wounded is predicted. The presence of the first review of history and its uniqueness relative to other Christian apocalypses would be explained by the theory that the work is a Christian redaction of an older Jewish composition. Unfortunately, there is no clear indication of date for either stage of the work.

The Testaments of Isaac and Jacob contain minor uses of *ex eventu* prophecy, but not in the form of a review of history. Test Jacob 2 refers to events in Jacob's past life. The function of these elements seems simply to be the enhancement of the literary fiction of pseudonymity.

More significantly, the Questions of Bartholomew refers to primordial events which have a paradigmatic significance for the present: the creation of the angels (4:25-35), the creation of Adam, the fall of Satan and his angels, and the deception of Eve (4:52-59).

The most striking difference between Christian and Jewish apocalypses of Type I (without a heavenly journey) is that the Christian works have a much more limited interest in the past. Only one Christian work, contrasted with six Jewish texts, has a review of history. Of the other three Christian works which have some interest in history, that interest is significant only in Ques Bart, where actually *pre*-historical events are recalled.

Type Ib: Apocalypses of Cosmic and/or Political Eschatology with Neither Historical Review Nor Otherworldly Journey

The only difference between this type and Type Ia is its lack of the review of history. Types Ib and Ic are distinguished in that Ib involves some form of public eschatology, whereas Ic entails only personal eschatology. Jacob's Ladder (the only Christian apocalypse of Type Ia) involves public eschatology in its expectation of the destruction of the world (8). No cosmic transformation is envisaged.

Five Christian apocalypses (probably six) belong to Type Ib. Two of these expect both cosmic destruction and cosmic renewal (Revelation and the Apocalypse of St. John the Theologian). Three predict cosmic destruction, but contain no indication of cosmic transformation (the Apocalypse of Peter, the Shepherd of Hermas, and the Testament of the Lord 1:1-14). The Book of Elchasai is tentatively included here since the allusion to the war of the angels of the north probably refers to a public, eschatological crisis (fr. 7).

Of the five apocalypses which clearly belong in this group, three are certainly early. Revelation dates to the first century, Apoc Peter and Hermas to the second century. The Book of Elchasai is also second century.

Type Ic: Apocalypses with Only Personal Eschatology (and No Otherworldly Journey)

Five of the early Christian apocalypses discussed in this essay belong to this type: 5 Ezra 2:42-48, Test Isaac 2-3a, Test Jacob 1-3a, Ques Bart and the Book of the Resurrection of Jesus Christ by Bartholomew the Apostle 8b-14a. These works are difficult to date. None of them has as yet been dated with persuasive arguments. 5 Ezra 2:42-48 is probably the earliest and has been assigned to the second or early third century. Ques Bart has been assigned to the third century.

As noted above, the most striking difference between this type (I) of early Christian apocalypse and the corresponding Jewish one is that the Christian apocalypses have a very limited interest in events of the past. Many of the Jewish apocalypses of the corresponding type have a clear interest in the politics of their times. The book of Revelation is the only one of this group of Christian apocalypses with such an interest.

As in the Coptic Gnostic apocalypses, there is a greater emphasis on dialogue and discourse as means of revelation in the Christian texts of Type I in comparison with the Jewish. However, the visionary element has not been eclipsed in these writings to the extent that it has in the Gnostic works.

Type IIa: "Historical" Apocalypses with An Otherworldly Journey

This type corresponds to Type Ia in the presence of an historical review and differs from it in containing the element of an otherworldly journey. No early Christian apocalypse belongs to

Type IIa since none of the apocalypses with an otherworldly journey has an historical review. There is some interest in history in the Christian apocalypses of Type II, similar to the expressions of such interest noted in those of Type I.

In the Ascension of Isaiah, there is an *ex eventu* prophecy of the descent, mission and ascent of Christ (9-11). This is the only example of an *ex eventu* prophecy in the otherworldly journeys.

In the Apocalypse of Paul, there is a prominent interest in telling the stories of primordial events or of certain historical figures with an apparently hortatory purpose (44-45, 49-51). In the Story of Zosimus, we find the Adam and Eve story told as a negative example (6, 19) and the history of the Rechabites as a positive example (7-9). Primordial and historical events are also recalled in the Apocalypse of Esdras (2:10-16, 19, 22; 3:10). In the Mysteries of St. John the Apostle and Holy Virgin, the primordial existence of water is mentioned (3b-4a) and the fall and expulsion of Adam from Paradise are recounted (4a-6b, 10a-13b). The story of Hezekiah turning his face to the wall is explained (13b-14b). The story of Adam's sin is also recounted in the Apocalypse of Sedrach (4:4-7:5).

Type IIb: Otherworldly Journeys with Cosmic and/or Political Eschatology

Four early Christian apocalypses belong to this type. One of these predicts both the destruction and transformation of the cosmos (Apoc Paul). The other three refer only to the destruction of the world (Asc Isa 6-11, Apoc Esdras, and the Apocalypse or Vision of the Virgin Mary).

Of these four works, the only one which, in its *present* form, can be assigned to the first three centuries of the common era with any likelihood is Asc Isa 6-11 (first or second century). An earlier form of the Apoc Paul may be dated to the third century. The dates of the other two works are uncertain.

Type IIc: Apocalypses with An Otherworldly Journey and Only Personal Eschatology

Eight of the early Christian apocalypses discussed in this essay belong to this type: Test Isaac 5-6; Test Jacob 5; Zosimus; the Apocalypse of the Holy Mother of God concerning the Punishments; the Apocalypse of James, the Brother of the Lord; The Mysteries of St. John the Apostle and Holy Virgin; Resurr (Bart) 17b-19b; and Apoc Sedrach.

All of these works are difficult to date. James assigned the present form of Zosimus (Greek version) to the fifth or sixth century, but believed that it is based on an older work. The opinions on the date of Apoc Sedrach have varied widely. James was of the opinion that it is older than Apoc Paul. The dates of the other works are even more uncertain. It is possible that none of the eight date to the first three centuries of the common era.

The early Christian apocalypses are clearly quite varied in type. Every type is represented except IIa ("historical" with otherworldly journey), which is very rare in any case. The most common types among Christian apocalypses are Ib, Ic, IIb and IIc. There is no indication of an historical development from the type lacking an otherworldly journey to the type characterized by such a journey. There are early examples of both: Revelation (no journey, first century) and Asc Isa 6-11 (otherworldly journey, first or second century). It is probable that the types involving only personal eschatology are somewhat later than those expressing cosmic and/or political eschatology. Of those involving public eschatology, one can be dated to the first century (Revelation); one to the first or second (Asc Isa 6-11); and two, possibly three to the second century (Apoc Peter, Hermas, Elchasai). Only one of the apocalypses expressing personal eschatology alone can be assigned to the second century (5 Ezra 2:42-48), and only one can be assigned to the third century (Ques Bart). We thus have four, possibly five, apocalypses with public eschatology dating to the first two centuries and only one with personal eschatology alone dating to the same period.

In spite of the variety of types, all of these works share the significant, basic characteristics expressed in the definition of an apocalypse given above. The similarities and variations are presented on the chart at the end of this essay. The chart is based on the master-paradigm given in the Introduction to this volume.

The similarities among the works fall under the three categories of manner of revelation, temporal elements and spatial elements. All of the works studied contain heavenly revelation communicated by a heavenly mediator. Most of the texts have a visionary element either in the form of a simple vision account or in the form of an otherworldly journey. Most of these also contain revelation in the form of a dialogue between seer and mediator or a discourse of the heavenly mediator. Only one work, the

Apocalypse of Sedrach, contains the auditory mode of revelation alone. In some works the heavenly mediator is Christ. Just as often this role is taken by one or more angels. Pseudonymity is not a constant factor. In Revelation, Hermas and the Book of Elchasai, the seer apparently uses his own name. Fictitious names are probably used in the story of Zosimus and in the account of Siophanes' journey to heaven (Resurr [Bart] 17b-19b). In the latter two cases, we do not find the use of the name of a well-known, venerable and authoritative figure as is the case in pseudonymous writing. The fundamental similarities between these works and the pseudonymous early Christian apocalypses lead to the conclusion that pseudonymity is not an essential characteristic of the genre "apocalypse" in the corpus of early Christian literature. The disposition and reaction of the seer are frequent but not constant elements. The transcendent character of the revelation and the seer's dependence on the heavenly world are often expressed by a description of the seer's ecstatic reaction or by his or her requests and questions addressed to the mediator.

Temporal elements involve an interest in the past and certain expectations of the future. As noted above, the more or less systematic review of history, so dominant in some forms of Jewish apocalypses, is virtually absent in the early Christian apocalypses. Such a review is found only in Jacob's Ladder, which is probably a Christian adaptation of a Jewish work. In Jacob's Ladder, as in the Jewish apocalypses which have a review of history, that review is part of the eschatological pattern. Events are narrated up to and including the final crisis and resolution. In other Christian apocalypses, certain past events are explicitly recalled as past and recounted as particularly significant for the present. They are selected and told apart from any systematic review of all history. The events most commonly selected are those involving Adam and Christ. This limited interest in the past occurs in Test Isaac 2-3a, Test Jacob 1-3a and Ques Bart (all Type Ic), in Apoc Paul and Apoc Esdras (Type IIb) and in Myst John and Apoc Sedrach (Type IIc). In the Asc Isa 6-11, we find an *ex eventu* prophecy of the descent, ministry and ascent of Christ (Type IIb).

There is considerable variety in the expectations of the future in early Christian apocalypses, but two groups can be distinguished.

(1) Ten, possibly eleven, texts have elements of both cosmic and personal eschatology. Three of these include both cosmic destruction and cosmic renewal--Revelation and Apoc Jn Theol

(both Type Ib) and Apoc Paul (Type IIb). Seven works predict only cosmic destruction--Jacob's Ladder (Type Ia); Apoc Peter, Hermas, Test Lord 1:1-14 (all Type Ib); and Asc Isa 6-11, Apoc Esdras and Apoc Mary (all Type IIb). The Book of Elchasai probably belongs here also in that it refers to a war of the angels of the north. By analogy with the book of Daniel this war may be understood as a public, political eschatological crisis. All of these works also expect personal salvation in some form of afterlife.

(2) In the thirteen other apocalypses, the elements of crisis and judgment/destruction, where present, refer to the past or to an ongoing process in the present, and future hope is limited to personal afterlife--5 Ezra 2:42-48, Test Isaac 2-3a, Test Jacob 1-3a, Ques Bart, and Resurr (Bart) 8b-14a (all Type Ic); and Test Isaac 5-6, Test Jacob 5, Zosimus, Apoc Moth God, Apoc James, Myst John, Resurr (Bart) 17b-19b and Apoc Sedrach (all Type IIc).

The only eschatological element which occurs in all twenty-four texts is the expectation of a personal afterlife.

The apocalypses in the form of an otherworldly journey are almost evenly divided into those which have cosmic eschatology and those which have only personal. Although one might expect the otherworldly journeys to be more individualistic, such is not the case. Type I is a form which is most often used for revelation concerned with the future of the world. It can, however, also be used to express a more personal form of future hope. This point is illustrated by Apoc Peter (Ib) which contains cosmic eschatology, but whose primary emphasis is on individual punishments after death. The otherworldly journey can be a vehicle for a variety of future expectations.

The spatial elements involve interest in heavenly or otherworldly realities. Such interest is characteristic of all texts discussed. The activities of angels and their influence on nature and human life is a common theme. Otherworldly entities are most prominent in the works of the journey type where the emphasis is on descriptions of the otherworldly regions and the rewards and punishments given there. A similar emphasis characterizes Apoc Peter, although it is not in the form of an otherworldly journey.

In the following discussions of individual writings, introductory question of date, provenance, and where necessary, attestation will be treated first. Then matters of form and content will be discussed. In the individual treatments of form and content, the master-paradigm given in the Introduction to this volume will not be repeated.

The early Christian apocalypses will be discussed in order of the types outlined above. Within each type, texts will be discussed in the probable order of composition, beginning with the earliest.

SURVEY

Type I: Otherworldly Visions and Auditions

Type Ia: "Historical" Apocalypses with No Otherworldly Journey

Jacob's Ladder

Jacob's Ladder is the only early Christian apocalypse of Type Ia. It is an account of a dream-vision of Jacob based on Gen 28:10-22. It is extant in two Slavonic recensions and is Christian in its present form. Only the last two sections, which appear only in the later recension (7-8), are clearly Christian. At the beginning of section 8 it is said that images of brass and stone would speak for three days as a sign of the Savior's birth. According to James (1920:102) this motif comes from a document of uncertain date called the "Wonders in Persia" or "The Dispute at the Court of the Sassanidae." The shorter recension may well represent an older, substantially Jewish work.

Revelation is mediated first of all in the form of a dream. This dream is recounted in section 1 which corresponds to Gen 28:10-15. The visionary element is expanded with a more detailed description of the ladder: there were twelve rungs with a human face at the ends of each rung (twenty-four in all). In section 3, an epiphany of the angel Sarekl to Jacob is described. Sections 4-6 (4-8 in the longer recension) comprise the revelatory discourse of Sarekl which interprets the dream.

Jacob's Ladder is the only early Christian apocalypse with a review of history. This peculiarity would be explained if a Jewish document has been adapted for Christian use. The review of history (4-6) is, of course, in the form of prediction. The motif of the periodization of history is also present: the twelve rungs represent the twelve times of this age. The review of history which follows, however, is not clearly based on this periodization. In its present form at least the review is rather obscure: section 4 refers to destruction of the temple and exile; section 5 to a violent king descended from Esau (the Romans?) who would force the people to worship idols and sacrifice to the dead; section 6 to bondage in a strange land and (in the longer recension only) to the destruction of the kingdom of Edom (Rome?) and all the Moabites. In the longer recension there is also a description of the descent and ministry of Jesus (7-8).

The element of persecution is present in the description of the violent reign of the heir of Esau (5), in the motif of exile (6) and in the allusion to the destruction of the temple (4). The punishment of sinners in a personal afterlife is presupposed by the comment that those who wounded him [Christ] will receive a wound which shall not be healed forever (8; long recension only). Both recensions expect judgment to come upon the oppressors of the people (6). The destruction of the world is alluded to in section 8 (when he is wounded...the end of all corruption draws near; long recension only). The coming one will destroy the power of the godless one (or evil one--Satan) and of idols and will cast all unrighteousness into the depths of the sea (8; long recension only). The personal afterlife of the just is implied by the statement that when he is wounded, the saving draws near, and his might and his years shall not fail forever (8; long recension only).

The work manifests a clear interest in angels. The Cherubim and Seraphim are described in Jacob's prayer and the song of the Seraphim is quoted (2). The divine intervention to judge the oppressors of the people is attributed to the prayers of the angels and archangels for the people (6; shorter recension only).

Type Ib: Apocalypses of Cosmic and/or Political Eschatology with Neither Historical Review Nor Otherworldly Journey

Five (probably six) early Christian apocalypses are of this type: Revelation, Apoc Peter, Hermas, (probably Elchasai), Apoc Jn Theol, and Test Lord 1:1-14.

Revelation

The NT book of Revelation in its present form is usually dated in accordance with a remark by Irenaeus ("at the close of Domitian's reign"--*Haer*. 5.30.3). On the basis of Irenaeus's comment and internal evidence, the book is dated by most commentators to 90-95 CE. The internal evidence points to the western part of Asia Minor as the provenance of the work. It is generally agreed that the author made use of earlier sources in parts of the book. This source material contains virtually no reliable indications of date. 11:1-2 and 17:10 might be dated prior to 70 CE, but these points are disputed.

The decision to include the book of Revelation might be disputed on the grounds that it is a letter, not an apocalypse. At the outset it should be noted that the book incorporates a variety of small units or forms. Most of the work consists of vision accounts. The vision form dominates 4:1-22:5, which is essentially a series of vision accounts. Chapter 1:9-3:22 is an epiphany of Christ. This epiphany contains a significant auditory element, a discourse in which Christ communicates seven messages to John. Many of the visions in 4:1-22:5 have an auditory element which takes a number of different forms: for example, doxologies (5:13; 7:12), acclamations (4:11; 5:9-10, 12), victory songs (12:10-12; 14:8; 19:1-2, 3), and beatitudes (14:13; 16:15; 19:9; 20:6). On one occasion, John and one of the elders engage in a brief dialogue (7:13-17). In Jewish apocalypses and other early Christian apocalypses, the seer typically asks the question and the revealer answers it. Here, the elder both asks and answers the question.

To determine the literary form of the book of Revelation as a whole, one must ask what the dominant literary form is or how all these smaller forms are integrated into a coherent whole. It has often been noted that the visions of the book of Revelation are enclosed within an epistolary framework, yet it would be an error of misplaced emphasis to say that the book of Revelation is primarily a letter in form. The epistolary form is subordinated to and in the service of the book's revelatory character. The work does not open immediately with the prescript of a letter, but with a preface or prologue which characterizes the book (in content at least) as an *apokalypsis* and a *prophēteia* (1:1, 3). There is no good reason to conclude that this preface was a later addition. Furthermore, the use of the letter form is quite superficial. The vision form is introduced already in 1:9. The seven messages do not follow the conventional letter form; they were never independent letters, but were composed for the present context--as messages of the revealer communicated in a vision (Yarbro Collins, 1976:6).

The dominant literary form in the book, as noted above, is the vision account. The otherworldly journey motif is not entirely absent, however. In 4:1 the visionary sees an open door in heaven and is told "come up hither!" In 17:1-3 and 21:9-10 he describes ecstatic translations in the spirit. The primary mode of revelation, nevertheless, is the vision supplemented by auditions and John is not led from region to region in the beyond as is typical in works of the journey type. Revelation thus belongs to Type I.

In two cases, the reception of revelation is linked to an otherworldly writing. The revelation of the events described in chapters 6:1-8:1 is directly linked to the opening of the scroll with seven seals introduced in chapter 5. The command issued by the mighty angel in 10:11, that the seer prophesy again, is linked to the seer's reception and consumption of a "little scroll" (10:10).

The ultimate source of the revelation is God (1:1), but it is mediated by Christ, angels and other heavenly beings (1:1; 5:5; 7:13-17; 10:1-11; 17:1-18; 19:9-10; 21:9-22:5; 22:6, 8-9, 10-11, 16).

Another argument for excluding Revelation from this study might be based on the fact that it is not pseudonymous. There is no indication that the author of Revelation is using a pseudonym. No attempt is made to link this John to the twelve nor to any other John for that matter. Further, no attempt is made to link this book to any other writings associated with the name John. Since pseudonymity is a typical feature of Jewish apocalypses, the apocalyptic character of Revelation has been questioned since it lacks this characteristic (Jones, 1968). It should be noted, however, that Jewish writings of the same period other than apocalypses were pseudonymous also, for example, the Wisdom of Solomon, the Psalms of Solomon and the Letter of Aristeas. Pseudonymity was a widespread phenomenon in the ancient world with a variety of functions (Metzger, 1972). The prior question then would be what the function of pseudonymity is in the Jewish apocalypses. John Collins has shown persuasively that the function pseudonymity had in the Jewish apocalypses is fulfilled in other ways in the book of Revelation (Collins, 1977a). As will become clear below, there are early Christian writings other than Revelation which fit our definition of an apocalypse and yet are not pseudonymous. Pseudonymity then does not seem to be an essential characteristic of early Christian apocalypses, although it is a common one.

The content of the revelation contained in the visions is primarily eschatological. I have shown elsewhere that chapters 6-22:5 consist of five series of vision accounts and that a common eschatological pattern is expressed in each series (Yarbro Collins, 1976: chap. 1). Salvation involves cosmic transformation (new heaven and new earth--21:1), resurrection (20:4-6, 13) and personal afterlife (6:9-11; 7:13-17). Those who will enjoy the blessings of salvation in their afterlives are those whose names are written in the book of life (3:5; 13:8; 17:8; 20:12, 15; 21:27).

Interest in otherworldly regions is expressed in chapter 4 in the description of the divine throne and its surroundings. The description of the heavenly Jerusalem (21:9-21) also belongs to this category. Interest in heavenly beings is expressed in the epiphany and visions of the exalted Christ (1:12-16; 5:6; 19:11-16) and the visions of Michael (12:7), the angel who has power over fire (14:18), the angel of the waters (16:5), and Satan (12:3-17; 16:13; 20:1-3, 7-10).

The seven messages which Christ dictates to John and which are directed to the seven churches consist primarily of exhortation (chaps. 2-3). The exhortation of the otherworldly mediator (Christ) focusses on the importance of standing firm in faith and love and enduring tribulation (2:2-5a, 9-10a, 13-16a, 19-21, 24-25; 3:1b-3a, 8, 10a). The exhortation is reinforced by eschatological threats and promises (2:5b, 7b, 10b, 11b, 16b, 17b, 22-23, 26-28; 3:3b-5, 9, 10b-12, 21).

The Apocalypse of Peter

This apocryphal Apocalypse of Peter is quite distinct from the Coptic Gnostic Apocalypse of Peter discovered at Nag Hammadi in 1946 and from the Arabic Apocalypse of Peter (Maurer: 664). The apocryphal Apocalypse of Peter is probably one of the earliest Christian apocalypses. Toward the end of the second century, Clement of Alexandria mentioned it as a writing of the apostle Peter. Thus the work must pre-date Clement by a period long enough for the establishing of such a tradition. The date of composition of 4 Ezra is given by Maurer (664) as a *terminus post quem* for the composition of Apoc Peter, since he believes Apoc Peter 3 to be dependent on 4 Ezra 5:33. It is not a case of a quotation, however, and the point of contact may be due rather to a knowledge of the same popular motif. Spitta has argued that the Apoc Peter is dependent on 2 Peter. The points of contact are an allusion to the Transfiguration on "the holy mountain" (Apoc Peter 15; 2 Pet 1:18) and the expectation of the destruction of the world by fire (Apoc Peter 5; 2 Pet 3:10-12). Here also, the points of contact can be explained as resulting from common tradition. There is no compelling reason to posit literary dependence. Weinel suggested (Maurer: 664) that the false Christ mentioned in Apoc Peter 2 is Bar Cochba. This is a plausible suggestion. The false Christ is associated with the fig tree which is identified as Israel. It is said that some will deny the Christ who was crucified and accept this false Christ. Others will reject him and he will slay them with the sword. According to Justin Martyr (quoted by Eusebius, *Eccl. Hist.* 4.8), Bar Cochba commanded that those Christians be punished severely who refused to deny that Jesus was the Messiah. According to Eusebius (*Chronicle*, Hadrian's year 17--Latin version), Bar Cochba, in Hadrian's year 17 (133 CE), killed Christians who refused to fight with him against the Romans. According to Apoc Peter 2, Enoch and Elijah will be sent to convict this false Christ. It seems then that the author associated the activity of Bar Cochba with the eschatological crisis and expected the end to follow soon. If this interpretation is correct, the work must have been composed not long after 133 CE.

Clement's knowledge and recognition of the work together with the condemnation of idols representing various animals (10) point to Egypt as the place of origin of Apoc Peter. The reference to animal idols, however, may be a later elaboration, since it is found in the Ethiopic but not in the Greek version.

The Apocalypse of Peter is extant in three Greek fragments, a number of patristic quotations and in an Ethiopic version. Most scholars have concluded that the Ethiopic version represents the original work substantially, although there are translation errors and possibly some later elaboration. The length of the Ethiopic text is only slightly longer than the length of the work given by the Codex Claromontanus and the Stichometry of Nicephorus (Hennecke-Schneemelcher: 1.46, 50).

At first the Apoc Peter seems to be a retelling of two incidents in the ministry of Jesus narrated in the first person by Peter and giving details not reported in the Synoptic gospels. The two incidents are the discourse about the end on the Mount of Olives (Mark 13 and pars.) and the Transfiguration (Mark 9:2-8 and pars.). The so-called Synoptic apocalypse is expanded to include a description of the places of punishment and the Transfiguration is supplemented with a vision of paradise. At the end of the Ethiopic version, however, it becomes apparent that the work is not a retelling of parts of Jesus' ministry. After the Transfiguration, instead of descending the mountain with his disciples, Jesus ascends to the second heaven with Moses and Elijah. This departure would seem to indicate that the setting of the work is after the resurrection of Jesus during the time he allegedly gave further instruction to his disciples. Since the Ethiopic version has been preserved as part of the Corpus Clementinum, it may be that the opening of the Apoc Peter once indicated such a setting more clearly than it does now.

As noted above, the work falls into two parts. Chapters 1-14 are set on the Mount of Olives. At the beginning of chapter 3 there is a brief vision account: "And he showed me in his right hand the souls of all (men) and...the image of that which shall be fulfilled at the last day...." The second part of the work (chaps. 15-17) is set "on the holy mountain" and includes two vision accounts: of Moses and Elijah as types of the righteous dead (15-16) and of paradise (16). These visions are complemented by revelation in auditory form. The brief vision of chapter 3 is followed by a long discourse of Christ on the last days emphasizing the punishments of hell. Most of chapters 1-3 consist of a dialogue between Christ and his disciples, primarily Peter. The visions of chapters 15-16 are clarified by a dialogue between Christ and Peter.

The content of the revelation in the Apoc Peter is primarily eschatological. In chapter 2 it is predicted that a false messiah will kill those (Christians) who refuse to recognize him as the Christ. In chapter 16, paradise is promised to those persecuted for Christ's "righteousness' sake." The conception of a general judgment and subsequent individual rewards and punishments is a prominent theme (6-14). The eternal punishments of the wicked are particularly emphasized (7-12). The destruction of the world by fire is described in chapter 5. The understanding of salvation includes the general resurrection at the end (4) and the personal afterlife of righteous individuals in Paradise in the meantime. Those whose names are written in the book of life are assured of their future bliss (17).

The interest in otherworldly regions is expressed in the description of the places of punishment (6-12), mention of the Elysian fields (14), and the brief vision of Paradise (16). Interest in otherworldly beings is expressed in the expectation that Enoch and Elijah would return (2), that an angel (Uriel) would be the agent of the general resurrection (4) and that various angels would execute the foreordained punishments (7-12).

The Shepherd of Hermas

Like Apoc Peter, the Shepherd of Hermas is one of the earliest Christian apocalypses. Vielhauer (1965:642) dates Herm to 120-140 CE on internal grounds. According to Goodspeed-Grant (30-33), at least parts of Herm go back to 95-100 CE because of (1) the reference to Clement (of Rome) in Vis II. iv. 3; (2) the fact that the work was composed in three stages and completed not later than 155 CE (the end of the episcopate of Pius in Rome; according to the Muratorian writer, Herm was composed in his time). The internal evidence indicates Rome as the place of origin (Vis I. i. 1). The reliability of this evidence has been questioned, but such skepticism has not won support (Vielhauer: 642).

There has been considerable debate whether Herm is an apocalypse or not. Since the primary interest of the book is how to deal with sins after baptism, some have argued that its use of the vision form has little relation to its content. Herm certainly fits part of our definition of an apocalypse: most of the work consists of revelation mediated by otherworldly beings.

In Vis I-II, Hermas is given a heavenly book to copy so that he can convey its message (recorded in Vis II. ii-iii) to the faithful. Hermas is commanded by the Shepherd to write down all which would be communicated to him (Vis V. 5-7). The remaining two sections of the book (the Mandates and the Similitudes) are thus, in effect, a heavenly book dictated by an angel.

Each of the epiphanies in the first section of the book consists of the appearance of an otherworldly being who mediates revelation in dialogue form. These mediators are the ancient lady, the Church (Vis I-IV) and a beautiful young man, who is probably an angel (Vis II. iv. 1; III. xi-xiii). In Vision V, an angel in the form of a shepherd appears, who takes the role of the otherworldly mediator in the rest of the book.

There is no indication that Hermas is a pseudonym. The author seems to have written quite simply in his own name (Vielhauer: 641-642).

Besides the great emphasis on heavenly modes of revelation, Herm also contains a strong eschatological interest. The word *thlipsis* is used both for persecution and the coming eschatological crisis (Vis II. ii. 7-8, iii. 4; III. vi. 5; IX. i. 1, ii. 5, iii. 6; Sim VIII. iii. 6-7). Those who died in persecutions are to be specially honored in the next world (Vis III. i. 9-ii. 1, v. 2; Sim VIII. iii. 6-7). Readiness for persecution and death is urged in a figurative manner in Sim I. 4-6. In one passage Hermas asks the heavenly mediator about the times ($kair\bar{o}n$), if the end (*synteleia*) were yet. The answer is that when the "tower" is finished, the end will come and that the tower will be quickly finished (Vis III. viii. 9). The eschatological orientation of the book is shown in the fact that repentance and forgiveness of sins after baptism are not accepted as a repeatable process. The book proclaims a new but *final* call for repentance which presupposes a short time until the end, during which the faithful can indeed remain sinless (Vis II. ii).

In the next world sinners and the heathen will be burnt (Sim IV. 4) and will be assigned to eternal destruction (Sim VI. ii. 3-4, v. 7; VIII. vi. 4,6, vii. 3,5,6, viii. 2-5, ix. 4, x. 2; IX. xiv. 2; X. ii. 4). The end involves the destruction of the world by fire and blood (Vis IV. iii. 3). The righteous after death will be with the angels (Vis II. ii. 7); they will receive great glory and eternal life (Vis II. ii. 6, iii. 2; III. ii. 1; IV. iii. 5). Those who are to be saved are inscribed in the heavenly books of life (Vis I. iii. 2; Sim II. 9).

The prominence of the heavenly world in Herm is evident in the major role played by heavenly beings. The ancient lady stands before the Father and gives an account of the deeds of the faithful (Vis III. ix. 10). This statement implies that she takes the role of the defender of the righteous in the heavenly court, where sinners can be accused now (Vis I. i. 5). Angels rule all creation, oversee the Church and protect individuals (Vis III. ii. 5, iv. 1-2; V. 2-4; Sim V. v. 3, vi. 2; VIII. iii. 3,5; IX. xii. 6). Angels of punishment act against sinners even in their earthly lives (Sim VI. ii. 5-iii. 6; VII. 1-7). Ethical struggles in the present are understood as struggles between heavenly beings (Man V. i. 2-4, ii. 1-8; VI. ii. 1-10; VII. 1-5; XII. iv. 6-7, v-vi.).

A considerable portion of Herm consists of exhortation and ethical instruction. Mandates I-XII contain such material spoken by the revealer figure to Hermas for his own benefit and for others (Man XII. iii. 2-3). Certain portions of the Similitudes are also given over to ethical instruction: in Similitudes I and II, the Shepherd instructs Hermas on the proper Christian attitude toward wealth, in Similitude V, on fasting and service.

Since Herm is characterized both by apocalyptic eschatology and by revelation mediated by otherworldly beings, there is no good reason to exclude it from the genre "apocalypse."

The Book of Elchasai

In one of the extant fragments of the Book of Elchasai (2), it is said that Elchasai came forth with his teaching in the third year of Trajan (101 CE). The work probably dates to about that time. It probably originated east of the Jordan and may have been composed in Aramaic (Irmscher: 745-747). The book is a sectarian work extant only in quotations by Hippolytus and Epiphanius.

The fragmentary nature of the surviving portions of the work makes determination of its literary form difficult. Fragments 1 (Epiphanius) and 3 are in the first person and indicate that the book may have been written in the first person originally. The work seems to have contained a vision account of two otherworldly beings; one (male in appearance) is identified with the Son of God. The other (female in appearance) is called the Holy Spirit (fr. 1--Hippolytus). The angel called the Son of God is said to have given the book to a certain Seres of Parthia, who gave it to Elchasai (fr. 1--Hippolytus). This angel is the otherworldly mediator of the revelation contained in the book.

It is possible that the name Elchasai is a sobriquet (Irmscher: 746). There is, however, no indication that this name or that of Seres was used pseudonymously.

Conclusions about the eschatological pattern must be tentative because of the fragmentary nature of the sources. There is a reference to persecution in fragment 8, but apparently as a repeatable phenomenon and not as the eschatological crisis. In fragment 7, a war between the godless angels of the north is predicted; this war is referred to in language reminiscent of the typical eschatological upheavals; because of this all kingdoms of godlessness are in disorder.

The cryptogram of fragment 9 refers to the day of the great judgment; the expectation of such a day presupposes the judgment of the wicked as well as personal afterlife. The promise of a share with the righteous (fr. 3) also implies belief in personal afterlife.

The astrological ideas of fragment 7 express interest in heavenly beings (the stars) and belief in their power over humanity. The reference to the war of angels in the same fragment expresses another kind of interest in heavenly beings and their activity. Like Daniel 10, this fragment apparently links angelic battles to earthly ones, since Trajan and the Parthians are mentioned in the context.

The Apocalypse of St. John the Theologian

The Apocalypse of St. John the Theologian, also referred to at times as the Questions of John, is extant only in Greek. The *terminus ante quem* is provided by the reference to a work of this title in the scholia on the Grammar of Dionysius Thrax which dates to the ninth century (Weinel, 1923:149). It is not certain, however, that the scholia refers to this particular work and not to another work of the same title. Bousset argued that the second half of the work shows connections with two works by Ephrem of Syria entitled Questions and Answers concerning the Last Judgment. Bousset suggested that the question and answer form of the Apoc Jn Theol derived from Ephrem's homilies, thus indicating 400 CE as an approximate *terminus post quem* for the work (1896:42). It is doubtful, however, that Ephrem's works were the immediate source of these elements. Apoc Jn Theol is clearly dependent on the book of Revelation, so about 100 CE is a reliable *terminus post quem*. The work contains no clear historical allusion; no compelling argument for fixing its date at any particular point after 100 CE has as yet been made.

Apoc Jn Theol is written as a first person account. Visions of heaven opened (2), the scroll with the seven seals (3), and the lamb (18) are recounted. The major way in which revelation is mediated is through dialogue between the seer and the ascended Christ. The seer is taken up to heaven on a brightly-shining cloud for the visions and dialogue (2), but he is not taken on a heavenly journey. Part of the revelation communicated is associated with the scroll with the seven seals (3-4, 18-19).

The eschatological crisis will involve famine (5) and the activity of the Antichrist (6-8). One of the most striking passages of this work is the physical description of the Antichrist (7). The wicked will be punished in the next world (21-24). Judgment will be executed on heaven and earth in their destruction (14, 19). Christ and his angels will be victorious over the Antichrist and all the unclean spirits who are in league with him; the latter will be judged and punished (16-20). Salvation includes the renewal of the earth (15, 25, 27), the general resurrection (10-12), and the deliverance of the elect at the end alive from the earth (13). Personal salvation involves rewards in the next world (23, 25).

An interest in otherworldly beings is expressed in the fascination with the Antichrist (6-8). Enoch and Elijah are expected to return to earth to convict the Antichrist and to be slain by him (8). All creation will be destroyed by the agency of Michael and Gabriel (9). Angels will take an active role in bringing about the events of the end (13-14, 17, 23). The just will dwell with angels in the next world (25). John questions Christ about the number of the angels (26).

Testament of the Lord 1:1-14

The Testament of the Lord is a fifth-century Syriac work on church order in the form of a discourse of the risen Lord to his disciples. Chapters 2-14 of book one treat the last things. This eschatological discourse was apparently independent at one time since it is attested independently of the Syriac church order. Another version of it appears as a prefix to the Ethiopic version of the Epistula Apostolorum. James (1893) published a fragment of a related if not identical work.

The date of the original independent apocalyptic discourse is difficult to determine. The Syriac church order provides a *terminus ante quem*. The Syriac version of the discourse mentions a king of foreign race who will arise in the west, a homicide and a persecutor (chap. 5; this allusion is lacking in the Ethiopic version). K. F. Neumann suggested that Maximinus Thrax (235-238 CE) is the emperor to whom reference is made (Weinel, 1923:145). The Latin fragment identifies the Antichrist with "Dexius" (James, 1893:188). This possible reference to Decius (249-251 CE) may be a third-century interpretation of an earlier form of the text.

The Syriac version begins with an epiphany of the risen Christ to his disciples. The time and place of the epiphany are not given. The manner of revelation is a discourse spoken by the risen Lord, who is thus in the role of the otherworldly mediator. The disciples are the pseudonymous recipients of the revelation. The Ethiopic version begins with a mysterious first person saying (1). There is no epiphany of the risen Lord. The discourse is simply introduced by the statement, "The word which our Lord Jesus spoke to his eleven disciples in Galilee, after he had risen from the dead, as he said:...."

The two versions differ rather significantly in content. The Syriac version seems to allow for a present state of salvation through knowledge. During the days of tumults in the church, Christ will send to the pure ones the understanding of knowledge, of truth and of holiness (8). The eschatological crisis is of major importance in both versions. Persecution as an aspect of the eschatological crisis is a major theme in the Syriac version (5, 8, 10), but is only briefly mentioned in the last, recapitulatory chapter of the Ethiopic (11). The greater part of both versions is devoted to descriptions of other sorts of eschatological upheavals. In the Ethiopic version, political upheavals (3, 5), cosmic signs and catastrophes (4), human strife (4), and the activity of the eschatological adversary (6) are expected. The Syriac version foretells famines and pestilences (3, 8), wicked rulers and human strife (4, 5), cosmic upheavals (6), strange births (7), the appearance and wars of the eschatological adversary (3, 9, 10) and tumults in the church (8). Both versions contain physical descriptions of the adversary (Ethiopic--6, Syriac--11). The Latin fragment also contains such a description.

The Ethiopic version predicts eternal fiery punishment for those who persecuted the righteous (8, 11). The Syriac refers to the "harvesting" of sinners in judgment, a probable allusion to an eschatological general judgment (12). The Ethiopic version also has more general references to the fiery punishment of sinners and/or unbelievers (2, 9--of wicked bishops and *pastophoroi*). The destruction of the world is predicted in the Ethiopic (11), but not in the Syriac. The Ethiopic seems to presuppose the resurrection of the just (4). The just will shine brighter than the sun, will dwell with or be like angels, and will enjoy a ten-thousand year time of rejoicing (7). The Syriac version mentions that the eschatological judge will be kind to those who have done [good] works (12). This comment implies belief in a personal afterlife for the just.

The importance of otherworldly beings in the Ethiopic version is manifested in the expectation that the angels will execute the cosmic catastrophes (4), in the eschatological activity of Satan (4) and of the adversary (6), and in the angelic character of salvation (7). Interest in otherworldly beings in the Syriac version is expressed in the anticipation of the eschatological adversary (3, 9-11).

The Ethiopic version ends abruptly with the last words of Christ's discourse (11). The disciples are not directly addressed. The Syriac version ends with paraenesis: the disciples are exhorted to be wise in order to persuade those who are in captivity to error and those sunk in ignorance to bring them to the knowledge of God.

These five (probably six) apocalypses constitute Type Ib of the corpus of early Christian apocalypses. They are distinguished by the lack of a review of history and an otherworldly journey and by the presence of both cosmic and personal eschatology. Two texts in this group expect both the destruction of the world and a cosmic transformation--Revelation and a work apparently modeled on it, Apoc Jn Theol. Three texts predict cosmic destruction only--Apoc Peter, Hermas, and Test Lord 1:1-14. The Book of Elchasai alludes to a public eschatological crisis.

Type Ic: Apocalypses with Only Personal Eschatology (and No Otherworldly Journey)

Five early Christian apocalypses belong to this type: 5 Ezra 2:42-48, Test Isaac 2-3a, Test Jacob 1-3a, Ques Bart and Resurr (Bart) 8b-14a.

5 Ezra 2:42-48

The passage normally referred to as 5 Ezra is identical with 2 Esdras 1-2 and is one of the Christian additions to the Jewish apocalypse designated 4 Ezra. There is no clear indication of date in 5 Ezra. Duensing places it about 200 CE (689); Myers (154), following Weinel and James, generally in the second century CE. Although Latin is the only language of antiquity in which 5 Ezra is extant, it is generally thought to have been composed in Greek.

The overall form of 5 Ezra is a collection of oracles of the Lord. Chapter 1:1-3 is a preface in the third person attributing the entire book (2 Esdras) to Ezra the prophet. In 1:4-2:8, Ezra (in the first person) communicates oracles of the Lord (by direct quotation). There is a shift to the third person in 2:10 ("This is what the Lord says to Ezra..."), but the direct quotation of an oracle of the Lord follows, just as in the preceding portion. In 2:33 the text shifts again to the first person, and this time Ezra addresses the readers directly.

Following Ezra's address to the readers (2:34-41) is a brief vision account, which is in the first person also (2:42-48). The vision is supplemented by a dialogue between the human recipient, Ezra, and an angel.

The vision is of the righteous dead being crowned and awarded palms by the son of God on Mount Zion. The description of the righteous implies that they have died because of their confession of the names of God and the Lord (vss. 45, 47). This description implies the expectation of persecution. The reference to immortal clothing (vs. 45) clearly expresses the hope of eternal life for the faithful.

The description of the son of God (vs. 43) and of his role in rewarding those who are faithful unto death (vss. 43-47) is an indication of interest in otherworldly beings.

Although the overall form of 5 Ezra is a collection of oracles, this vision account is a small apocalypse which serves as a transition to the vision accounts of 4 Ezra.

Testament of Isaac 2-3a

The ancient lists of apocryphal works contain no reference to a Testament of Isaac. The allusion to the apocryphal books of the three patriarchs in the Apostolic Constitutions (6:16) may include a reference to this work. Following M. R. James, Delcor (78-79) holds that Test Isaac is dependent on the Jewish Testament of Abraham. Test Isaac is clearly Christian in its present form (Delcor: 79). Delcor, following P. Nagel, dates the Sahidic version of Test Isaac to about 400 CE. Delcor is inclined to accept Nagel's theory of a Greek original and to date it, along with the Test Abraham, to about the turn of the era. K. H. Kuhn argued that there is insufficient evidence for positing a Greek original or for dating the work. Test Isaac is extant in two Coptic versions (Sahidic and Bohairic), in Arabic and Ethiopic.

The Test Isaac is introduced as an account of the death of Isaac. It is then said that Isaac wrote his testament and passed on his teaching to his son, Jacob. The rest of chapter 1 is devoted to exhortation, perhaps intended as a sample of Isaac's teaching. The actual account begins in chapter 2 with the appearance of Michael to Isaac. The angel informs him of his impending death, the sort of afterlife he can expect and about the future of Jacob and his descendants. Chapter 3 and the beginning of chapter 4 contain a narrative account of Isaac's activities after the epiphany. The rest of chapter 4 is devoted to Isaac's hortatory address to the multitudes gathered around him. Following his discourse, Isaac was taken on a heavenly journey (5-6). Upon his return, he gave Jacob one final exhortation and then died (7). Chapters 8-9 constitute a kind of epilogue which encourages veneration of Abraham and Isaac.

As the preceding summary of the form and content of Test Isaac shows, it belongs to the genre "testament" rather than "apocalypse," when viewed as a whole. Test Isaac contains not only an account of the patriarch's death, but also the leave-taking and exhortation typical of the genre "testament" (chaps. 4, 7). Within the larger work, however, are two passages which fit our definition of an apocalypse: chapters 2-3a and 5-6. The former passage belongs to our Type Ic and will be discussed immediately below. The latter is an account of a heavenly journey and will be discussed later with the other texts of Type II.

Like the Jewish Testament of Abraham, the Test Isaac centers on the death of the patriarch and involves a heavenly journey which he experiences *before* death. Unlike Test Abraham, Test Isaac does not contain the motif of the reluctance of the patriarch to die when called.

Test Isaac 2-3a is an epiphany in which revelation is mediated in dialogue form by the angel Michael. The revelation mediated by Michael includes a brief *ex eventu* prophecy: that the descendants of Jacob would become a great people consisting of twelve tribes (chap. 2). The revelation also treats the glorious afterlife awaiting the righteous (chap. 2). The importance of otherworldly beings in this passage is indicated by the remark that Isaac was accustomed to converse with angels daily (2). The angels and other inhabitants of the heavens are reported to have spoken the "amen" to Isaac's blessing of Jacob (2).

Testament of Jacob 1-3a

Like Test Isaac, the Testament of Jacob is not mentioned in the ancient lists of apocrypha, but may be alluded to in the Apostolic Constitutions 6:16. Test Jacob appears to have been modeled on Test Isaac and is also Christian in its present form. Unlike Test Isaac, Test Jacob alludes frequently to passages of the Genesis narrative recounting episodes of the patriarch's life (for example, to Gen 46:30 at the end of chap. 1). There is no clear indication of date. Test Jacob is extant in Coptic (Bohairic), Arabic and Ethiopic.

Like Test Isaac, Test Jacob belongs to the genre "testament" when viewed as a whole. Test Jacob contains the leave-taking (chap. 4, end of chap. 5) and the exhortation by patriarch to his son (chap. 7) typical of testaments, as well as an account of the patriarch's death (end of chap. 5). However, like Test Isaac, Test Jacob contains two passages each of which fits our definition of an apocalypse: chapters 1-3a and 5. The former passage belongs to our Type Ic and will be discussed here. The latter is a heavenly journey and will be treated later with other texts of that type.

Test Jacob 1-3a is an epiphany in which revelation is mediated primarily in the form of a discourse by the angel Michael. There is a minor element of dialogue. In the initial portion of Michael's discourse, there is explicit recollection of certain key incidents in the patriarch's past life, for example, his dream of the heavenly ladder (2). The discourse also contains a very brief reference to the fact that Jacob and others will be called patriarchs until the end of the ages. The expectation of personal afterlife is reflected in Michael's discourse: The just will have eternal life in the kingdom of the heavens, in a place of light and joy (2).

Interest in heavenly beings is expressed in the remark (similar to the one concerning Isaac in Test Isaac 2) that Jacob had daily contact with angels (1). Michael tells Jacob that he has accompanied him since his infancy and aided him at crucial moments (2). Jacob is said to have seen God face-to-face and to have contemplated his army of angels at the time of his vision at Bethel (2).

Questions of Bartholomew

Jerome (*Commentary on Matthew*, prologue) and the Gelasian Decree (Hennecke-Schneemelcher: 1.47) mention a gospel of Bartholomew among apocryphal writings. There is evidence for two distinct works associated with the apostle Bartholomew in surviving manuscripts. One is a work extant only in Coptic and is entitled the Book of the Resurrection of Jesus Christ by Bartholomew the Apostle. That work contains two small apocalypses which will be discussed below. The other work is called the Questions of Bartholomew and is extant in Latin, Greek and Slavonic. Both of these works are classified as gospel literature in Hennecke-Schneemelcher. Actually, the Questions of Bartholomew is an apocalypse according to the definition given above and in the Introduction to this volume.

There is no clear internal indication of date. Scheidweiler (488) places the original form of the work in the third century, but gives no reasons for this dating.

The framework of the book is composed in the third person. Several visions are reported by Bartholomew in the first person: of angels worshipping Jesus on the cross (1:6), of the dead, including Adam, arising and worshipping Jesus on the cross (1:21-22), of angels before Adam (1:23) and of an avenging angel (1:24-25). It is reported briefly that the apostles were shown the abyss (3:7-9), but what they saw is not described. Ques Bart begins with a brief reference to an occasion during the earthly life of Jesus on which the apostles asked Jesus to show them the secrets of the heaven. Jesus' response was that he could reveal nothing until he had put off his body of flesh (1:1-2). After the resurrection of Jesus, the apostles experienced an epiphany of him (1:3). Later in the work an epiphany of Beliar is described (4:12-16, 18-60). In connection with one of the vision accounts, Bartholomew reports the audition of Jesus' voice (or simply "voices") in the underworld, of a great wailing and gnashing of teeth (1:7).

As in the Apoc Peter, the major way in which revelation is mediated in Ques Bart is through dialogue between the resurrected Christ and his disciples. The dialogue form is also used for a revelatory exchange between Beliar and Bartholomew (4:22-59). Besides the risen Lord, the angels of the west (3:7-9), Michael (4:12) and Beliar (4:15) function as otherworldly mediators of revelation.

Ques Bart manifests considerable interest in primordial events: the creation of the angels (4:25-35), the creation of Adam, the fall of Satan and his angels, and the deception of Eve (4:52-59). There is no review of history, but there is an allusion to the belief that all history constitutes six thousand years (1:16/17). The wicked will be punished after death (4:37-44). The eschatological judgment has already occurred in Christ's victory over Beliar, Hades, the Devil and/or Beelzebub (1:10-21). The righteous can expect personal salvation; their souls sojourn in Paradise after leaving the body (1:28-29).

In one of the Greek recensions, the gates and bars of Hades are mentioned (1:18). In one of the Latin and in the Slavonic recension, these physical features of Hades are elaborated somewhat (1:10-20). The abyss is shown to the apostles (3:7-9), but it is not described. One of the instruments of punishment

for the wicked is brought up from Hades and shown to Bartholomew
(4:40-42). The work shows a very strong interest in angels, their
names and their activities: the avenging angels before the Father's
throne (1:26), the angels of the west (3:7), the angels of the
underworld (4:12), angels who influence human beings (4:30, 44)
and those who control nature (4:31-35, 45). Michael (4:12, 29,
53-55) and Beliar (1:10-21; 4:7-60) play prominent roles. A number of other angels are also named (4:29, 47).

The Book of the Resurrection of Jesus Christ by Bartholomew
the Apostle 8b-14a

The Book of the Resurrection of Jesus Christ by
Bartholomew the Apostle was mentioned above in the discussion of
the Questions of Bartholomew. Three Coptic recensions of the Book
of the Resurrection are known. Two of these are extant only in
fragments and the beginning of the more or less complete recension
is missing (four or five leaves according to the editor--Budge,
1913:xvii). Like the Questions of Bartholomew, the Book of the
Resurrection is usually treated as gospel literature. Since the
beginning of the work is missing, it is difficult to determine its
literary form with any precision. Much of the work is narrative
in the third person, but there are occasional shifts into the
first person when Bartholomew speaks. The manuscript edited by
Budge begins with brief reference to the crucifixion, burial and
resurrection of Jesus and goes on to describe Jesus' victory over
Hades. There are indications that a more detailed crucifixion
narrative was contained in the beginning of the document (Hennecke-
Schneemelcher: 1.505-506). In any case, the greater part of the
work by far deals with events after the resurrection. This fact
makes its designation as a gospel rather questionable.

There are no clear indications of date in the work.
James says that Coptic literature of this class is usually supposed to belong to the fifth and sixth centuries. He conjectures
that this document is of such a date, or at latest of the seventh
century, but he gives no arguments (1924:186). Schneemelcher
agrees with James' date for the present form of the work, but
thinks that at least some of the traditions on which it is based
go back to the third or fourth century (Hennecke-Schneemelcher:
1.508).

The Book of the Resurrection contains two brief apocalypses, 8b-14a and 17b-19b. The first of these belongs to Type Ic.
The second is an otherworldly journey and will be discussed below.
In 8b, there is a description of the Savior's ascent to heaven
followed by the sons of Adam whom he had redeemed from Hades.
Further description is given in 9a of his arrival with many angels
in the seventh heaven and his coronation by the Father. There
follow remarks of Bartholomew in the first person indicating that
he had seen these events. There is also a warning to Bartholomew's
son Thaddaeus to avoid letting the book come into the hands of any
unbeliever, heretic or impure person (9a-9b). This aside may be
an indication that the opening of the book characterized it as a
discourse of Bartholomew to his son. One cannot be sure of this
since the ending is in a third person narrative style.

Following these personal comments of Bartholomew is
further description of the enthronement of Christ (9b-10a). In 10a
we find the typical visionary formula "I saw," followed by a reference to the Savior at the right hand of the Father and a list of
angels and other heavenly beings. The description of the vision

continues with an account of the reconciliation of Adam and Eve with the Father (11a-11b). The vision continues with the arrival of Abraham, Isaac, Jacob, Job, Moses and Noah to greet Adam (13a). The vision closes with the remark that Adam was then stationed by God at the Gate of Life to salute the righteous men as they enter Jerusalem, the city of Christ, and Eve to greet the women (13b).

Bartholomew's remarks (9a) indicate that Christ had ordered Michael to enable Bartholomew to see these mysteries. Thus both Christ and Michael function as otherworldly mediators.

The expectation of personal afterlife is expressed in the statement that the righteous will shine brighter than the sun and will dwell in the [heavenly] Jerusalem (13a-13b).

The Resurr (Bart) 8b-14a manifests considerable interest in heavenly beings: the Seraphim (8b), Archangels, Cherubim, Seraphim, Powers, Dominions, the Twelve Virtues of the Holy Spirit, the twenty-four Elders, and the seven Aeons (10a), Michael (11a, 11b, 12b), the Powers and the Virgins (11b), and Raphael and six other angels of light who are also named (12a). The quotation of the various hymns implies an interest in the heavenly liturgy which may have been correlated with the liturgy of the author's community. Michael and all the angels are said to intercede for the children of Adam (12b).

Summary of Type I

The twelve works discussed so far all describe revelation mediated by an otherworldly being to a human recipient in the form of visions and auditions. These works are: Jacob's Ladder, Revelation, Apoc Peter, Hermas, Elchasai, Apoc Jn Theol, Test Lord 1: 1-14, 5 Ezra 2:42-48, Test Isaac 2-3a, Test Jacob 1-3a, Ques Bart and Resurr (Bart) 8b-14a.

Only Jacob's Ladder has *ex eventu* prophecy in the form of a review of history. The review of history is part of the eschatological pattern in that it leads into the catastrophic events of the end. Ques Bart refers to past, primordial events which have significance for the present.

Seven of these works express cosmic eschatology as well as personal eschatology: Jacob's Ladder, Revelation, Apoc Peter, Hermas, Elchasai, Apoc Jn Theol, and Test Lord 1:1-14. The other five contain personal eschatology only: 5 Ezra 2:42-48, Test Isaac 2-3a, Test Jacob 1-3a, Ques Bart, and Resurr (Bart) 8b-14a. Thus, the non-journey type of apocalypse is used more frequently to express expectations regarding the future of the world, although it is often used to express purely personal hopes as well.

There are notable differences between the Christian apocalypses of the non-journey type and the corresponding Jewish ones. *All* the Jewish apocalypses of this type have *both* a review of history *and* cosmic eschatology as well as personal eschatology. Many of the Jewish texts have a prominent interest in the contemporary politics. Revelation is the only Christian text of this type where such an interest is clearly present.

Type II: Otherworldly Journey

The texts of this group have the same basic characteristics as those of Type I: (1) heavenly or mysterious revelation which is mediated by an otherworldly being, (2) an eschatological pattern usually involving crisis, judgment or destruction and salvation, and (3) an emphasis on otherworldly realities. The distinguishing mark of this group is that the primary manner in which the revelation is mediated is the heavenly or otherworldly journey rather than the more simple modes of vision and audition.

Type IIb: Otherworldly Journeys with Cosmic and/or Political Eschatology

Four early Christian apocalypses belong to this type: Asc Isa 6-11, Apoc Paul, Apoc Esdras and Apoc Mary.

Ascension of Isaiah 6-11

The Ascension of Isaiah is extant in an Ethiopic version, two recensions of the Latin version, in a Slavonic recension, and in Coptic and Greek fragments. There is also a related Greek legend. The most debated issue has been the question of unity. Burkitt and Burch (see Flemming-Duensing, 643) have argued that Asc Isa is a unified composition and that the original work was substantially identical with the extant Ethiopic version. Most other commentators have taken the position that Asc Isa is a compilation of two or more documents. There are two main arguments against unity: (1) one Latin recension and the Slavonic version contain only the vision or ascension of Isaiah (roughly chaps. 6-11 of the Ethiopic) and (2) there are certain anomalies in the present text which seem to be the result of editing. The address of Isaiah to Hezekiah in 4:1 is awkwardly placed given the announcement of Hezekiah's death in 2:1. The account of Isaiah's martyrdom in chapter 5 is the logical continuation of his arrest in 3:12. It is also odd that the announcement (1:1-4) that Hezekiah would tell his son about his own vision is not fulfilled in the work. It is thus probable that there were originally two independent documents: a Christian vision or ascension of Isaiah corresponding more or less to chapters 6-11 of the Ethiopic (there is disagreement on whether 11:2-22 is original or not) and a martyrdom of Isaiah. It is difficult to determine whether the martyrdom was originally Jewish or Christian. It is generally agreed that chapters 2:1-3:12 and 5:2-14 belonged to the legend of the martyrdom. How much, if any, of chapter 1 belonged to it is disputed. The rest of the material (chap. 4; 5:1, 15-16; parts of chap. 1) is Christian and was either composed or added from other sources at the time the legend and the vision were combined. It is not obvious that 3:13-31 and 4:1-18 originally belonged together. Each passage is indirectly characterized as a vision (3:31; 4:19), but they are not mediated revelation and thus differ in a fundamental way from the visions of the works discussed above. They do contain eschatological material and so will be discussed below with related types of literature.

The independent Ascension of Isaiah (chaps. 6-11) contains no historical allusions to aid in determining its date. A *terminus ante quem* is provided by Epiphanius' reference to *to anabatikon Hēsaiou* (*Haer.* 40.2). Charles assigned the work to the end of the first century (xlv) and Flemming-Duensing to the second century (643), but there is no compelling reason to favor either position over the other.

Chapter 6 begins with the statement that Isaiah and his son went to Hezekiah in Jerusalem in the twentieth year of the king's reign. The narrative continues in the third person describing Isaiah holding forth to Hezekiah, the princes of Israel, the eunuchs, the king's councillors, and forty prophets. Isaiah then fell into a trance "for he saw a vision" (6:12). The narrative portion concludes by saying that afterward Isaiah communicated his vision to Hezekiah, to his (Isaiah's) son and to the other prophets. In 7:2 a first person account begins. The introductory formula "I saw" is used frequently in the account to introduce descriptions of the regions and beings seen by the prophet on his journey (7:9, 14 and passim). The first vision described is of "a sublime angel" (7:2). Isaiah asks the angel who he is and a short dialogue follows (7:3-8). During the journey there are more such dialogues in which the angel explains to Isaiah what he is seeing (7:16-17, 25-27 and passim). The audition of angelic voices and hymns and even the words of the Most High are reported (10:1-3, 6-16).

The climax of the revelation imparted to Isaiah is an *ex eventu* prophecy of the descent, mission and ascent of Christ, "the Beloved" (9:12-18; 10:7-11:33). In the recensions which have 11:2-22, the account of the descent of the Beloved is expanded with legendary material about his birth and infancy. The descent of the Beloved is the eschatological turning point which will be followed by the destruction of the world (10:12; 11:37). The mission of the Beloved includes making "spoil of the angel of death" (9:16) and the judgment and destruction of Satan and his angels (7:12; 10:12). The only form of salvation mentioned is personal immortality (7:23; 9:7-9, 24-26).

The emphasis on otherworldly realities is highlighted by the heavenly journey motif. The journey provides opportunity for descriptions of the seven heavens, the different kinds of angels, thrones and praises in each of the heavens, and particularly the inhabitants of the seventh heaven. In the present time it is the wicked angel Sammael and the angels of the firmament who determine events on earth; the strife on earth reflects the strife among the angels (7:9-12). There is also mention of the heavenly books in which human deeds are recorded (9:19-23).

The Apocalypse of Paul

The oldest and best witness to the text of the Apocalypse of Paul is a Latin manuscript published by James (1893). There are a number of other Latin recensions, a summarizing and interpolated Greek text, as well as Coptic, Syriac, Armenian and Slavonic versions. The Apoc Paul seems to have been the most popular and widespread of the Christian apocryphal apocalypses.

At the beginning of the work (in the Syriac version at the end), the story of its own discovery is given in the third person. This account mentions the names of the current consuls and James' calculation of the date is 388 CE. The present form of the book thus can be dated to the period immediately following that date. The many doublets show that the author made use of earlier, overlapping materials. Origen apparently knew an Apocalypse of Paul and it may have been an earlier form of this work (Duensing: 755). Casey (28) argued that the work, apart from the secondary story of its discovery, dates to 240-250. His arguments are the mention of an Apoc Paul by Origen and the fact that the work does not reflect the great persecutions of Decius, Valerian and Diocletian nor the doctrinal controversies of the fourth century. He also noted that the type of monastic life reflected in the work was already common in Origen's time.

The *incipit* of the work characterizes it as "the revelation of the holy apostle Paul" and alludes to 2 Cor 12:2-4. The result is that the entire work is designated as the revelation Paul received on his journey to the third heaven.

The overall framework of chapters 3-10 is an address of Paul to "this people," which he is instructed by the Lord to deliver. Chapters 4-6 comprise a series of dialogues between God and the various natural elements who complain about human sin. Chapters 8-10 contain two dialogues. One is between God and the angels from those who have renounced the world; the other between God and the angels from sinners.

The greater portion of the work (chaps. 11-51) is an account of Paul's otherworldly journey. On this journey, an angel served as his guide and interpreter (11, 19, 21, 22 and passim).

Apoc Paul contains no systematic review of history, but there is a prominent interest in retelling the stories of certain figures of the past, probably for a hortatory purpose. The story of Jesus' passion is retold in such a way as to exhort to repentance (44). The brief reference to the sufferings of the prophets and others has the same function (44). The story of Adam and Eve's sin (45), the legendary deaths of Isaiah, Jeremiah, Ezekiel, the stories of Lot, Job and others (49-51) have similar functions.

Personal afterlife is presupposed in the Apoc Paul, which means judgment and punishment immediately after death for sinners (15-18, 31-42). The great day of judgment is still expected (end of 16, end of 18) and the destruction of the world (21). Salvation will include a new earth, the land of promise which will come down from heaven to replace the old (21-22). A general resurrection is expected (14, 15). Until the general resurrection, the righteous will rejoice in Paradise (14) or in the city of Christ (22-30).

Interest in otherworldly realities is very pronounced in Apoc Paul. The heavenly journey format provides the opportunity for extensive descriptions of otherworldly regions.

There is also a clear interest in otherworldly beings. According to chapter 7, angels protect each human being and each people and report all human deeds to God at the beginning of every day and night (see also chaps. 9-10). As in Asc Isa 7:9-12, the idea is expressed in chapter 11 that human behavior reflects the dynamics and values of lower heavenly beings who dwell under the firmament of heaven. It is thought that two groups of angels (good and bad) meet each soul at the time of death; one or the other group takes charge of the soul depending on its deeds (11-12). The punishments are executed on sinners by angels (16, 34). Michael is called the angel of the covenant (14, 43-44).

Emphasis on heaven is also expressed in the idea that every human deed is recorded in a heavenly book (17) and that the names of all the righteous are listed on heavenly tablets (19). Earthly worship is thought to reflect the liturgy of the seventh heaven (29).

The Apocalypse of Esdras

The Apocalypse of Esdras was edited by Tischendorf from one Paris manuscript in 1866. Denis (91) indicated that a second manuscript had become known. Otto Wahl (1977) has produced a new critical edition based on the two manuscripts and Tischendorf's text. There are Latin, Armenian and Ethiopic documents which are either recensions of the Apoc Esdras or closely related works. The Apoc Esdras is literarily independent of 4, 5 and 6 Ezra except for the fact that the later work (Apoc Esdras) is modeled to some extent on 4 Ezra. The same pseudonym is used, the dialogue element is imitated and some of the same theological motifs appear. The Latin version of Apoc Esdras (Visio beati Esdrae) was edited by Mercati in 1901. There is another Latin work attributed to Ezra and published in the same volume which is of a quite different nature (Revelatio quae facta est Esdrae et filiis Istrahel de qualitatibus anni); it is an astrological work of some sort (Denis: 94-95).

In its present form, Apoc Esdras is clearly Christian. James (1893:113) remarks that the work is "Byzantine" in character and that any more precise date is difficult to assign. He suggests the ninth century. Batiffol dated the work in its present form to the fifth-eighth centuries. Riessler (1273) assumes that the present work is an interpolated version of an originally Jewish composition. Denis (92-93) thinks that the Jewish portions of the work could be nearly as old as 4 Ezra. Müller (88-90) takes a position similar to Riessler's. His main argument is that the particularly Christian elements of the work can be shown to be interpolations because of the literary inconsistencies and sudden shifts in the work. It is certainly true that there are such literary problems in Apoc Esdras. It is not at all obvious, however, that they were introduced by a combination of Jewish passages on the one hand with Christian ones on the other. For example, one of the most striking inconsistencies is a constant movement from the first person (Ezra speaking) to the third (first person in 1:2-9; 2:1-2; 4:7-27; 5:2-10, 16-17; 5:21-6:3; 7:2-3; elsewhere, the third person is used). There are Christian elements in both groups of passages (for example, 1:6 and 1:19). It is quite probable that Apoc Esdras contains several literary stages, but these have not yet been sorted out convincingly.

The work is introduced as the discourse and revelation of Ezra the holy prophet (1:1). The date of his experiences is given (1:2) as the thirtieth year (probably after the destruction of Jerusalem; see 2 Esdras 3:1) and the twenty-second of the month (the month is not named).

Prior to the otherworldly journey of Ezra, he experienced a vision which is only summarily reported: "I saw the secrets of God and his angels" (1:5). Most of the revelation given to Ezra is mediated in the context of his otherworldly journey. The first stage of the journey is to the first heaven (1:7). Here Ezra sees an army of angels, places of punishment, Michael, Gabriel and all the apostles (see above). It is also here that he has the first two of his dialogues with God. Next Ezra travels downward to Tartarus (4:8) where he sees various types of sinners being punished and hears their cries. Here the third dialogue between Ezra and God takes place; it concerns the Antichrist (4:28-5:1). According to 5:7, Ezra is removed by a cloud to heaven. He sees places of punishment here, presumably similar to those mentioned in 1:7. The fourth dialogue of Ezra with God takes place here

(5:12-19). In 5:21, Ezra is taken to "the East" (presumably Paradise, see 5:20). There he sees the tree of life, Enoch, Elijah, Moses, Peter, Paul, Luke, Matthew, all the just and the patriarchs. He also sees further punishments of sinners. Surprisingly, we read in 5:27 that he was led deeper into Tartarus. This confusion may be due to the joining of sources. The return of Ezra to earth is not described.

On his journey, Ezra is guided by angels (1:7). Michael, Gabriel and thirty-four other angels take him into Tartarus (4:7). The angels mediate revelation to him in dialogue form in the course of the journey.

There is no review of history in Apoc Esdras, but certain events of the past are recalled: the creation of Adam and the sin of Adam and Eve (2:10-16), the destruction of Sodom and Gomorrah (2:19), the destruction of Jerusalem (2:22) and the promise of God to Abraham (3:10). The usual eschatological woes are expected (3:11-14), including the activity of the eschatological adversary (3:15; 4:25-37, 43). The punishment of individual sinners in the afterlife is a major theme (1:7-11, 24; 4:9-24; 5:2-5, 8-11, 23-28). The judgment and destruction of the world is expected (2:27-30; 3:3, 6; 4:38-39). The expected salvation includes a general resurrection (4:36) and personal afterlife (1:9, 12, 14; 6:17, 21; 7:2-3).

The Apocalypse of the Virgin Mary

The Apocalypse or Vision of the Virgin Mary is extant only in Ethiopic. The editor of the text was of the opinion that the original language was Greek and that the Ethiopic is a translation of the Arabic version (which, he thought, was based upon the Greek; Chaine: 43).

Much of this Apoc Mary is similar to certain portions of the Apoc Paul in content and sometimes also in wording. The similarities are all with passages in Apoc Paul 13-44. A tentative *terminus post quem* of 388 CE may be set on the basis of this literary relationship. The possibility must be left open for the moment that the author of the Apoc Mary knew an earlier form of the Apoc Paul than that known today. Schneemelcher suggested a seventh century or later date, but gave no evidence to support his suggestion (Hennecke-Schneemelcher: 2.754).

Apoc Mary begins with an invocation of the Father, the Son, the Holy Spirit and the Virgin Mary. The work proper is then introduced as a treatise by John, the son of Zebedee. He is quoted and he quotes Mary. The greater portion of the work is the first person account of Mary concerning her otherworldly journey. The first stage of the otherworldly journey is the epiphany of Christ to his mother (Chaine, Latin translation: p. 45, line 19). A dialogue between the two follows immediately (45,19-46,3). The dialogue form is a major mode of revelation through the work (48,22-25; 49,19-26; 51,23-52,3 and passim).

The visionary and auditory modes of revelation are encompassed by the framework of the otherworldly journey. The journey begins on Golgotha at midday on the sixth day of the week. Clouds transport Mary above the third heaven (45,16-19). From there she travels to Paradise (51,5-10) and then is led from place to place within Paradise (52,4, 18, 31; 53,15; 56,31-34 and passim). Next she is led to the West, to the ends of heaven and earth where sinners are punished (61,19-20). Her return to earth is not described. Her son, the exalted Christ, is her guide and interpreter on this journey.

Personal afterlife for sinners is expected to involve punishments. The specific punishments for particular sins are described (61,19-67,35). The judgment of the entire world on the last day is mentioned (47,32-33). A general resurrection is apparently expected (47,33-34; 50,32-33). After death the just soul is taken by angels of light to heaven and given a garment of light. It then dwells with Abraham in Paradise (47,9-32; 51,5-7). There are special rewards for particular virtues: some will dwell in the city of Paradise (52,11-16), others at the river of wine, of honey or of milk (52,18-53,23). Various other places of rest are described (55,3-5; 56,31-35; 57,12-16; 58,3-9) including the heavenly Jerusalem with its temple (59,11-19) and the city of the Lord (60,1-15).

These four apocalypses constitute Type IIb of the corpus of early Christian apocalypses. They are distinguished by the combination of an otherworldly journey with cosmic (as well as personal) eschatology. One text in this group expects both the destruction of the world and a cosmic renewal--Apoc Paul. The other three texts predict cosmic destruction but no renewal--Asc Isa 6-11, Apoc Esdras and Apoc Mary.

Type IIc: Apocalypses with An Otherworldly Journey and Only Personal Eschatology

Eight early Christian apocalypses belong to this type: Test Isaac 5-6, Test Jacob 5, Zosimus, Apoc Moth God, Apoc James, Myst John, Resurr (Bart) 17b-19b and Apoc Sedrach.

Testament of Isaac 5-6

Another portion of the Testament of Isaac (2-3a) was discussed above as an example of an apocalypse of Type I. The second small apocalypse of this work (5-6) is an account of Isaac's journey to heaven before his death.

The only eschatological element present is the expectation of personal afterlife. The wicked are punished by wild beasts and fire after death (5). The righteous enjoy eternal life in heaven, joy and light (6). Interest in otherworldly realities is shown in the rather detailed description of the punishments of sinners; the river of fire and several pits are described where sinners are tortured. Several otherworldly beings are mentioned: Abtelmoluchos, who presides over punishments (5), the Cherubim, Seraphim, Michael and other angels (6).

Testament of Jacob 5

Another portion of the Testament of Jacob (1-3a) was discussed above as an example of an apocalypse of Type I. Like Test Isaac, Test Jacob also contains a second brief apocalypse, the account of Jacob's journey to heaven before his death (5). The heavenly journey in Test Jacob comprises a relatively smaller portion of the entire work than is the case in Test Isaac.

As in Test Isaac 5-6, the patriarch is shown both the punishments of sinners and the rewards of the righteous in their personal afterlives. Interest in otherworldly beings is expressed in the description of those who torment sinners in the next world. No description of the seer's return to earth is given.

The Story of Zosimus

The story of Zosimus is extant in Greek, in Syriac (under the title The Legend of the Sons of Jonadab, Son of Rechab, and the Blessed Isles), in Ethiopic (The History of the Blessed Men Who Lived in the Days of Jeremiah the Prophet), Slavonic and Arabic. This group of related traditions is quite distinct from the Visions of Zosimus, which is an encyclopaedic treatise on alchemy attributed to Zosimus of Panopolis (third century CE; see Denis: 95). The different versions of the narrative vary considerably; the discussion of literary form and content below is based on the Greek text as published by James (1893).

According to Nau (1898:264), the form of the work common to all the Syriac manuscripts could not be earlier than the fifth century, because it speaks with insistence of the holy Trinity, the blessed virgin Mary as mother of God, and of hierarchies of angels and archangels. According to James (1893:93-95), the present form of the Greek text dates to the fifth or sixth century, but behind that text stands an earlier work, perhaps a Jewish apocalypse. That work, or at least traditions also found in it, existed prior to 250 CE, since such traditions are found in Commodian.

The work refers to itself as a testament in chapter 21, but its only feature similar to the testament form is the fact that Zosimus' death is described near the end. The issue is complicated by indications of several literary stages in the work. The last chapter (22) is in the first person, but written by someone other than Zosimus, who calls himself "one of those who (are) in the desert." The last sentence of chapter 21 (which contains the testament reference) and chapter 1 are in the third person. Chapters 2-21a comprise a first person narrative of Zosimus. The minimal resemblance to the testament form and the occurrence of the self-designation as testament in a third person portion of the work make it unlikely that this designation is original.

The journey format includes of course a visionary element--what the traveler saw on his journey. The typical introductory formula of a vision, "I saw," occurs only occasionally. This formula introduces the first account of what Zosimus saw when he entered the land of the blessed ones--a naked man sitting there (4). The formula is also used to introduce the man's manifestation to Zosimus of the glory of his face (like that of an angel) and of his true clothing (5). A number of epiphanies are recounted in a rather matter-of-fact manner--before, during and after the otherworldly journey. Prior to the journey, the epiphany of an angel to Zosimus is described (1). Two angels appear to Zosimus and the blessed ones to assure the blessed ones that their visitor was sent by God and thus not to be feared (5). An angel appears to Zosimus to assist him in the last stage of his return journey (18). After his return Satan appears to Zosimus, once alone (19) and once with 360,000 demons (20). After their departure, the angel who assisted Zosimus on his return journey reappears to him (20).

The major way in which revelation is mediated in this work is by Zosimus' miraculous journey to another world, the land of the blessed ones. The climax of the journey occurs when the blessed ones write down for Zosimus, with their fingernails on stone tablets, the story of how they came to the blessed land (7-9), how they live there and their manner of death (10-15). Zosimus thus takes back with him a "heavenly book" which is intended to be a model for life in this world (this is what disturbs Satan--19).

Zosimus' journey is made possible by divine power acting through a camel (2, 17), a storm wind (2, 17), and two trees (3, 16). An angel is his guide on the last stage of the journey (18--see above). The transcendent character of the journey and of the mysterious land is indicated by the blessings spoken over Zosimus by the storm wind, the camel (17) and the angel (18) on his return journey. Even more strikingly, the blessed land is surrounded by a river which no flying creature, no wind can cross. The sun cannot pass over it; not even "the one who tempts in this world" is able to cross this river (2).

There is no reason to think that the name Zosimus was used pseudonymously. No specific date, time nor place, other than the desert, is given for the initial angelic epiphany nor the starting point of the journey.

Two events of the past are explicitly recalled. One is the sin and fall of Adam and Eve which functions as a negative example for the righteous living in the present (6, 19). The other is the past history of the blessed ones. They, the Rechabites, alone heeded Jeremiah's call to repentance and were rewarded by removal to this Paradise-like place (7-9). The eschatological crisis has become an on-going struggle with Satan ("the tempter"--chap. 2, see above; see also chaps. 4, 6, 18-20, 21a). There is a brief reference to the end (*to telos*), when human beings from the world would join the Rechabites in the blessed land (5). This reference probably implies the destruction of the world, but this is not certain. The victory over Satan is not described as a once-and-for-all event of the future to be executed by God, Christ or their angels. Rather, it is described as an accomplishment of Zosimus with heavenly assistance (18a, 20b). Zosimus says that he himself sent the devil (*ho diabolos*) and the demons with him into the eternal fire (20). Such a victory is theoretically possible for all, especially those who live ascetically in the desert (21a). Personal afterlife is presupposed.

The Apocalypse of the Holy Mother of God concerning the Punishments

The Apocalypse of the Holy Mother of God concerning the Punishments is an account of the otherworldly journey of the mother of Christ, on which she sees the places of punishment for sinners after death. The work is extant in Greek, Slavonic and Ethiopic and is distinct from the Apocalypse or Vision of the Virgin Mary, extant only in Ethiopic. The latter was discussed above. James (1893) simply printed the oldest Greek manuscript of the Apoc Moth God known to him. Many other Greek manuscripts are available (three of which were mentioned and quoted by Tischendorf), but they have not yet been compared. According to a Venice manuscript quoted by Tischendorf, the seer also viewed the pious ones in Paradise, but Tischendorf (xxix) indicated that the passage dealing with Paradise is very brief and in the nature of an appendix. The work probably treated only the places of punishment originally.

The only firm *terminus ante quem* is provided by the date of the Greek manuscript edited by James, eleventh-twelfth century (109). In James' opinion, Apoc Esdras is dependent on this work (113), but the Apoc Esdras is also very difficult to date. The question of a *terminus post quem* needs to be investigated further. James suggested that the Apoc Moth God is literarily dependent on the Apoc Peter and the Apoc Paul, and that the very idea of attributing an apocalypse to the Mother of Christ only arose in connection with the development of the Assumption legend and literature (111-112).

The overall framework of the Apoc Mother God is in the third person. The opening scene is the Mount of Olives. The time is not stated, but it gradually becomes clear that it is after the resurrection of Christ. Revelation is mediated in a variety of ways. There is a pronounced visionary element: a vision of those being punished in Hades (3), of a great darkness and the souls there (4) and of various methods of punishment (13, 14, 15 and passim). The initial revelatory experience is an epiphany of Michael the archangel (1). The dialogue form is used extensively; most often involving the Mother of God and Michael (2, 3, 4, 5-8 and passim). Near the end is a dialogue between the Theotokos and God the Father, in which she intercedes for Christian sinners, her children (26-28). Much of the work is devoted to the Theotokos' otherworldly journey. She is taken first of all to the South where certain sinners are punished (5-10), then to the West (11-21) and to the regions of Paradise on the left (22-25) where other sinners are punished. Finally, she is taken to the height of heaven (26-30).

The only eschatological elements in this work are the expectations of eternal punishment for the wicked and salvation for the just. Most of the work is devoted to the description of particular punishments related to particular sins (3, 4, 5, 9, 10, 13 and passim). The expectation of a general resurrection is briefly alluded to (1). The Theotokos is told that she will rest in Paradise (25). Presumably other righteous individuals will enjoy the same afterlife.

The Apocalypse of James, the Brother of the Lord

The Apocalypse of James, the Brother of the Lord is quite distinct from the two Apocalypses of James discovered at Nag Hammadi. It has not survived as an independent work, but is contained in a Coptic Encomium on St. John the Baptist attributed to St. John Chrysostom. The date is uncertain, but must be prior to 985 CE, the date of the Coptic manuscript in which it is contained (Budge, 1913:li). The passage in question is quoted by the author of the encomium from an old document which he says he found in the library in Jerusalem. The title of the document is not given. The title used above is inferred from the fact that the relevant passage (10a-16b) is a first person account of James, the brother of the Lord (see 11b; Budge apparently translated "John" by mistake; the Coptic has *Iakkōbos*).

James says that the apostles were gathered on the Mount of Olives with the Savior after his resurrection from the dead. The overall framework of the mediated revelation is a heavenly journey. During the journey the apostles as a group (13b) and certain individual apostles (14b, 15b) engage the Savior in dialogue. The apostles are transported through the seven heavens, but are allowed to enter only the third. The Savior is the mediator of revelation; he transports the apostles and interprets what they see. James, the brother of the Lord, is the pseudonymous recipient of revelation.

Personal afterlife is presupposed. The wicked go to Amente (the underworld) after death and punishment, which includes passing through a river of fire (12b, 13a). In the third heaven the apostles are shown the good things prepared as rewards for the just; they are also shown John the Baptist and his parents who dwell there. Those who commemorate John the Baptist will be transported by him after death across the river of fire in a golden boat, taken by him to the third heaven, arrayed in celestial apparel and will dwell there in the Paradise of the third heaven as members of Christ's kingdom (12a-13a, 14a-15a).

The dominant concern in this passage is to encourage the veneration of John the Baptist. The emphasis is on the rewards promised to those who engage in such veneration. Given the nature of the document in which this passage occurs, it is not improbable that the reference to an ancient document from Jerusalem is a literary device employed by the author of the encomium to enhance the prestige of John the Baptist.

The Mysteries of St. John the Apostle and Holy Virgin

The Mysteries of St. John the Apostle and Holy Virgin is an account of the heavenly journey of John the beloved disciple and the revelation which he received on that occasion. The work is extant only in Coptic in a manuscript published by Budge (1913), which also contains the life and conversation of Pisentius, a bishop and anchorite. The manuscript was written in 1006 CE (Budge: xxxii). There is no other clear indication of date. The work is distinctive in its extensive adaptation of Egyptian mythology (Budge: lxvii-lxx) and in its conception of a direct relationship between heavenly beings and their activities, on the one hand, and the fertility of the earth, on the other.

Near the beginning of the work, the epiphany of an angelic being ("a Cherubim") is described (1b-2a). What John sees on his journey is usually introduced with the formula "I saw" (2b and passim). These descriptions are followed by dialogues in which the visions are explained (2b and passim). John travels to the first (2b) and the seventh heavens (6b) and to Paradise (9b). The work opens with Christ's return to the Mount of Olives after his resurrection. He miraculously (by a cloud) gathers the apostles to himself there. Christ (with the Father's permission) is the ultimate mediator of revelation. It is the Cherubim who actually takes John on his journey and serves as his interpreter (1b, 2b). John the beloved disciple is the pseudonymous recipient of revelation (1a-1b).

There is no systematic review of history in Myst John, but there are references to the past. The account of the primordiality or pre-existence of water reinforces its sacrality (3b-4a). The story of the heavenly or even divine origin of wheat is told: it is created by heavenly beings for Adam after his expulsion from Paradise; he is taught how to cultivate it so that he would not starve (4a-6b). The story of the fall of Adam, which contains a number of aetiological elements, is told (10a-13b) and the story of Hezekiah turning his face to the wall is explained (13b-14b). There is no clear evidence that a future crisis is expected; there is instead the idea of an ongoing conflict between

Michael and the angel of wrath. The outcome of each phase of this conflict determines whether fertility or famine comes upon the earth (8b-9b). Personal afterlife is presupposed. When people die, each one is taken to the place of which he is worthy (18b).

Interest in otherworldly regions is expressed in the brief description of the first heaven (2b). John is told how earth and heaven are supported (16a) and about the stars (19a-19b). The main emphasis of the Myst John is on heavenly beings who affect human life on earth. Twelve "men" and Michael in the first heaven control the process whereby the earth brings forth fruit. These are the twelve rulers of the worlds of light and each rules for one year at a time (2b-3a). The Father controls the time and amount of the water's coming upon the earth. The angels pray that he will allow the water to flow (3a-3b). Michael and the angels of the seventh heaven cause the dew to fall on earth (6b-7a). Angels regulate the wind, dew and fertility (15a-15b), the passing of the hours of the day and the sunset (16a-16b).

The Book of the Resurrection (Bartholomew) 17b-19b

Another portion of the Book of the Resurrection of Jesus Christ by Bartholomew the Apostle (8b-14a) was discussed above as an example of an apocalypse characterized by mediated heavenly revelation with no heavenly journey (Type I). The second apocalyptic passage of this work (17b-19b) is an account of the death, otherworldly journey, and finally resurrection of Siophanes, the son of Thomas the Apostle. Although the account of Siophanes' experiences involves his death, the accounts of otherworldly journeys are usually in a rather realistic mode, so that this peculiarity is less significant than might be expected. The journey passes through a river of fire (18a-18b) into heaven, where the seer must be immersed three times in Lake Acherusia. He then enters Paradise and is taken to the "tabernacle of the Father" (18b). Michael is the seer's guide and interpreter on the journey (18b-19a). Siophanes is the human recipient of the revelatory experience, as already noted. He may be a fictitious character, but there is no reason to conclude that the name of some well-known figure is being used pseudonymously.

The only eschatological element in this document is the expectation of personal afterlife. Siophanes' fate is typical of a righteous person after death: he is led through various trials to heaven by Michael. The souls of the righteous will dwell in the Paradise of heavenly life (18a-18b). The emphasis in the document is on the special rewards (thrones, crowns, robes) of the Twelve Apostles in Paradise (18b-19a).

The Apocalypse of Sedrach

The Apocalypse of Sedrach is a brief work recounting the heavenly journey of the seer, his dialogues with God and his death. The work is known to be extant only in a single Greek manuscript dating to the fifteenth century and published by James (1893:127-137). Opinions have varied widely on the date, unity and original provenance (Jewish or Christian) of the work. Weinel thought the work was of medieval origin because of the late form of Greek in which the manuscript is written (1923:158-159). James (127) believed that the Apoc Sedrach was older than the Apoc Paul. Apoc Sedrach is clearly Christian in its present form. A number of scholars have concluded that the work was originally Jewish (Denis: 98-99). Apoc Sedrach is similar to 4 Ezra in its concern for theodicy. In fact, this theme is the dominant interest of the work. It shares with the Testament of Abraham the motif of the seer's refusal to die.

Apoc Sedrach opens with a preface identifying itself as the discourse of the holy Sedrach. A brief discourse on love follows (chap. 1). Sedrach then hears "a voice" and engages in a dialogue with it (2:1-3). A large portion of the work is devoted to Sedrach's dialogues with God (3:1-8:12; 10:1-6; 12:2-5; 14:3-16:8). The "voice" that Sedrach hears takes him to the third heaven (2:4). The intended identity of the seer is unclear. "Sedrach" could be a form of Esdras, the Greek form of the name of one of Daniel's companions, or a form of the name Sirach. The pseudonymous use of the name is probable, but uncertain.

The theodicy issue is raised in part by means of retelling of the story of Adam's sin (4:4-7:5). There is a brief allusion to the Antichrist (15:5). Punishment of the wicked after death and reward of the righteous are presupposed (16:5). When Sedrach resists death, he is told that he will live in Paradise after death (12:1). Presumably, the same destiny is presupposed for all the just. Sedrach prays to the archangel Michael for help and asks him to intercede for the world (14:1-2).

These eight apocalypses constitute Type IIc of the corpus of early Christian apocalypses. They are distinguished by the combination of the otherworldly journey with purely personal eschatology.

Summary of Type II

The twelve texts discussed in the preceding portion of this essay all describe revelation mediated by an otherworldly being to a human recipient by means of an otherworldly journey. These works are: Asc Isa 6-11, Apoc Paul, Apoc Esdras, Apoc Mary, Test Isaac 5-6, Test Jacob 5, Zosimus, Apoc Moth God, Apoc James, Myst John, Resurr (Bart) 17b-19b and Apoc Sedrach.

None of the Christian apocalypses of Type II contains a review of history. Asc Isa 6-11 is the only apocalypse of this group which has an *ex eventu* prophecy. The "prophecy" is of the descent, mission, and ascent of Christ (9-11). This "prediction" functions analogously to the reviews of history in the Jewish apocalypses. Just as the reviews of history in the Jewish apocalypses lead up to the catastrophes of the end, in Asc Isa 11:36-38, the mission of Christ and "the end of this world" will both take place "in the last generation."

The past is used in other ways in the otherworldly journeys also. Primordial and/or historical events are recounted to illuminate the present or for an hortatory purpose in Apoc Paul, Zosimus, Apoc Esdras, Myst John, and Apoc Sedrach.

Four of the otherworldly journeys express both cosmic and personal eschatology: Asc Isa 6-11, Apoc Paul, Apoc Esdras and Apoc Mary. The other eight express only personal eschatology: Test Isaac 5-6, Test Jacob 5, Zosimus, Apoc Moth God, Apoc James, Myst John, Resurr (Bart) 17b-19b and Apoc Sedrach. Thus, the otherworldly journey is used more frequently to express expectations regarding personal afterlife, although it can also be used as a vehicle for cosmic hopes as well.

Other Christian Apocalypses

A number of Christian apocalypses have been excluded from this study because of their late date. As was noted above, those works which are clearly later than 260 CE have been omitted. The various apocalypses of Daniel have been excluded because they contain historical allusions to events after that date. While they do make use of earlier tradition, it does not seem possible to isolate earlier documents used by them (see Denis: 309-314 and Berger: 6-7). The Evernew Tongue, an Irish apocalypse based on a lost Latin Apocalypse of Philip, has been excluded because of the probable late date of even the lost Latin document (see McNamara: 115-118).

Other works have been omitted because they do not fit the definition of an apocalypse adopted above. An apocalypse of Zechariah is mentioned among the apocrypha in the Catalogue of the Sixty Books, but so far only legendary material has been discovered attached to the name of Zechariah, who appears in these legends as the father of John the Baptist, not as the OT prophet (see Hennecke-Schneemelcher: 1.50, 52; 2.752-753 and James, 1920:74-75).

A "Revelation, called of Stephen" is condemned in the Gelasian Decree (Hennecke-Schneemelcher: 1.48). Sixtus Senensis says that the Apocalypse of Stephen, the first martyr, who was one of the seven deacons of the apostles, was prized by Manichaean heretics as Serapion witnesses. James could find no such reference in Serapion (1924:564). P. von Winterfeld suggested that the work mentioned in the Gelasian Decree is actually the account of the finding of the relics of Stephen contained in the letter of the priest Lucian (literature given in Hennecke-Schneemelcher: 2.754). I. Franko noted that the letter has little in it which might evoke a condemnation and published a Slavonic romance which he suggested reproduces the original beginning of Lucian's narrative. James gives a paraphrase of this romance (1924:565-568). This narrative contains a brief discourse of Stephen which is characterized by apocalyptic eschatology. It has the form of an oracle, however, rather than one of the forms of mediated revelation characteristic of apocalypses. The title "Apocalypse of Stephen" is thus as inappropriate for this narrative as for the letter of Lucian. Either the reference in the Gelasian Decree is the result of a misunderstanding, as von Winterfeld suggested, or the work referred to there has not yet been discovered.

Related Types

There are a number of texts which only partially fit the definition of an apocalypse given at the beginning of this essay and in the Introduction to this volume. In most cases, some form of eschatology is present, but the mediated character of the revelation is lacking. These texts are often included in studies of early Christian apocalypticism and thus are discussed briefly below. Most of the works in question are oracles.

Oracles

Mark 13 and Parallels

Mark 13 and parallels are often referred to as the Synoptic apocalypse(s). Formally speaking, Mark 13 is a discourse of Jesus with a dialogue-like introduction and a brief narrative setting. Whether this text and its parallels fit our definition of an apocalypse depends on whether Jesus is to be understood as an otherworldly mediator. The judgment one makes on this issue depends on one's understanding of the Christology of each Synoptic gospel. The decision not to include Mark 13 pars. with the apocalypses in this essay is based on the judgment that the Jesus of the Synoptic gospels, in the portions prior to the resurrection accounts, is not an otherworldly being in the same sense as the resurrected Christ and the angels are, who appear as mediators in the apocalypses. Thus, the role of Jesus in Mark 13 pars. is more appropriately defined as oracle-giver or prophet than as otherworldly mediator.

The eschatological crisis is expected in the form of persecution (vss. 9, 11-13) and other typical eschatological woes (vss. 6-23). Judgment, and possibly destruction, is described in terms of cosmic disturbances and the coming of the Son of Man (vss. 24-26). The gathering of the elect is a form of public salvation, which certainly implies individual afterlife (vs. 27). The importance of heavenly realities is expressed in the expectation that angels will have a role in the eschatological drama (vs. 27).

Sibylline Oracles 1-2

The first two books of the Sibylline Oracles constitute a unified collection of oracles, originally a Jewish composition which was later edited and expanded by a Christian. Geffcken (1902b:49) dated both the Jewish work and the Christian redaction to the third century CE. Kurfess (1941) dated the Jewish stage to about the turn of the era and the Christian stage prior to 150 CE. The *terminus ante quem* for the Jewish stage is about 300 CE, since Sib Or 7:7, 9-12 is apparently dependent on 1:183, 193-196 and Sib Or 7 was known to Lactantius. The last datable historical allusion in the Christian portion of the work is the destruction of Jerusalem.

The manner of revelation here is direct inspiration of the oracle-giver, the Sibyl. Like most early Christian apocalypses, this work is pseudonymous. Like some Jewish apocalypses and unlike the vast majority of Christian apocalypses, Sib Or 1-2 contains a systematic review of history. This review begins with creation (1:5-21) and the creation and fall of Adam and Eve (1:22-64). In the Jewish original, subsequent history was divided into ten generations. The accounts of the first five generations (including the flood) are in the past tense; that is, they are presented as explicit recollections of the past. The account of the sixth generation begins in the past tense (1:283, 288-290), but then shifts to the future (1:291-306). The account of the seventh generation (1:307-323) is also in the future tense. These two accounts seem to be examples of *ex eventu* prophecy. In the present form of the work, the account of the first seven generations is followed by a description of the incarnation, ministry and resurrection of Christ (1:324-386) and the destruction of Jerusalem (1:387-400). These accounts are also *ex eventu* prophecies. Then follows the eschatological account of the tenth generation (2:6-38).

The eschatological crisis involves persecution (2:46-47; a reference to martyrs) and woes similar to those of Mark 13 (2:190-192; see also 2:154-173, 194-195). The destruction of the world by fire is expected (2:196-213). Salvation involves the general resurrection of the dead (2:221-229), personal immortality (1:350; 2:46-53, 336-337) and cosmic transformation (2:319-329). Punishment of individuals in the next world is also expected (1: 350; 2:254-312). Angels are expected to have a role in the eschatological drama (2:214-219, 227-237, 242).

Sibylline Oracles 7

The *terminus ante quem* for Sib Or 7 is provided by Lactantius' reference to 7:123 in *Div. Inst.* 7.17.13. There are no conclusive data for fixing the date any more precisely. Geffcken (1902b:36) and Kurfess (1951:313-314) prefer the second century; Rzach (1923:2142) the third.

Like Sib Or 1-2, Sib Or 7 is a collection of Greek hexameter oracles, pseudonymously attributed to the Sibyl. Again, pseudonymity is the only characteristic relating to the manner of revelation which is shared with any of the Christian apocalypses.

The reference to testing by false prophets is probably to be understood as the eschatological crisis (132-138). The destruction of the world by fire is expected (118-125, 129-131). Salvation involves the transformation of the world (146-149). Personal afterlife is presupposed (126-129). The importance of the heavenly world is expressed in the reference to angels who oversee natural phenomena and watch over cities (33-35).

Sibylline Oracles 8

Book 8 of the Sibylline Oracles consists of two parts: 1-216 (Jewish originally, except for the pagan oracle in 131-138 and the Christian in 194-216), which dates to about 175 CE, and 217-500 (Christian). The second part was known to Lactantius.

Book 8 opens with a highly summarizing review of history (1-216). The review begins with the recollection of the tower of Babel incident (4-5) and of seven kingdoms of the past, from Egypt to Macedonia (5-8). The text then shifts to *ex eventu* prophecy with the prediction of the rise of the Italian kingdom (9). The rest of the review of history alternates between *ex eventu* and eschatological prophecy.

The eschatological crisis involves eschatological adversaries (Nero, 139-141 and a woman ruler, 194, 199-200) and typical woes (84-94, 174-175, 217). The destruction of the oppressor, Rome, is predicted (37-49, 73-80, 95-106, 123-130, 141-159) as well as the destruction of the world by fire (15-16, 225-226). Salvation involves resurrection of the dead (205, 227-228, 310-311, 314), eternal life (255, 409-411) and the transformation of the earth (424-428).

6 Ezra

The passage normally referred to as 6 Ezra is identical with 2 Esdras 15-16, another Christian addition to 4 Ezra. 6 Ezra is extant in Latin and, in fragmentary form, in Greek. There is no conclusive evidence of date. Myers (349-351), following Riessler, suggests the third century.

6 Ezra, for the most part, is a series of oracles of the Lord. The oracles in 15:28-33 and 34-45 have a visionary element, but they are not, strictly speaking, vision accounts. There is no otherworldly mediator and Ezra is not explicitly mentioned.

The eschatological crisis includes persecution (15:8b-10a, 21-22, 53, 56; 16:69-74) and other woes (15:19; 16:17-35). Judgment on the world (15:5-6, 27a), on oppressors (15:7-13, 20-22; 15:28-16:11) and on nations (15:15b-18) is expected, as well as the destruction of the world (15:14-15a, 23a; 16:12-16). Personal afterlife is not explicitly mentioned but is implied (16:68b-75).

The Apocalypse of Elijah

The so-called Apocalypse of Elijah is actually a series of oracles. The work is attributed to Elijah only in the title. No human recipient of the oracles is mentioned. The text itself is completely anonymous. Several hortatory passages occur among the oracles: 1:2-3, 8-11, 12-21 and 22-26. The rest of the work is extended narrative prediction in the future tense. Several oracles are explicitly characterized as oracles of the Lord (1:1, 8b-10, 16, 20; 2:1). One of these opens the work and, in effect, designates the entire book as the word of the Lord.

The Apoc Elijah (the commonly used title is adopted here for convenience) is extant only in Coptic, but was originally composed in Greek. The hypothesis that the Coptic is a translation from the Greek is supported by the existence of a brief Greek fragment of the work. The Apoc Elijah is clearly Christian in its present form. There is disagreement on whether the work is a Christian composition which made use of Jewish traditions (Schürer) or a Christian edition and expanded version of one or more Jewish documents (Bousset, Rosenstiehl). The passage which most clearly reflects an historical situation is 2:23-45, especially 32-45. The so-called "Assyrians" have control over Egypt and are led by a king from "the city of the sun." The "Assyrians" and the "Persians" are portrayed as enemies. Bousset argued that the only Syrian king who was notably an enemy of the Persians (that is, the Sasanians) was Odenath, ruler of Palmyra (d. 267 CE). Thus, he reasoned, the "city of the sun" refers to Palmyra rather than to Heliopolis. Bousset argued that this passage is a Jewish composition, because of its favorable attitude toward the Persians. Schürer also linked this passage to the period of Palmyrene domination of Egypt in the second half of the third century CE. Rosenstiehl (61-67) follows Bousset and Schürer on the date of the present form of Apoc Elijah. He argues (75-76), however, that the document was merely updated at that time, and that the greater part of the work is an Egyptian Jewish document with Essene characteristics written in the first century CE. The arguments adduced by Rosenstiehl for this first century source are not conclusive. There is also a Hebrew Apocalypse of Elijah which is related to the Coptic Apoc Elijah, especially in its physical description of the eschatological adversary. Its editor, Buttenwieser, dated it to 260 CE. Weinel was of the opinion that it was written in the third or fourth century CE (1923:166). The Hebrew Apoc Elijah is discussed in the essay by A. Saldarini in this volume.

The eschatological pattern occurs in Apoc Elijah in its full form. At least part of 2:2-45 is a review of history in the form of prediction. The eschatological crisis includes the threat of false teachers (1:12-14), typical eschatological woes (2:23-31, 37-38; 3:62-63), and the activity of the eschatological adversary (2:33-34; 3:1, 5-55, 64-80), which involves persecution and death for the saints (3:40-54, 79-80). Judgment and destruction are expected in various forms: the defeat of oppressors (the "Assyrian" king, all pagans and all the wicked--2:40), the defeat and destruction of the eschatological adversary by the returned Enoch and Elijah (3:91-96), the destruction of evil spirits (*diaboloi*-- 3:83) and the destruction of the world (1:2; 2:1; 3:97). The Lord will judge the angels (3:90). Salvation involves personal afterlife for the faithful (1:3, 8, 10) with the angels (3:99), resurrection (3:48), special honor in heaven for those killed by persecution (3:48-50), the rescue of the just from the wrath of the eschatological adversary and their translation to a kind of Paradise (3:56-61), cosmic transformation (3:98) and a thousand-year messianic reign (3:99). The judgment and punishment of individual sinners after death is also expected (1:11; 3:86-88, 90).

Heavenly realities have primarily a future role in Apoc Elijah; for example, angels will do battle against the eschatological adversary in the end time (3:81).

The Apocalypse of Thomas

The so-called Apocalypse of Thomas is extant in two Latin recensions, the shorter of which is generally accepted as more original (de Santos Otero: 798-799). There is no internal indication of date. The only guideline is the date of the oldest manuscript containing the shorter recension, namely, the Cod. Vindob. Palatinus 16. This manuscript dates to the fifth century.

Formally speaking, the work is a discourse of "the Son of God the Father," "the father of all spirits," "the Savior." These titles imply that the transcendent, exalted Christ is meant. The work is entirely in the first person (Christ speaking). The discourse is addressed to "Thomas," presumably the apostle. No indication is given of time or place. In fact, there is no narrative framework whatsoever. No response from Thomas is mentioned. Because of the lack of a narrative framework and thus of a description of the mediation of the revelation, the work is better classified as an oracle than as an apocalypse.

The discourse is completely devoted to eschatological matters and relates the signs of the end of the world which will take place during the seven last days. Salvation involves the resurrection of the righteous dead on the sixth day. Before that time their souls remain in Paradise. After their resurrection they will be like the angels and will be borne into the presence of the Father by angels. On the seventh day the righteous still living will be delivered from the world by angels. Apoc Thomas manifests a pronounced interest in angels throughout.

Testaments

The Testament of Adam and the Penitence of Adam

A Testament of Adam is extant in Ethiopic and Arabic versions. Two Syriac fragments, representing two Syriac recensions of the same work, have survived. In the Arabic manuscripts, the Testament of Adam is appended to the Book of the Cave of Treasures. A Greek work, related to one of the Syriac fragments and containing a liturgy of the hours of the day and night, is extant under the name of Apollonius [of Tyana]. A related form of the Greek work was known to George Cedrenus, a Byzantine chronicler. The way Cedrenus refers to this work implies that its title was the Apocalypse of Adam or the Penitence of Adam.

The Ethiopic and Arabic Testament of Adam begins abruptly with a discourse on prayer at fixed intervals. Human prayer is to be coordinated with the prayers of various parts of the natural realm and of the angels. The discourse is addressed to "my son," and in the next portion of the discourse it becomes clear that the speaker is Adam. This second portion is an *ex eventu* prophecy of the birth and ministry of Jesus and of the Flood. The discourse closes with references to the end of all things, the destruction of the world by fire, the sanctification of the earth, and God's presence on it. The work closes with the statement that Seth wrote down and sealed "this commandment." This work is most appropriately to be categorized as a testament. It is related to the apocalypses in its eschatology and in the interest in the heavenly world expressed in the opening portion of the discourse.

The work known to Cedrenus seems to have involved the manner of revelation characteristic of apocalypses: certain things were revealed to Adam through Uriel, the angel who is over repentance. According to Cedrenus, the work expressed an interest in present heavenly realities similar to that of the Arabic-Ethiopic Test Adam and contained predictions of the Watchers and the Flood. It is not clear whether the work also contained eschatological expectations; Cedrenus does not mention any. It is thus not clear whether the work known to Cedrenus ought to be categorized as an apocalypse.

The Testaments of Isaac and Jacob were discussed above. Although the controlling form of these works is the testament, they each contain two small apocalypses, one of each major type.

Individual Related Works

Didache 16

Didache 16, the so-called "little apocalypse" of the Didache, is instruction about the last things with a hortatory introduction (vss. 1-2). The passage is anonymous apart from the title of the work, which attributes its teaching to the Lord through the twelve apostles. Chapter 16 does not belong to the portion of the work which Audet dated to about 70 CE (9:1-11:2), but was probably added, with the rest of the work, not long afterwards--around 90 CE (Grant-Goodspeed: 13) to 100-110 CE (Vielhauer in Hennecke-Schneemelcher: 2.627).

The eschatological crisis is expected in the form of a fiery trial (vs. 5). In the Greek text of the Didache itself, the eschatological judgment is only implied in the reference to the coming of the Lord on the clouds. In the version of this passage which appears in Apost Const 7, it is said that he will judge the world deceiver, the devil, and requite each according to his deeds (Audet: 73). Salvation involves the resurrection of the saints (Did 16:6). The concept of resurrection of course includes the expectation of personal afterlife.

Ascension of Isaiah 3:13-4:18

The question of the unity of the Ascension of Isaiah was discussed above in the treatment of Asc Isa 6-11. The conclusion reached there was that Asc Isa is a composite work, based mainly on a narrative about the martyrdom of Isaiah (to which at least 2:1-3:12 and 5:2-14 belonged) and the clearly Christian account of Isaiah's heavenly journey (6-11). Chapter 3:13-31 and 4:1-18 are

Christian passages added, probably but not certainly, at the time
the two main documents were combined. It is not obvious that
3:13-31 and 4:1-18 were composed together.

Chapter 3:13-31 begins as a third person summary of the
revelation announced by Isaiah concerning the descent, death and
resurrection of Christ, the establishment of the church, and the
discord within the church during the last days. In verse 31 there
is a sudden shift to the first person and a reference to the preceding summary as "these my visions." Chapter 4:1-18 is an account
of the end of the world characterized by the appearance of the
eschatological adversary--Beliar in the form of Nero. This passage
is a simple oracle spoken by Isaiah in the first person to Hezekiah
and Jasub (4:1). Verse 19 refers indirectly to what precedes as a
vision. Since 4:1-18 makes use of the Nero legend, it most probably dates to the period from 68 to 120 CE.

The summary of the descent and ministry of Christ in
3:13-31 is a kind of review of history in the form of prediction,
though of course it is not an attempt to give a complete or systematic overview of history. The latter part of the passage describes various disorders in the church as a characteristic of the
"last days," thus probably as part of the eschatological crisis.

In 4:1-18 we find the eschatological crisis in the form
of persecution of the faithful by the eschatological adversary
(vss. 2-13). The defeat and punishment of Beliar and his hosts by
Christ and his angels is expected (vs. 14), as well as the destruction of the world and the evil angels (vs. 18). The defeat
of Beliar (and "his kings"--vs. 16) implies the defeat of Rome,
since Beliar is identified here with Nero. Thus the judgment has
political as well as spiritual meaning. Salvation involves the
resurrection of the faithful dead and the translation to heaven
of those still alive (vss. 15-17). The importance of heavenly
realities in the future is shown in the expectation that angels
will take part in the eschatological drama (vs. 14).

Neither of these passages has been included with the
apocalypses because they lack the characteristic of a mediated
manner of revelation. The references to these passages as visions
are superficial and possibly secondary.

The Apocalypse of John the Theologian attributed to John Chrysostom

The Apocalypse of John the Theologian attributed to John
Chrysostom or the second Greek apocryphal Apocalypse of St. John
is actually a simple dialogue between "John" and "the Lord." The
work contains no definite evidence of date. Nau, who published
the text, suggested a date from the sixth to the eighth century,
but gave no clear reasons for his suggestion.

Like most Christian revelation dialogues, it is not a
true dialogue but a series of questions and more extensive answers.
The stylized form of the opening statements of the answers is
similar to that of the first Greek apocryphal Apocalypse of St.
John. This second work is entirely in the third person, while the
other is in the first person. The second so-called Apocalypse of
St. John was not included among the apocalypses above because
there is no indication that heavenly, transcendent revelation is
involved. No indication of time or place is given; nor any hint

that Christ is in the role of heavenly mediator. He is not described as exalted in any way, nor is there any indication that the setting is after his resurrection.

The only element of the eschatological pattern present in this work (hereafter Ques Jn Theol) is the expectation of personal afterlife. Sinners will be punished after death like Judas in a river of fire (3). The righteous will be honored by the Lord before angels and men (6, 42) and will be in heaven after death (14). Interest in the heavenly world is expressed in the statement that fasting makes possible an ascent to the heavenly realm and allows life with the angels (12). This seems to refer to present mystical experience as much as to life after death.

Ques Jn Theol should not be categorized as an apocalypse because it lacks the characteristic of mediated, heavenly revelation. It does, however, show traces of apocalyptic eschatology and the interest in the heavenly world typical of apocalypses.

APOCALYPSES	1.1.1 Visions	1.1.2 Epiphanies	1.2.1 Discourse	1.2.2 Dialogue	1.3 Otherworldly journey	1.4 Writing	2. Otherworldly mediator	3.1 Pseudonymity	3.2 Disposition of recipient	3.3 Reaction of recipient	4.1 Theogony/cosmogony	4.2 Primordial events	5.1 Recollection of past	5.2 Ex eventu prophecy	6. Present salvation	7.1 Persecution	7.2 Upheavals	8.1 Judgment of wicked	8.2 of world	8.3 of otherworldly beings	9.1 Cosmic transformation	9.2.1 Resurrection	9.2.2 Afterlife	10.1 Otherworldly regions	10.2 Otherworldly beings	11. Paraenesis by mediator	12. Instructions to recipient	13. Narrative conclusion
Apoc Sedrach			x	x			x	x*	x		x				x	x						x		x				
Resurr(Bart) 17b-19b	x		x	x	x														x	x	x		x					x
Myst John	x	x	x	x		x	x	x	x		x	x				x*			x*	x	x						x	x
Apoc James	x		x	x	x		x	x	x	x					x					x	x	x						x
Apoc Moth God	x	x		x	x		x	x	x	x					x				x	x	x	x						
Zosimus	x	x	x	x	x	x	x		x	x	x	x						x	x			x	x	x				x
Test Jacob 5	x			x			x	x							x							x		x				x
Test Isaac 5-6	x		x	x			x	x		x					x							x	x	x				x
Apoc Mary	x	x	x	x			x	x	x	x					x	x			x	x	x	x						x
Apoc Esdras	x	x	x	x			x	x	x	x	x	x		x	x	x			x	x	x	x						x
Apoc Paul	x	x	x*	x	x		x	x			x	x			x	x		x	x	x	x	x					x*	x
Asc Isa 6-11	x			x	x		x	x		x			x				x	x		x	x	x					x	x
Resurr(Bart) 8b-14a	x						x	x		x										x		x						x
Ques Bart	x	x		x			x	x		x			x	x*			x		x			x	x	x	x	x		
Test Jacob 1-3a		x	x	x*			x	x					x	x*								x			x		x	x
Test Isaac 2-3a		x		x			x	x		x				x								x		x			x	
5 Ezra 2:42-48	x			x			x	x		x					x*							x		x			x	
Test Lord 1:1-14		x	x				x	x							x	x	x	x	x		x	x			x	x	x	
Apoc John Theol	x			x	x*	x	x	x	x	x						x	x	x	x	x	x	x			x		x	x
Elchasai	x				x	x									x*	x						x			x			x*
Hermas	x	x	x	x		x	x		x	x						x		x	x	x				x		x	x	x
Apoc Peter	x		x	x			x	x		x						x	x	x			x	x	x	x				x
Revelation	x	x	x	x*	x*	x	x		x						x	x	x	x	x	x	x	x	x	x	x	x	x	
Jacob's Ladder	x	x	x				x	x		x				x			x	x	x	x				x		x		

Asterisks indicate either (1) that an element is possibly, but not certainly, present, or (2) is implicit, or (3) is present in a very minor way.

Yarbro Collins: Early Christian Apocalypses 105

RELATED WORKS	1.1.1 Visions	1.1.2 Epiphanies	1.2.1 Discourse	1.2.2 Dialogue	1.3 Otherworldly journey	1.4 Writing	2. Otherworldly mediator	3.1 Pseudonymity	3.2 Disposition of recipient	3.3 Reaction of recipient	4.1 Theogony/cosmogony	4.2 Primordial events	5.1 Recollection of past	5.2 Ex eventu prophecy	6. Present salvation	7.1 Persecution	7.2 Upheavals	8.1 Judgment of wicked	8.2 of world	8.3 of otherworldly beings	9.1 Cosmic transformation	9.2.1 Resurrection	9.2.2 Afterlife	10.1 Otherworldly regions	10.2 Otherworldly beings	11. Paraenesis by mediator	12. Instructions to recipient	13. Narrative conclusion
Ques Jn Theol			×																			×			×	×		
Asc Isa 4:1-18															×		×	×	×			×	×		×			
Didache 16																×		×*				×	×					
Penit Adam				×	×				×															×				
Test Adam	×			×			×										×	×					×					×
Apoc Thomas	×						×*									×		×				×	×	×				
Apoc Elijah									×		×	×	×	×	×	×	×	×				×	×*					
6 Ezra																×	×	×	×				×*					
Sib Or 8				×							×	×			×	×	×			×	×	×						
Sib Or 7				×											×*		×			×	×	×						
Sib Or 1-2				×						×	×	×	×		×	×	×	×*			×	×	×		×			
Mark 13		×	×*													×	×	×*	×*				×		×			

Asterisks indicate either (1) that an element is possibly, but not certainly, present, or (2) is implicit, or (3) is present in a very minor way.

SELECT BIBLIOGRAPHY

GENERAL

Batiffol, P.
1926   "Apocalypses apocryphes." Pp. 756-767 in *Dictionnaire de la Bible*. Vol. 1. Ed. F. Vigouroux. Paris: Letouzey.

Berger, Klaus
1976   *Die griechische Daniel-Diegese: Eine altkirchliche Apokalypse*. Leiden: Brill.

Bousset, Wilhelm
1896   *The Antichrist Legend*. Trans. A. H. Keane. German ed., 1895. London: Hutchinson.

Charlesworth, J. H.
1976   *The Pseudepigrapha and Modern Research*. SBLSCS 7. Missoula: Scholars Press.

Denis, Albert M.
1970   *Introduction aux pseudépigraphes grecs d'Ancien Testament*. SVTP 1. Leiden: Brill.

Ernst, J.
1967   *Die eschatologischen Gegenspieler in den Schriften des Neuen Testaments*. Regensburg: Pustet.

Goodspeed, Edgar J.
1966   *A History of Early Christian Literature*. Rev. and enlarged by Robert M. Grant. Chicago: University of Chicago.

Hennecke, Edgar
1963, 1965   *New Testament Apocrypha*. 2 vols. Ed. W. Schneemelcher. Trans. and ed. R. McL. Wilson. Philadelphia: Westminster.

James, M. R.
1893   *Apocrypha Anecdota*. Texts and Studies 2/3. Cambridge: Cambridge University.

1920   *The Lost Apocrypha of the Old Testament*. London: SPCK.

1924   *The Apocryphal New Testament*. Oxford: Clarendon.

Lindblom, Johannes
1968   *Gesichte und Offenbarungen: Vorstellungen von göttlichen Weisungen und übernaturlichen Erscheinungen im ältesten Christentum*. Skrifter utgiva av Kungl. Humanistiska Vetenskapssamfundet i Lund 65. Lund: Gleerup.

McNamara, Martin
1975   *The Apocrypha in the Irish Church*. Dublin: Dublin Institute for Advanced Studies.

Metzger, Bruce M.
1972   "Literary Forgeries and Canonical Pseudepigrapha." *JBL* 91: 3-24.

Riessler, Paul
1928   *Altjüdisches Schrifttum ausserhalb der Bibel*. Darmstadt: Wissenschaftliche Buchgesellschaft (reprint, 1966).

Tischendorf, C. von
  1866   *Apokalypses apocryphae: Mosis, Esdrae, Pauli, Johannis,
              item Mariae dormitio.* Leipzig: Mendelssohn (reprint, 1966).

Vielhauer, P.
  1965   "1. Introduction." Pp. 608-642 in "Apocalyptic in Early
              Christianity." Hennecke-Schneemelcher, 2.608-683.

Weinel, Heinrich
  1923   "Die spätere christliche Apokalyptik." Pp. 141-173 in
              Eucharistērion 2. Festschrift für Hermann Gunkel. Ed. H.
              Schmidt. Studien zur Religion und Literatur des Alten und
              Neuen Testaments NF 19/2. Göttingen: Vandenhoeck & Ruprecht.

APOCALYPSES

Jacob's Ladder

Translation

English
James, M. R.
  1920   *The Lost Apocrypha of the Old Testament.* Pp. 96-103.

German
Bonwetsch, [G.] N.
  1900   *Die apokryphe "Leiter Jakobs."* Pp. 76-87 in Königliche
              Gesellschaft der Wissenschaften, Göttingen. Nachrichten,
              Philologisch-historische Klasse. Göttingen: Vandenhoeck &
              Ruprecht.

Introduction
Charlesworth, J. H.
  1976   *The Pseudepigrapha and Modern Research.* Pp. 130-131.

Denis, A. M.
  1970   *Introduction.* Pp. 34-45.

The Book of Revelation

Böcher, Otto
  1975   *Die Johannesapokalypse.* Erträge der Forschung 41.
              (Contains a 500-entry bibliography). Darmstadt: Wissen-
              schaftliche Buchgesellschaft.

Collins, John J.
  1977a   "Pseudonymity, Historical Reviews and the Genre of the
              Apocalypse of John." *CBQ* 39: 329-343.

Jones, Bruce W.
  1968   "More about the Apocalypse as Apocalyptic." *JBL* 87: 325-327.

Yarbro Collins, Adela
  1976   *The Combat Myth in the Book of Revelation.* HDR 9.
              Missoula: Scholars Press.

Apocalypse of Peter

Greek Text

Klostermann, Erich
  1903   *Apocrypha I. Reste des Petrus-evangeliums, der Petrus-
              apokalypse und des Kerygma Petri.* . . Kleine Texte für
              Vorlesungen und Übungen 3. Bonn: Marcus (2nd ed., 1908).

Ethiopic Text

Grébaut, Sylvain
1910 "Littérature éthiopienne pseudo-Clémentine." *Revue de l'Orient Chrétien* 15: 198-208, 307-316, 425-433.

Translation

Duensing, H. and Hill, David
1965 Hennecke-Schneemelcher, 2.668-683.

Studies

Dieterich, Albrecht
1913 *Nekyia: Beiträge zur Erklärung der neuentdeckten Petrusapokalypse.* Leipzig. Reprint; Darmstadt: Wissenschaftliche Buchgesellschaft, 1969.

Maurer, Ch.
1965 Hennecke-Schneemelcher, 2.663-668.

Spitta, F.
1911 "Die Petrusapokalypse und der zweite Petrusbrief." *ZNW* 12: 237-242.

Vielhauer, Philipp
1975 "Die Petrus-Apokalypse." Pp. 507-513 in *Geschichte der urchristlichen Literatur: Einleitung in das Neue Testament, die Apokryphen und die Apostolischen Väter.* Berlin: de Gruyter.

Shepherd of Hermas

Greek Text

Whittaker, Molly
1956 *Der Hirt des Hermas. Die apostolischen Väter.* Vol. 1. GCS 48. Berlin: Akademie.

Text and Translation

Lake, Kirsopp
1930 "The Shepherd of Hermas." Pp. 1-305 in *The Apostolic Fathers.* Vol. 2. LCL. London: Heinemann.

Translation and Commentary

Dibelius, Martin
1923 *Der Hirt des Hermas.* HNT suppl. vol. Tübingen: Mohr.

Snyder, Graydon
1968 *The Shepherd of Hermas. The Apostolic Fathers.* Vol. 6. Ed. Robert M. Grant. Camden: Nelson.

Studies

Bauckham, R. J.
1974 "The Great Tribulation in the Shepherd of Hermas." *JTS* NS/25: 27-40.

Giet, Stanislas
1963 *Hermas et les pasteurs.* Paris: Presses Universitaires de France.

O'Hagan, A. P.
1961 "The Great Tribulation to Come in the Pastor of Hermas." *Studia Patristica* 4: 305-311.

Reiling, J.
  1973   *Hermas and Christian Prophecy*. Leiden: Brill.

Vielhauer, P.
  1975   "Der Hirt des Hermas." Pp. 513-523 in *Geschichte der urchristlichen Literatur*.

Book of Elchasai
Greek Text
Hilgenfeld, Adolf
  1881   *Hermae Pastor*. Pp. 227-240 in Novum Testamentum extra canonem receptum 3/2. 2nd ed. Leipzig: Weigel.

Translation and Introduction
Irmscher, J. and Wilson, R. McL.
  1965   Hennecke-Schneemelcher, 2.745-750.

Studies
Strecker, G.
  1959   "Elkesai." *RAC* 4.1171-1186. Stuttgart: Hiersemann.

Apocalypse of St. John the Theologian
Greek Text
Tischendorf, C.
  1866   *Apocalypses apocryphae*. Pp. 70-94.

Studies
Bousset, W.
  1896   *The Antichrist Legend*. Pp. 42-43.

Tischendorf, C.
  1866   *Apocalypses apocryphae*. Pp. xviii-xix.

Weinel, H.
  1923   "Die spätere christliche Apokalyptik." Pp. 149-151.

Testament of the Lord
Syriac Text
Lagarde, P. A. de
  1865   *Reliquiae juris ecclesiastici antiquissimae syriace*. London: William and Norgate.

Rahmani, Ignatius
  1899   *Testamentum Domini nostri Jesu Christi*. Moguntiae: Kirchheim (with Latin translation).

Latin Fragment
James, M. R.
  1893   *Apocrypha Anecdota*. Pp. 151-154.

Ethiopic Text
Guerrier, Louis
  1913   *Le Testament en Galilée de notre seigneur Jesus-Christ*. Patrologia orientalis 9/3. Paris: Firmin-Didot.

Translation

English
Cooper, James and Maclean, Arthur
    1902   *The Testament of Our Lord* (from the Syriac with introduction and notes). Edinburgh: Clark.

German
Wajnberg, I.
    1919   "Apokalyptische Rede Jesu an seine Jünger in Galiläa." Pp. 47*-66* in *Gespräche Jesu mit seinen Jüngern nach der Auferstehung: Ein katholisch-apostolisches Sendschreiben des 2. Jahrhunderts.* TU 43. Ed. Carl Schmidt. (Translation is from the Ethiopic). Leipzig: Hinrichs.

Studies

Achelis, H.
    1907, 1913 "Testamentum domini nostri Jesu Christi, eine Kirchenordnung des 5. Jahrhunderts." Pp. 557-559 in *Realencyclopädie für protestantische Theologie und Kirche* 19. Leipzig: Hinrichs. "Nachtrag," 24.560.

Fascher, Erich
    1934   "Testamentum domini nostri Jesu Christi." Pp. 1016-1020 in PW 2/5a. Stuttgart: Metzler.

5 Ezra

Latin Text

Bensly, R. L.
    1895   *The Fourth Book of Ezra.* Texts and Studies 3/2. Cambridge: Cambridge University (reprint, 1967).

Translation and Introduction

Duensing, H. and Hill, David
    1965   Hennecke-Schneemelcher, 2.689-695.

Translation and Commentary

Myers, Jacob
    1974   *I and II Esdras.* AB 42. Garden City: Doubleday.

Studies

Daniélou, J.
    1972   "Le Ve Esdras et le judéo-christianisme latin au 2e siècle." Pp. 162-171 in *Ex orbe religionum: Studia Geo Widengren.* Vol. 1. Studies in the History of Religions (Supplements to Numen) 21. Leiden: Brill.

Testament of Isaac

Coptic Text

Guidi, I.
    1900   *Il testo copto del Testamento di Abramo: Il Testamento di Isacco e il Testamento di Giaccobo.* Rendiconti della Reale accademia dei Lincei, classe di scienze morali, storiche, e philologiche 5/9. Rome: Tipografia della Accademia (Bohairic).

Kuhn, K. H.
    1957   "The Sahidic Version of the Testament of Isaac." *JTS* NS/8: 225-239.

Translation

English

Gaselee, S.
1927   "Appendix." *The Testament of Abraham.* (From Coptic). Ed. G. H. Box. London: SPCK.

Kuhn, K. H.
1967   "An English Translation of the Sahidic Version of the Testament of Isaac." *JTS* NS/18: 325-336.

German

Riessler, P.
1928   *Altjüdisches Schrifttum.* Pp. 1135-1148.

French

Delcor, M.
1973   *Le Testament d'Abraham.* SVTP 2. Leiden: Brill. From Bohairic by M. Chaîne (pp. 196-205), Ethiopic by Chaîne and A. Caquot (pp. 224-233), and Arabic by Chaîne and P. Marçais (pp. 252-261).

Studies

Charlesworth, J. H.
1976   *The Pseudepigrapha and Modern Research.* Pp. 123-125.

Delcor, M.
1973   *Le Testament d'Abraham.* Pp. 78-83.

Testament of Jacob

Coptic Text

Guidi, I.
1900   (Above under Test Isaac)

Translation

English

Gaselee, S.
1927   (Above under Test Isaac)

French

Delcor, M.
1973   (Above under Test Isaac). From Bohairic, pp. 205-213; Ethiopic, pp. 233-241; Arabic, pp. 261-267.

Introduction

Charlesworth, J. H.
1976   (Above under Test Isaac: 131-133)

Questions of Bartholomew

Greek Text

Vassiliev (= Vasil 'ev), A.
1893   "Quaestiones sancti Bartholomaei apostoli." *Sbornik pamiatnikov vizantiiskoĭ literatury.* Anecdota Graeco-Byzantina 1. Moscow: Sumptibus et typis Universitatis caesareae.

Wilmart, A. and Tisserant, E.
1913   "Fragments grecs et latins de l'Evangile de Barthélemy." *RB* NS/10=22: 161-190, 321-368 (a different Greek recension from that published by Vassiliev).

Latin Text
Moricca, U.
    1921, 1922   "Un nuovo testo dell' 'Evangelo di Bartholomeo.'" *RB* 30: 481-516, 31: 20-30 (Latin text with apparatus criticus; made use of all recensions).

Translation and Introduction
Scheidweiler, F. and Schneemelcher, W.
    1963   Hennecke-Schneemelcher, 1.484-503.

Book of the Resurrection of Jesus Christ by Bartholomew the Apostle

Coptic Text
Budge, E. A. W.
    1913   *Coptic Apocrypha in the Dialect of Upper Egypt.* Pp. 1-48 and plates I-XLVIII (a third recension). London: Printed by order of the Trustees.

Lacau, P.
    1904   "Fragments d'apocryphes coptes." *Mémoires publiés par les membres de l'Institute français d'archéologie orientale du Caire* 9: 39-77 (two recensions).

Translation
English
Budge, E. A. W.
    1913   (See above). From recension published by Budge, pp. 179-215; from two recensions published by Lacau, pp. 216-230.

Introduction
Schneemelcher, W.
    1963   Hennecke-Schneemelcher, 1.503-508.

Ascension of Isaiah

Ethiopic, Latin Texts, Greek Fragments and Related Greek Legend
Charles, R. H.
    1900   *The Ascension of Isaiah* (also contains a Latin translation of the Old Slavonic version and an English translation). London: Black.

Coptic Fragments
Lacau, P.
    1946   "Fragments de l'Ascension d'Isaie en copte." *Muséon* 59: 453-467.

Lefort, L. Th.
    1938   "Coptica Lovaniensia (suite)." *Muséon* 51: 24-30 (with a French translation).

    1939   "Fragments d'Apocryphes en copte-akhmîmique." *Muséon* 52: 7-10 (with a French translation).

Translation or Translation and Introduction
English
Box, G. H.
    1919   *The Apocalypse of Abraham and the Ascension of Isaiah*. Translations of Early Documents. London: SPCK.

Charles, R. H.
1900 (See above)

Flemming, J., Duensing, H., and Hill, D.
1965 Hennecke-Schneemelcher, 2.642-663.

French
Tisserant, Eugène
1909 *L'Ascension d'Isaïe.* Paris: Letouzey.

German
Hammershaimb, Erling
1973 "Das Martyrium Jesajas." Pp. 15-34 in *Jüdische Schriften aus hellenistisch-römischer Zeit* 2/1. (Chaps. 1-5 only). Gütersloh: Mohn.

Studies

Caquot, A.
1973 "Bref commentaire du 'Martyre d'Isaïe.'" *Sem* 23: 65-93.

Flusser, David
1953 "The Apocryphal Book of Ascensio Isaiae and the Dead Sea Sect." *IEJ* 3: 30-47.

Helmbold, A. K.
1972 "Gnostic Elements in the Ascension of Isaiah." *NTS* 18: 222-226.

Philonenko, M.
1967 "Le *Martyre de 'Esaïe* et l'histoire de la secte de Qoumrân." Pp. 1-10 in *Pseudépigraphes de l'Ancien Testament et manuscrits de la mer Morte.* Vol. 1. Ed. M. Philonenko. Paris: Presses Universitaires de France.

Vielhauer, P.
1975 "Die Himmelfahrt Jesaias." Pp. 523-528 in *Geschichte der urchristlichen Literatur.*

Apocalypse of Paul
Latin Text

James, M. R.
1893 *Apocrypha Anecdota.* Pp. 11-42.

Silverstein, Th.
1935 *Visio sancti Pauli.* Studies and Documents 4. London: Christophers.

1959 "The Vision of St. Paul. New Links and Patterns in the Western Tradition." *Archives d'histoire doctrinale et littéraire du Moyen Age* 34: 199-248.

Greek Text

Tischendorf, C.
1866 *Apocalypses apocryphae.* Pp. 34-69.

Coptic Text

Budge, E. A. W.
1915 *Miscellaneous Coptic Texts in the Dialect of Upper Egypt.* London: Printed by order of the Trustees.

Syriac Text

Ricciotti, G.
1932   *L'apocalisse di Paolo siriaca.* Vol. 1, *Introduzione, testo e commento.* Vol. 2, *La cosmologia della Bibbia e la sua trasmissione fino a Dante.* Brescia: Morcelliana.

1933   "Apocalypsis Pauli syriace." *Or* 2: 1-24, 120-149.

Translation and Introduction

Duensing, H. and Hill, D.
1965   Hennecke-Schneemelcher, 2.755-798.

Studies

Casey, R. P.
1933   "The Apocalypse of Paul." *JTS* 34: 1-32.

Apocalypse of Esdras

Greek Text and Introduction

Wahl, Otto
1977   *Apocalypsis Esdrae, Apocalypsis Sedrach, Visio Beati Esdrae.* PVTG 4. Leiden: Brill.

Latin Text

Mercati, G.
1901   "Visio beati Esdrae." Pp. 70-73 in *Note di letteratura biblica e cristiana antica.* Studi e Testi 5. Rome: Vatican.

Ethiopic Text

Halévy, J.
1902   *Tĕ'ĕzâza sanbat (Commandements du sabbat), accompagné de six autres écrits.* Pp. 57-79. Bibliothèque de l'Ecole des hautes études. . . Sciences historiques et philogiques 137. Paris: Bouillon.

Translation

German
Müller, U. B.
1976   "Die griechische Esra-Apokalypse." Pp. 85-102 in *Jüdische Schriften aus hellenistisch-römischer Zeit* 5/2. Gütersloh: Mohn.

French
Halévy, J.
1902   (See above: 178-195)

Studies

Batiffol, P.
1926   "Apocalypses apocryphes." P. 765.

Denis, A. M.
1970   *Introduction.* Pp. 91-96.

James, M. R.
1893   *Apocrypha Anecdota.* Pp. 112-113 (brief comment on the date).

Apocalypse of the Virgin Mary

Ethiopic Text

Chaîne, Marius
1909   "Apocalypsis seu Visio Mariae Virginis." Pp. 51-80 in *Apocrypha de B. Maria Virgine*. Part 1, *Textus*. Corpus Scriptorum Christianorum Orientalium. Scriptores Aethiopici 1/7. Rome: Luigi.

Translation

Latin
Chaîne, M.
1909   "Apocalypsis seu Visio Mariae Virginis." Pp. 43-68 in *Apocrypha de B. Maria Virgine*. Part 2, *Versio*. (See above)

English Summary
James, M. R.
1924   *The Apocryphal New Testament*. Pp. 563-564.

Studies

Schneemelcher, W.
1965   Hennecke-Schneemelcher, 2.754.

Story of Zosimus

Greek Text with Apparatus Criticus

James, M. R.
1893   *Apocrypha Anecdota*. Pp. 96-108.

Syriac Text

Nau, F.
1899   "La légende inédite 'Des fils de Jonadab, fils de Réchab, et les îles Fortunées--texte syriaque (attribué à Jacques d'Edesse) et traduction francaise." *Revue sémitique d'épigraphie et d'histoire ancienne* 7: 54-75.

Ethiopic Text

Budge, E. A. W.
1896   "The History of the Blessed Men Who Lived in the Days of Jeremiah the Prophet." Pp. 355-376 in *The Life and Exploits of Alexander the Great*. Vol. 1. London: Clay.

Translation

English
Budge, E. A. W.
1896   (See above: Vol. 2, pp. 555-584)

Craigie, W. A.
1951   "The Narrative of Zosimus concerning the Life of the Blessed." Pp. 220-224 in *The Ante-Nicene Fathers*. Vol. 10. Ed. Allan Menzies. Grand Rapids: Eerdmans.

French
Nau, F.
1899   (See above: 136-146)

Studies

Charlesworth, J. H.
1976   *The Pseudepigraph and Modern Research*. Pp. 223-228.

McNeil, B.
1978   "The Narration of Zosimus." *JSJ* 9: 68-82.

Nau, F.
1898   (See above: 6: 263-266)

Picard, J. C.
1967   "L'*Histoire des Bienheureux du temps de Jérémie* et la *Narration de Zosimi:* arrière-plan historique et mythique." Pp. 27-43 in *Pseudépigraphes de l'Ancien Testament.* (See above, Philonenko entry under Asc Isa).

Apocalypse of the Holy Mother of God concerning the Punishments

Greek Text

James, M. R.
1893   *Apocrypha Anecdota.* Pp. 115-126.

Dawkins, R. M.
1948   "Krētikē Apokalypsis tēs Panagias." *Krētika Chronika* 2: 487-500 (a Cretan version).

Bibliographical Information on Slavonic Versions

Kozak, E.
1892   "Bibliographische Uebersicht der biblisch-apocryphen Literatur bei den Slaven." *Jahrbücher für protestantische Theologie* 18: 127-158.

Translation

Rutherfurd, A.
1951   "The Apocalypse of the Virgin." Pp. 169-174 in *The Ante-Nicene Fathers.* Vol. 10. (See above, Craigie entry under Story of Zosimus).

Studies

James, M. R.
1893   *Apocrypha Anecdota.* Pp. 109-113.

Schneemelcher, W.
1965   Hennecke-Schneemelcher, 2.753-754.

Tischendorf, C.
1866   *Apocalypses apocryphae.* Pp. xxvii-xxx.

Weinel, H.
1923   "Die spätere christliche Apokalyptik." Pp. 156-157.

Apocalypse of James

Introduction, Coptic Text and English Translation

Budge, E. A. W.
1913   *Coptic Apocrypha* (see above under Book of the Resurrection). Pp. 1-lvi, lxx-lxxii; 128-145 (especially 136-143); 335-351 (especially 343-350).

Studies

James, M. R.
1924   *The Apocryphal New Testament.* Pp. 37, 504.

Mysteries of St. John the Apostle and Holy Virgin

Introduction, Coptic Text and English Translation

Budge, E. A. W.
1913   *Coptic Apocrypha* (see above under Book of the Resurrection). Pp. xxxii-xli, lxvii-lxx, 59-74, 241-257.

Apocalypse of Sedrach

Greek Text and Introduction

Wahl, Otto
1977   (Above under Apoc Esdras)

Translation and/or Introduction

Charlesworth, J. H.
1976   *The Pseudepigrapha and Modern Research.* Pp. 178-182.

Rutherfurd, A.
1951   (Above under Apoc Moth God: 175-180)

RELATED TYPES

Mark 13

Studies

Gaston, Lloyd
1970   *No Stone on Another: Studies in the Significance of the Fall of Jerusalem in the Synoptic Gospels.* Leiden: Brill.

Hartman, Lars
1966   *Prophecy Interpreted: The Formation of Some Jewish Apocalyptic Texts and of the Eschatological Discourse Mark 13 Par.* Coniectanea Biblica. New Testament Series 1. Lund: Gleerup.

Lambrecht, Jan
1967   *Die Redaktion der Markus-Apocalypse.* Rome: Päpstliches Bibelinstitut.

Pesch, Rudolf
1968   *Naherwartungen: Tradition und Redaktion in Mark 13.* Düsseldorf: Patmos.

Sibylline Oracles 1-2

Greek Text

Geffcken, Johannes
1902a   *Die Oracula Sibyllina.* GCS 8. Leipzig: Hinrichs.

Rzach, A.
1891   *Oracula Sibyllina.* Leipzig: Freytag.

Translation and Introduction

Kurfess, A. M. and Wilson, R. McL.
1965   Hennecke-Schneemelcher, 2.703-745.

Studies

Geffcken, Johannes
   1902b   *Komposition und Entstehungszeit der Oracula Sibyllina.*
                Texte und Untersuchungen zur Geschichte der Altchristlichen
                Literatur N.F. 8/1. Pp. 47-53. Leipzig: Hinrichs.

Kurfess, A.
   1941   "Oracula Sibyllina I/II." *ZNW* 40: 151-165.

Rzach, A.
   1923   "Sibyllinische Orakel." *PW* 2A: 2146-2152.

Sibylline Oracles 7

Text and Translation

                (Above under Sib Or 1-2)

Studies

Geffcken, Johannes
   1902b   (Above under Sib Or 1-2: 33-37)

Gager, J. G.
   1972   "Some Attempts to Label the Oracula Sibyllina, Book 7."
                HTR 65: 91-97.

Kurfess, A. M.
   1951   *Sibyllinische Weissagungen.* Berlin: Heimeran.

Rzach, A.
   1923   (Above under Sib Or 1-2: 2141-2142)

Sibylline Oracles 8

Studies

Geffcken, Johannes
   1902b   (Above under Sib Or 1-2: 38-46)

Rzach, A.
   1923   (Above under Sib Or 1-2: 2142-2146)

6 Ezra

Latin Text

Bensly, R. L.
   1895   (Above under 5 Ezra)

Greek Fragment

Hunt, A.
   1910   *The Oxyrhynchus Papyri.* Part 7. P. 11 (= 15: 57-59).
                London: Egypt Exploration Fund.

Translation, Introduction and Commentary

Duensing-Hill
   1965   (Above under 5 Ezra)

Myers, Jacob
   1974   (Above under 5 Ezra)

Apocalypse of Elijah

Coptic Text

Schmidt, C.
1925 — *Der Kolophon des Ms. orient. 7594 des Britischen Museums: Eine Untersuchung zur Elias-Apokalypse.* Sitzungsberichte der Preussischen Akademie der Wissenschaften, phil.-hist. Kl. Berlin: de Gruyter.

Steindorff, G.
1899 — *Die Apokalypse des Elias, eine unbekannte Apokalypse und Bruchstücke der Sophonias-Apokalypse.* Texte und Untersuchungen zur Geschichte der Altchristlichen Literatur NF 2/3a. Leipzig: Hinrichs.

Greek Fragment

Wessely, C.
1924 — *Les plus anciens monuments du Christianisme écrits sur papyrus.* Vol. 2. Patrologia Orientalis 18. Paris: Firmin-Didot.

Related Hebrew Text with German Translation

Buttenwieser, M.
1897 — *Die hebräische Elias-Apokalypse.* Leipzig: Pfeiffer.

Translation

English
Houghton, H. P.
1959 — "Sahidic 'Sophonias Apocalypse'" (transliteration of the Coptic text and English translation of the Sahidic version of Apoc Elijah—so Rosenstiehl, p. 23; see below). Pp. 43-67 in "The Coptic Apocalypse." *Aegyptus* 39: 43-91, 179-210. "Akhmîmice (*sic*): 'The Apocalypse of Elias.'" Ibid., 179-210.

French
Rosenstiehl, Jean M.
1972 — *L'apocalypse d'Elie.* Introduction, Traduction et Notes. Paris: Geuthner.

German
Steindorff, G.
1899 — (See above)

Riessler, P.
1928 — *Altjüdisches Schrifttum.* Pp. 114-125, from Coptic; pp. 234-240, from Hebrew.

Studies

Rosenstiehl, Jean M.
1972 — (See above)

Apocalypse of Thomas

Latin Text

Bihlmeyer, R.
1911 — "Un texte non interpolé de l'Apocalypse de Thomas." *Revue Bénédictine* 28: 270-282.

Wilhelm, Friedrich
1907 — *Deutsche Legenden und Legendare.* Longer recension. Leipzig: Hinrichs.

Translation and Introduction

James, M. R.
    1924   *The Apocryphal New Testament.* Pp. 555-562 (gives translation of longer recension also).

Santos Otero, A. de and Best, E.
    1965   Hennecke-Schneemelcher, 2.798-803 (shorter recension only translated).

Testament of Adam and Penitence of Adam (Cedrenus)

Ethiopic and Arabic Texts

Bezold, C.
    1906   "Das arabisch-äthiopische Testamentum Adami." Pp. 893-912 in *Orientalische Studien Th. Nöldeke zum 70. . . .* Vol. 2. Ed. Carl Bezold. Giessen: Töpelmann.

Syriac Text

Kmosko, M.
    1907   *Patrologia syriaca* 1/2. Appendix. Ed. R. Graffin. (Two Syriac versions with a Latin translation). Paris: Firmin-Didot.

Greek Text

Nau, F.
    1907   *Patrologia syriaca* 1/2. Appendix. (See above)

James, M. R.
    1893   *Apocrypha Anecdota.* Pp. 139-144 (includes the Greek text of the relevant Cedrenus passage, p. 139).

Translation

English

Budge, E. A. W.
    1927   "Testamentum Adami." Pp. 242-248 in *The Book of the Cave of Treasures.* London: The Religious Tract Society.

James, M. R.
    1920   *The Lost Apocrypha of the Old Testament.* P. 2. (Translation of Cedrenus passage).

Studies

Denis, A. M.
    1970   *Introduction.* Pp. 7-8, notes 23, 24 and 26; pp. 9-14.

Renan, E.
    1853   "Fragments du livre gnostique intitulé 'Apocalypse d'Adam,' ou 'Penitence d'Adam,' ou 'Testament d'Adam,' publiés d'après deux versions syriaques." *Journal asiatique* 5/2: 427-471.

Didache 16

Greek Text

Bihlmeyer, K. and Schneemelcher, W.
    1956   *Die apostolischen Väter.* 2nd ed. Tübingen: Mohr.

Text and Translation
Lake, Kirsopp
  1912 "Didache." Pp. 303-333 in *The Apostolic Fathers*. Vol. 1. LCL. Cambridge: Harvard University (reprint, 1965).

Translation and Commentary
Kraft, Robert A.
  1965 *Barnabas and the Didache. The Apostolic Fathers*. Vol. 3. Ed. Robert M. Grant. New York: Nelson.

Studies
Audet, J. P.
  1958 *La Didachē: Instructions des apôtres*. Etudes Bibliques. Paris: Gabalda.

Bammel, E.
  1961 "Schema und Vorlage von *Didache* 16." *Studia Patristica* 4: 253-262.

Apocalypse of John the Theologian attributed to John Chrysostom (Ques Jn Theol)

Introduction, Text and Translation
Nau, F.
  1914 "Une deuxième Apocalypse apocryphe grecque de Saint Jean." *RB* 23: 209-221.

THE GNOSTIC APOCALYPSES

Francis T. Fallon
University of Kansas

SYNOPSIS

The purpose of this essay is to introduce gnostic apocalypses to those who are interested in studying the genre "apocalypse" across a wide spectrum of literature. The writings considered will include, first of all, those of the recently found Nag Hammadi codices and, secondly, those of the previously known Coptic gnostic codices, i.e., the codices Askew, Berlin, and Bruce, which date from the fourth to the sixth century CE. Excluded from our consideration will be the Hermetic writings from Nag Hammadi, since they are to be treated in the essay by Attridge on "Greco-Roman Apocalypses" in this volume.

Perhaps a word concerning the Nag Hammadi codices is in order at this point. These codices derive from the latter half of the fourth century CE, and the tractates contained within them were probably written from the first to the fourth century CE and translated from Greek into their present Coptic. In referring to the tractates, we shall use the conventions adopted by the UNESCO-sponsored International Committee for the Nag Hammadi Codices (see Robinson, 1974). These tractates are now available in a one-volume English translation, *The Nag Hammadi Library* (see Robinson, 1977).

To date, not many studies have been devoted to the specific issue of genre in gnostic apocalypses or revelations. In his essay on apocalypses in general, Vielhauer turned his attention to the gnostic writings and noted the difference in content between Jewish apocalypses and these gnostic writings, i.e., eschatological-apocalyptic material versus cosmological and soteriological material. As a result, he suggested that the term "apocalypse" in the title of gnostic writings should not be considered as a designation of literary genre but rather in a more general sense as the revelation of the redeeming gnosis (Vielhauer: 599). Rudolph concurred in this judgment and devoted a careful study to a specific type of gnostic revelation, the revelation dialogue. He considered the revelation dialogue to be an original gnostic creation, but its roots he traced back to the Platonic dialogue and the *erotapokriseis* literature of Hellenism (Rudolph, 1968:106-107; 1969:156). In his dissertation, Parrott has analyzed Jewish, Christian and gnostic revelatory writings, which contain dialogue or discourse but do not contain visions, dreams or cryptic modes of speech (Parrott, 1970). Contrary to Rudolph, he finds the origins of this literary genre in the Jewish Wisdom tradition. In another dissertation, to which I am gratefully indebted throughout this paper, Perkins studied the gnostic revelation dialogue and concluded that its origins are to be found in Jewish apocalyptic literature (Perkins, 1972). However, in its development Perkins would concur with Rudolph that the genre has been subjected to wider Hellenistic influence. In our essay, we shall introduce not only these revelation dialogues but also the other types of gnostic revelatory writings, and then in a final section we shall present some related categories of gnostic documents.

Contrary to the view of Vielhauer and Rudolph, we shall use the term "apocalypse" to refer to a literary genre when speaking of gnostic writings. The basis for this usage is a phenomenological study of the characteristics present in Jewish, Christian, Greco-Roman, and Persian, as well as gnostic, writings that may be identified as apocalypses. We shall see that eschatological material is also present in the gnostic apocalypses. The usage of the term "apocalypse" for gnostic writings is not meant to decide the question of the historical origin and derivation of gnostic apocalypses from Judaism or the Greco-Roman world. Further specialized studies will be needed to answer the question of derivation. For the present, we shall restrict ourselves to the phenomenological level and to the common characteristics that have emerged from our joint study of the genre "apocalypse" across a broad sweep of literature.

In his Introduction to our essays, Collins has summarized the characteristics which have emerged in his definition of an apocalypse as "a genre of revelatory literature with a narrative framework, in which a revelation is mediated by an otherworldly being to a human recipient, disclosing a transcendent reality which is both temporal, insofar as it envisages eschatological salvation, and spatial, insofar as it involves another, supernatural world." Further, in the Introduction Collins has set forth a master paradigm which includes all the elements of the definition as well as other, significant elements. In addition, he has suggested that there are two main types of apocalypses: those without (Type I) and those with (Type II) an otherworldly journey; and that three sub-types may be distinguished within each: those with an historical review (a), those with cosmic eschatology (b), and those with only personal eschatology (c). We shall analyze the gnostic apocalypses in the light of this definition and see that they fulfill its requirements. Further, we shall also see that gnostic apocalypses can be divided into the same types and sub-types, with the exception that there are no historical apocalypses (Ia or IIa).

At the outset, some observations can be noted. In the gnostic apocalypses, what is prominent is the spoken word. The revelation is usually transmitted through discourse or dialogue. There is little emphasis upon vision other than the sight of the revealer, although there are some exceptions (e.g. ApocPeter, PS IV, ApocPaul). There are no allegorical visions.

The otherworldly mediator is an angel or pleromatic being or, more frequently in Christian revelations, the Lord. The epiphany of the revealer is presented. It is frequently but not always associated with light, involved with a self-predication, and placed upon a mountain. For the revelations by Christ, the time is usually after the resurrection (see, however, the ApocPeter). As far as the human recipient is concerned, all the seers are pseudonymous. Very frequently, some perplexity on the part of the seers is mentioned (ApocPaul is an exception), as well as their reaction to the revealer.

Concerning the content on a temporal axis, it can be noted that very often the origin of man and his fall are recounted. However, this is not true in every case (e.g. ApocPeter). Particularly distinctive about the gnostic apocalypses and present in each of them is their emphasis upon present salvation through knowledge. It may be said to be a defining characteristic of the gnostic apocalypse. In addition to this emphasis upon present salvation, there can also be found in the gnostic apocalypses the ascent of the soul or the divine element to the divine realm above, i.e., an interest in personal afterlife, in eschatological salvation. Occasionally, this interest is accompanied by an interest in the consummation, i.e., the dissolution of the cosmos and the return of all the divine elements to the divine realm (e.g. NatArch, PS I-III, ParaShem). Obviously, there is no interest in these gnostic apocalypses in cosmic transformation at the end of time, since the cosmos is in principle evil.

Concerning the content on a spatial axis, it can be stated that the heavens are always important in the gnostic apocalypses and more developed in the later works (e.g. PS). The distinctive element in gnostic apocalypses is that the heavens and/or their rulers are evil. Only above them is found the divine realm or the pleromatic realm, which is good. Each of the gnostic revelations considered has this dual system, and it too may be considered a defining characteristic of the gnostic apocalypse.

In presenting the gnostic apocalypses, we shall first introduce those without an otherworldly journey and then those with an otherworldly journey. Since there has been scholarly discussion on the issue of the dialogues, we shall also distinguish in our presentation those which involve discourse and those which involve dialogue. Further, we shall distinguish and introduce the non-Christian before the Christian apocalypses.

SURVEY

The Apocalypses

Type I: Otherworldly Revelations but No Otherworldly Journey

Discourses

The Apocalypse of Adam CG V,5 (ApocAd)

The ApocAd in its overall literary genre is a testament, a testament of Adam to his son Seth (64[58].1ff), in which Adam reports a revelation which he has received (65[59].24-66[60].14 and 67[61].14ff). The revelation contains a prediction concerning future destructions by flood and by fire and then the future coming of an enlightener into the world. Scholars have been divided upon the origins of this document. Some have proposed a Christian-gnostic origin for the work (Daniélou; Schenke), but because of the lack of explicit references or explicit allusions to Christian ideas, a Jewish gnostic origin is more probable for the document (Boehlig and Labib; MacRae). Although the tractate is difficult to date precisely, a date as early as the first century CE has been suggested (Robinson, 1974: 13f.). Because of the importance of Seth within the document, it probably stems from Sethian gnostic circles (Wisse, 1972:606).

The revelation occurs in the form of a dream vision. Adam "slept in the thought of his heart" and saw three men before him whose image he could not recognize (65[59].24-29). Adam then reports to Seth the things revealed to him by these three men (67[61].14ff). The three men from the upper realm are the otherworldly mediators and are presumably angelic figures (65[59].25-31). Adam and Eve sign in their hearts in response to the presence of the three men (66[60].9-14).

There is a review of history. However, it is the primordial history of Genesis, which is discussed by means of a prediction of a future flood (69[63].1-17), and fire (75[69].9-16), and then the prediction of the coming of a revealer figure is made (76[70].8-15). These predictions should probably be associated with the *ex eventu* prophecies of Jewish apocalypses, although the distinction between history and primordial history should be noted. In its soteriology, ApocAd states that those who possess the true knowledge are not to perish (76[70].21-23) but are to live forever (83[77].11-17). In contrast, the peoples without knowledge recognize and confess that they will perish since their works are evil (83[77].23-84[78].3).

As present heavenly realities, the document presents the ruler of the heavens as an evil ruler who brings about the flood and seeks to end the seed of those who have knowledge. Beyond him is the true God.

In its concluding elements, the recipients are to transmit the revelation in that the race of those men who are chosen is to enlighten the entire aeon (83[77].1-4). There is no account of the departure of the revealer, but such is probably implicit in the arrival of the lower deity (66[60].14-23). There is at least a reference to the pursuit of the gnostic by evil forces, if not to persecution by other men (84[78].23-27).

The Allogenes CG XI,3 (Allog)

The tractate Allog is an apocalypse with discourse in which the seer Allogenes records for his son Messos the revelations which he has received. In the first part (45.1-57.27), he receives a revelation from the revealer Youel and then in a second part (57.27-69.20) he is taken up in an otherworldly journey to receive further revelations. Thus there is a mixture here of both categories of apocalypses.

Allogenes probably sees the revealer and also the other figures of the world above (cf. 57.24-38); later, he sees Autogenes, the Savior, Barbelo and the other holy powers (58.7-60.12).

The origin of the otherworldly figures is presented in 45.6-57.24. The saving significance of the revelation which Allogenes receives is also emphasized (e.g. 50.24-35; 52.7-34; 59.10-60.12; 60.28-61.22). Those who are judged are judged from themselves for their failure to know (64.13-36). There is no explicit discussion of personal afterlife. However, such may be implicit in the reference to the escape (50.24-35) and the permanent strengthening (60.28-61.22) of Allogenes. The figures of the world above are clearly transcendent (e.g. 51.6-11). There is no direct discussion of the evil nature of the world below. However, such is probably implicit in the need for escape from this lower world (50.24-35).

Concerning the concluding elements, at the end of the first part Allogenes is instructed to seek the good that is within him and told that he will receive a further revelation after 100 years (56.15-35). At the end of the second part, he is instructed to write down his revelations in a book and to leave the book upon a mountain (68.16-23). The first part concludes with the departure of the revealer Youel (57.24-27). In the second part Allogenes writes the book which he then transmits to Messos (68.24-69.20) after the departure of the revealer.

The Second Apocalypse of James CG V,4 (2 ApocJas)

Having introduced the non-Christian apocalypses, we now turn to a Christian apocalypse with discourse but no dialogue. The 2 ApocJas is a tractate in which a Jewish priest named Mareim recounts the trial and martyrdom of James the Just, the brother of the Lord. This Jewish priest is said to be a kinsman of James' father Theuda and to have served as a juror in the law court where James was tried. In his trial, James delivers a speech in which he recounts that the risen Jesus appeared to him and gave to him the secret revelation.

Because of the different interests of the martyrdom section and the apocalypse section, Brown has suggested that the apocalypse section has been added to the original martyrdom legend by a gnostic redactor (Brown, 1972:156; 1975:236). He has also disputed the association of the document with Jewish Christianity, just because of the prominence of James (Boehlig, 1967:135-138), but proposed that the 2 ApocJas stems from the Syria-Palestine area circa 200 CE.

After the resurrection, Christ comes through the door to James and his mother (50[44].5-10). As the otherworldly mediator, in his self-predication, Jesus announces that he is the stranger who is not known by men (51[45].6-11). In the speech of Jesus, there is no questioning or response by the seer. Rather, Jesus' speech has within it a call to hear and know (51[45].6-22). The speech of Jesus here seems to take on the characteristics of the revelatory discourse, which we shall discuss under "Related Types."

James had been thinking for some time (50[44].5-7) and then is perplexed at being addressed as brother by the Lord; the difficulty is then answered by the mother (50[44].13-17).

There is a discourse on the evil intentions of the demiurge to continue to entrap and afflict the gnostics (53[47].1-21). Within this context, Jesus presents the original creation of man and the entrapment of the divine within him by the demiurge (54[48].10-20). Jesus speaks of his own work to reveal the truth and commissions James as an enlightener and redeemer who is to bring revelation to others (55[49].17-18). In its eschatology, 2 ApocJas asserts that the time of the evil rule of the demiurge is limited and thus implies a judgment or destruction of him, but the Father's time is eternal (53[47].12-29). Christ also issues the call to know all things that one might go out of the body like him (57[51].6-10).

As one would expect in a gnostic document, the present heavenly rulers are evil (53[47].1-21). It is only beyond the heavens that one reaches the realm of the true God.

Concerning the concluding elements, in an interesting passage Jesus disappears as James tries to embrace him (57[51].10-12). James as the recipient of the revelation is then martyred.

Melchizedek CG IX,1 (Melch)

The tractate Melch is very fragmentary in nature and thus assessment of it must remain tentative at present, until scholars have had an opportunity to analyze it at greater length. However, it does seem to be a Christian apocalypse with discourse rather than dialogue and to possess some Sethian elements. In the tractate Melchizedek receives revelations from heavenly messengers concerning the future death and triumph of Jesus Christ and his own identification with him.

There may be a reference to the origin of the lower world and its powers in 9.1-25. There also seems to be a discussion of Adam and Eve and their trespass in 9.25-10.25. In the third section of the tractate, Melchizedek seems to be identified with Jesus Christ, whose future fate is then told (18.7-27.4). Melchizedek in a prayer to the Father expresses thanks for the revelation which has brought him from death to life (14.15-15.15). There are scattered references to the destruction of the evil powers (6.20-25; 14.1-10; 26.1-27.4).

The messengers are from the realm of light above in contrast with the evil powers below.

For its concluding elements, the recipients are told not to reveal the revelations unless so instructed (27.4-8). The messengers are then taken up to heaven (27.8-10).

These tractates (ApocAd, Allog, 2 ApocJas and Melch) are the only gnostic revelations without an otherworldly journey in which there is a discourse but no dialogue. We turn next to the apocalypses with dialogue but without an otherworldly journey. We shall consider first those whose sources are proposed to be non-Christian before we introduce the Christian documents.

Dialogues

The Sophia of Jesus Christ CG III,4 and BG 8502 (SJC)

Our first tractate, the SJC, appears both in the Nag Hammadi documents and in the Berlin codex. It is a revelation by the risen Christ to his twelve disciples and seven women, in which he discloses the mystery of the origin of the aeons, the origin of the cosmos, and the nature of his own salvific work. The content of the revelation is closely related to another work found twice in the Nag Hammadi corpus, i.e., the *Letter of Eugnostos*, CG III,3 and V,1 (Eug). This letter of Eug is a dogmatic epistle with no Christian references. Scholars are divided concerning the exact relationship between these two works. Some have argued that SJC is the earlier work and has been pruned of Christian references by the author of Eug (Schenke); others have proposed more probably that Eug is the earlier work and has been incorporated into the Christian apocalypse frame (Krause; Perkins: chap. 1). It is difficult to associate the work with a particular sect, and only an approximate date, the late second or third century CE, can be given (Puech: 248).

The Savior appears after the resurrection like a great angel of light (BG 78.11-79.9). Rather than a self-identification but probably as a modification of it, the Savior greets his disciples with the words "Peace be with you." The location is that of a mountain in Galilee. The twelve disciples and the seven women interrupt the discourse of the Savior with their questions, to which the answers of the discourse are loosely attached. Before the appearance of the Savior, the disciples are perplexed concerning the mysteries of the pleroma and of salvation (BG 78.2-10). At his appearance, they are also amazed and afraid (BG 79.11-12).

The discourse of the Savior reviews pre-history: the highest God (BG 84.1ff), the theogony, i.e., the origin of the pleroma (BG 93.15ff), and implicitly the cosmogony (BG 116.2-14). In its soteriology, SJC states that the Savior came to unite the gnostics with the Spirit and make them one and that the person who knows these mysteries and knows the Father will enter into the Father and rest (BG 122.1-123.19). The discourse ends by describing the various places where the souls will go after death depending upon their knowledge (BG 123.1ff). Those who know the Father in a faulty manner will remain in the fault and come to rest in the eighth But those who know the Father with a holy knowledge will enter to the Father and come to rest in him.

The heavenly realities are presented in terms of instruction concerning the divine pleromatic realm and concerning the evil rulers of the lower heavens, who entrap the gnostics. There is an exhortation in that the gnostics are exhorted to destroy the graves of the evil rulers, to suppress their *pronoia*, to break their yoke, and to awaken what is the Lord's (BG 126.5-12).

For its concluding elements, after the instruction the Savior is said to disappear from the seers (BG 126.17-127.1). The recipients are then said to preach the Gospel (BG 127.1ff).

The Apocryphon of John CG II,1; III,1; IV,1; BG 8502 (ApocryJn)

Our second document, the ApocryJn, is an apocalypse with dialogue in which, after the resurrection, Jesus appears to John, the son of Zebedee, on the Mount of Olives and reveals to him the secrets of the pleroma, the origin of the world, the future fate of souls, and then commissions him to communicate this knowledge to others. The ApocryJn must have been widely used for we find three copies of it at Nag Hammadi as well as one copy in the Berlin codex. Among the four copies there are two recensions: a long recension present in CG II,1 and CG IV,1, and a short recension present in BG and CG III,1. Scholars are divided as to whether the long (Giversen) or the short (Kasser) recension is prior. The ApocryJn is also clearly related to the account in Irenaeus, *Adversus haereses* 1.29, and thus the traditions of ApocryJn, if not the books we possess, date from the second century CE and stem from the broad stream of Barbelo or Sethian gnosticism (Wisse, 1971:209). The cosmogonic and soteriological myth also shows traces of Christianization of a previously non-Christian myth (Perkins: chap. 2).

Christ appears to John in a stream of light as a child with the form of an old man (BG 20.19-21.6). With the *egō eimi* formula, Christ identifies himself as the Father, Mother and Son (BG 21.19-22.2). Before the appearance of Jesus, John is sad of heart (BG 20.6) and brooding over questions concerning the Savior, his Father, the Aeon to which he would go (BG 20.8-19). At the appearance of the light, John became afraid and fell down (BG 21.1-2).

There is a review of both pre- and primordial history. After a description of the highest God, Christ reveals the theogony, i.e., the origin of the pleroma (BG 25.18-36.15), and then the cosmogony. Along with the cosmogony, a gnostic interpretation of Genesis is also given (BG 36.16-64.13). Those will be saved who have received the spirit of life in this existence and have known the All (BG 65.3-8 and 68.4-16). There is great concern in the presentation for personal eschatology, for the fate of souls after they come out of the flesh. Those saved are led up to the rest of the aeons (BG 68.12-13), those who have not known the All are returned until they achieve knowledge (BG 68.13-69.13), and those who knew and turned away are kept for the day of punishment (BG 70.8-71.2).

The focus of interest is upon the cosmogony as the story of the origin of the present evil cosmos and evil rulers of the heavens. Only the pleroma is evaluated positively.

In its concluding elements, John is to write down these mysteries and give them to the same spirits (BG 75.15-19). Jesus is said simply to depart from John (BG 76.17f), and then John begins to communicate these mysteries by recounting them to the other disciples (BG 77.1-2).

The Gospel of Mary BG 8502 (GMary)

Our next document, the GMary from the Berlin codex, is a document with two apocalypses with dialogue. Unfortunately, the first six pages of the work are missing, and thus the character of the first apocalypse is not fully clear. Within the second apocalypse, pages 11-14 of the document are also missing so that the character of this apocalypse is also obscured. In what remains of the first apocalypse Peter, probably accompanied by other disciples, questions the Savior concerning the fate of matter and the sin of the world. After his command to preach the Gospel, the Savior departs. The disciples then turn to Mary in their perplexity to learn from her the words which the Savior had given to her alone. She then reports to them a vision of the Savior to her in which he recounted the fate of the souls after death.

Scholars have proposed that there were originally two independent documents behind the GMary (Till: 26), which may have been non-Christian (Wilson: 102). Since what remains of content in the two parts of GMary is not repetitious or contradictory but rather complementary, it seems more probable that one non-Christian document may have been broken up and placed in this dual frame (Perkins: chap. 3). It is with difficulty assigned to any gnostic sect but probably dates from the second century CE (Puech).

In what remains of part one, we can see that the Savior is the otherworldly mediator (2), who responds to the questions of Peter as the pseudonymous seer (3.1). The Savior then commands his hearers (BG 8.12-22) to preach the Gospel.

The interest in soteriology is expressed in the revised saying of Jesus: "The Son of Man is within you. Follow him. Those who seek will find him" (8.18-21). After the lacuna, the subject of the discussion is the soul in its ascent through the several heavens and their powers (15.1ff), the soul's freedom at that point from desire and ignorance (16.16ff), and its possession of rest for the duration of the aeon (17.4-7). The eschatology is thus personal but with a possible allusion to the end of the aeon and its destruction.

The revelation discloses the evil powers who rule the heavens and impede the ascent of the soul to the divine realm.

For its concluding elements, the disciples are commanded to preach the Gospel in the first part (8.21-22). The only departure of the revealer is reported at the end of the first part

(9.5). Then the disciples begin to preach the Gospel at the end of the document, and they fear persecution as they do so (19.1-12).

The Nature of the Archons CG II,4 (NatArch)

Our next document, the NatArch, is a treatise with a Christian introduction and two parts, a gnostic version of Genesis and an apocalypse with dialogue. Bullard in his edition and commentary on the treatise suggested that the two parts were originally independent and had not at that time been Christianized. Later scholars argued that the two parts formed a whole (Perkins: chap. 7) or that the apocalypse in its present form reflects a Christian concern and probably dates from the latter half of the second century, from Sethian and/or Ophite circles (Fallon).

The angel Eleleth is presented as coming down from heaven (93[141].8). Eleleth then identifies himself by means of the *egō eimi* formula as "Wisdom, the Great Angel who stands in the presence of the Holy Spirit" and "Understanding" (93[141].8 and 19). The time is just prior to the Flood and the place is that of Mount Seir (92[140].14). The seer is Norea, a female figure, who seeks to board the ark with Noah (92[140].14-18). The occasion for the appearance of Eleleth is not that of perplexity by Norea but rather conflict with the evil archons of the world (93[141]. 1-2). The seer Norea then asks questions of Eleleth, to which he replies.

In the revelation section of the treatise there is told the story of the fall of Wisdom and the resultant creation, i.e., the cosmogony (94[142].4ff). There is also a review of early history in the gnostic version of Genesis, which occurs in the first part of the treatise. For its soteriology, the revealer foretells that after three generations "that seed" will appear and then the Spirit of truth will teach the gnostics about everything and anoint them with eternal life (97[145].1-3). In its eschatology, NatArch states that those who have been taught will go up to the Infinite Light and know the Father (97[145].7-8 and 13-20), while the evil powers will be destroyed. While the interest here is still upon personal afterlife, it is to be noted that the final consummation is referred to in the destruction of the evil powers.

The seven heavens are controlled by Sabaoth, the son of the evil demiurge Ialdabaoth. It is only above the heavens, above the veil, that one reaches the realm of light.

Concerning the concluding elements, the persecution referred to within the context of the apocalypse is the persecution by the demonic rulers (93[141].1-2). The treatise as a whole begins with a reference to the fight with the evil powers.

Now that we have considered those apocalypses with dialogues with proposed non-Christian sources, we shall turn to the Christian apocalypses with dialogue.

The First Apocalypse of James CG V,3 (1 ApocJas)

Our first document here, the 1 ApocJas, contains two apocalypses of Jesus to James. The first takes place prior to Jesus' death. In it he reveals in a dialogue the highest God, his own death, the coming martyrdom of James, the seventy-two heavens and the reason for his descent into the world; he then promises another revelation. The disciples are perplexed at the death of

Jesus. After the resurrection Jesus appears to James on Mount Gaugela. James embraces him and kisses him. Then Jesus reveals that he had not suffered at his death and what the soul is to say in its ascent after death. James is told to give the revelation to Addai, and after the departure of Jesus he goes to the twelve.

Scholars have disputed whether the document shows Jewish-Christian affinities (Boehlig) or not (Brown, 1972:70), but have agreed that one section (33.5-36.11) shows Valentinian influence. Thus the present document should be dated circa 200 CE (Brown, 1972:270). The two dialogues should probably be taken as complementary to one another rather than as previously independent documents.

Jesus presents the highest God (24[18].18-20) and a brief account of the origin of the pleroma (24[18].25-25[19].1), with a lengthier treatment on the origin of the seventy-two heavens (26[20].2-27[21].12). Concerning soteriology, Jesus proclaims that he has brought forth the image of that which is, so the sons of that which is should know what is theirs and what is alien (25[19].2-5) and that only when they cast off blind thought will they reach what is (27[21].1-7). Jesus reveals to James what is to be said to the powers in the ascent of the soul after death (33[27].2-24). The interest is again in personal eschatology.

The heavens are again considered as the locus of evil powers, who prevent the ascent of the soul (33[27].2-24) to the divine realm. James is exhorted to cast away from himself all lawlessness (40[34].19-22).

For its concluding elements, James is to transmit the revelation to Addai, who will write it down (36[30].15-16). At the end of the first dialogue, Jesus says simply, "Now I shall go" (30[24].7). At the end of the second dialogue, James preaches the revelation to the twelve (42[36].20-22). James is also to be martyred (25[19].10-19 and 32[26].17-22); such is ultimately the work of the evil archons.

The Apocalypse of Peter CG VII,3 (ApocPet)

The ApocPet is another Christian apocalypse with dialogue. It takes place before the death of Jesus and in it the Savior discusses with Peter the blindness and dumbness of the priests and scribes, the variety of souls, the imitation fellowship which will arise and oppress the brothers, and the correct understanding of the crucifixion, i.e., that the Savior did not really suffer.

It would seem that the "imitation fellowship" must be the orthodox church, and the reference to persecution by it would bespeak a later date in the gnostic movement for this writing.

At the beginning of the tractate, Peter has a vision of light descending upon the Savior, to which he responds with fear and joy (72.21-26). There is no account of the Savior's appearance to Peter from heaven, evidently because the dialogue is set in a context prior to the death and resurrection. Rather, the vision of the light descending upon the Savior probably functions as the appearance motif. Later, Peter has a vision of the Savior as if seized and upon a cross and also as if above the tree and laughing (81.5-24). The interpretation of this vision is then given by the Savior (82.17-83.15).

The real soteriological concern is for the immortal souls who have a correct understanding of the Savior and his crucifixion as opposed to the imitation fellowship with their incorrect understanding. In its eschatology, the ApocPet shows an interesting differentiation. The souls of the imitation fellowship will be cast into outer darkness and will not enter in with the sons of light at the coming of the Savior (77.24-78.30).

The present heavens are ruled by evil archons (77.1-20) as well as by angels of error (77.22-78.1). Above them is the realm of light (78.20-21).

For its concluding elements, Peter is to become perfect and a ruler of the remnant called to understanding (71.15-21) and to entrust what he has seen to those of another race (83.16-24). Rather than a departure account of the revealer, the Savior promises to be with Peter (84.6-13). In Apoc Pet's interesting version of persecution, the brothers are oppressed by the imitation sisterhood (79.11-12).

The Letter of Peter to Philip CG VIII,2 (PetPhil)

PetPhil is a gnostic writing which is related to the stream of Sethian or Barbelo gnosticism (Wisse, 1970:209 n. 22) and in which a number of literary genres are found: first, a letter from Peter to Philip; second, an apocalypse in which Jesus appears at the Mount of Olives and dialogues with the apostles; third, a narration which includes a sermon of Peter and tells of the preaching of the apostles.

The disciples gather at the suggestion of Peter, since they are unsure of the way in which to preach Jesus in the world. The origin of the lower evil powers and the lower world is briefly treated in the discourse concerning the foolishness of the mother, who in other tractates is named Sophia, and the arrogance of Authades, the evil archon (135.8-136.15). The reason for the appearance of Jesus in the world was that the seed which was lost from the pleroma might recognize him and strip off what is corruptible (136.16-137.9). The purpose for the coming of Jesus is to gather the lost seed of the pleroma and ultimately to return it (136.16-137.4).

The instruction by Jesus explains the origin of the evil powers and the reason for their fighting against the disciples, as well as the pleroma from which the disciples come.

For its concluding elements, the disciples are instructed to fight the evil powers by teaching in the world (137.20-138.5). The document concludes with the report that the disciples began to preach about Jesus in Jerusalem, that Jesus appeared again to promise to be with them, and that then the disciples went forth to preach.

Hypsiphrone CG IX,4 (Hyps)

The tractate Hyps appears to be a revelation of some sort, but the fragmentary nature of the text makes it difficult to ascertain the exact nature of the document and its gnostic affiliations.

Pistis Sophia (PS)

The Askew Codex, in which PS is found, has been known to the scholarly world since the eighteenth century. The manuscript itself dates from the second half of the fourth century. Within the PS there are four books. Scholarly analysis has shown that book IV is a separate and older work, which probably dates from the first half of the third century. Books I-III form another, later work, which probably derives from the second half of the third century. Both works, however, came from Egypt (Schmidt and Till, 1954:xxiiif.); and although they cannot be ascribed with certainty to a particular sect, the books show a relation to the same stream of gnosticism witnessed in ApocryJn.

Book IV of PS, like Allog, has a mixture of both categories of apocalypses. There is an appearance of the Lord Jesus after the resurrection to the disciples.

There is also a report of a vision of a great powerful light and a vision of fire, water, wine and blood in c. 141. After his appearance, the Lord Jesus addresses a magical prayer to the Father. At first, the disciples, who question Jesus continuously, are at the West and South, and Jesus is at the altar of offering. Then he takes them in the air on an otherworldly journey into the way of the middle place (c. 136). Later, Jesus and his disciples are said to be on a mountain of Galilee (c. 141).

There is a small section recounting the origin of those of the middle and those of the lower spheres (c. 136-137). Concerning soteriology, the Lord promises at the opening of the revelation to present all knowledges and all mysteries to the disciples so that they might be perfect and children of the pleroma (c. 138). The main focus of the document is upon personal eschatology: reward or punishment. Those who have all knowledges and all mysteries will be able to pass through all the aeons to the light treasury (c. 138), whereas punishment awaits the evil souls in the ways of the middle (c. 139-140). As a result, there is concern for the forgiveness of sins and knowledge of the name to protect the soul in its ascent (c. 142-143). There follows then a discussion of the different punishments for the various types of sinners (c. 144-148).

The aeons of the middle are the places for the punishment for the souls which do not have all knowledges and all mysteries (c. 138-148), whereas the light treasury is the ultimate destiny of those who do.

PS I-III is another Christian apocalypse with dialogue. In it, Jesus speaks on the Mount of Olives with the disciples after the resurrection for eleven years, ascends, and then returns to appear in light to them. The disciples are fearful at the disappearance and reappearance of Jesus. In response to their questions, Jesus explains how in his ascent he readjusted the fates so that souls might pass through and how Wisdom repented of her fault at his ascent. Then he commissions the disciples to preach the repentance necessary to receive the mysteries (c. 102) and explains the fate of various types of souls after death.

Although the myth of Wisdom's fall is not recounted, it is presupposed in the account of her repentance (c. 30ff). The concern of PS is not for the salvation of the world but for the salvation of souls. The ascent of Jesus through the aeons is

considered as a service to this end (c. 22-23) so that those who
now receive the mysteries (c. 85) may enter into the light (c.
135). In addition to its concern for the ascent of the number of
perfect souls of the inheritance of the light (c. 86), PS also
shows a concern for the consummation of the aeon, the dissolution
of the All, and the punishment of sinners (e.g. c. 23, 86, 119).

PS is interested in portraying the evil, lower spheres
and the various aeons through which the soul must pass and the
mysteries necessary to pass through them before the soul can reach
the light.

For its concluding elements, the disciples receive the
command to preach the repentance, which will make men worthy to
receive the mysteries (c. 102). The threat of persecution which
the disciples receive is from the archons of the world (c. 7).

With PS I-III, we come to the last of the gnostic apocalypses which do not involve an otherworldly journey (although we
have noted some mixed genres: Allog and PS IV). In contrast to
the Jewish apocalypses, noticeable in the gnostic writings is the
lack of emphasis upon visions and the prominence of dialogue.
What was a minor mode of communication in the Jewish apocalypses
(see Collins) has become the most frequent mode in gnostic revelations. In matters of substance, as we suggested at the start of
this essay, the gnostic emphasis upon present salvation through
knowledge is also strikingly different from the emphasis in the
Jewish apocalypses upon a future salvation, although the gnostic
apocalypses do retain a future element to the salvation.

Type II: Otherworldly Revelation and Otherworldly
Journey

Discourses

The Paraphrase of Shem CG VII,1 (ParaShem)

Our second main category of gnostic apocalypses consists
of those which have an otherworldly revelation and an otherworldly
journey. Here, too, we shall consider first those apocalypses
which involve a discourse but no dialogue. Subsequently, we shall
consider those with dialogue.

Our first example, ParaShem, is a report by Shem of how
he was snatched up out of his generation by his mind and brought
up to the edge of creation (1.2-11). There his mind separated
from his body as in sleep; he saw no earthly image, since light
was there; implicitly then Shem saw the light and heard a revelation of Derdekeas concerning the origin of the world and of men,
the destruction by flood, and the future fate of the world (1.12ff).
Derdekeas predicts the destruction of Sodom, the coming of a revealer and a final destruction of the end.

To date, scholars have noted that ParaShem has no Christian references and that Hippolytus in his *Refutatio omnium
haeresium* 5.19 has a similar account of the origins of the world,
which he attributes to the Sethians and which shows a Christianized version. Thus, the ParaShem can probably be dated to the
second half of the second century (Wisse, 1970:139).

There is an extensive discussion of the original principles--light, darkness, and unbegotten Spirit in the middle--and the origin of the cosmos from them. There is a prediction of a primordial event, i.e., the destruction of Sodom (28.34-29.33). As in ApocAd, this prediction should probably be associated with the *ex eventu* prophecies of Jewish apocalypses, although here too the concern is with primordial history rather than simply history. According to the soteriology of ParaShem, the seed of Shem is the special race of gnostics who are to receive this revelation from him (25.12-15; 26.21-24) in order that light within them might be rescued (26.21-24 and 28.27-30). The revealer too is to come in order to open the gates (36.2-6). The eschatology focuses more on the consummation. The cosmos is to be destroyed (48.19-22) and thought will be separated from darkness and enter into the indescribable light of the unbegotten Spirit (48.21-27).

The forces of the present universe, i.e., the three basic principles and the derived powers, are revealed. The powers which derive from darkness are evil in that they prevent the return of the thought to the Spirit.

For its concluding elements, the need to transmit or preach the revelation is frequently emphasized in the document (26.17-25; 28.34-29.6; 41.2-5; 48.30-49.9). There is no account of the revealer's departure; rather, Shem wakes up as from a long sleep (41.21-22). After the awakening of Shem there is another hearing of the voice of Derdekeas to assure that the revelation will be transmitted after the departure of Shem (47.32-49.9). Within the discourse it is said that Shem and his race are to be persecuted by darkness and nature (29.7-12).

As we previously mentioned, Allog includes in its first section a discourse of the revealer Youel to the seer Allogenes but in its second section an otherworldly journey of Allogenes without a question and answer pattern. Allog in this second section is the only other example of an apocalypse with otherworldly journey which contains discourse rather than dialogue. We turn now to those with dialogue.

Dialogues

Zostrianos CG VIII,1 (Zost)

Our first document, the tractate Zost, is an apocalypse in which, after a period of questioning and perplexity by Zostrianos, an angel of the knowledge of the eternal All appears to him. The angel then guides him on an otherworldly journey, and Zostrianos has a vision of the various aeons in his ascent. At each stage of the ascent Zostrianos is informed of the names of those who dwell in the aeon and he is baptized in their name. The principal figures in this system are the triple-powerful, invisible Spirit, the virgin Barbelo, and the aeons Kalyptos, Protophanes, and Autogenes. When the revelations are finished, Zostrianos returns to the perceptible world.

Sieber has noted already that there are no discernible Christian traits in the document. Further, the names of the figures in the gnostic system relate Zost to such other documents as ApocAd, 3 StelesSeth, Allog, ApocryJn and GEgypt. Lastly, this tractate Zost seems to be the work which Porphyry says was refuted by Plotinus' disciple Amelius in his *Life of Plotinus* 16 and therefore must antedate 270 CE.

The fall of Sophia and the resultant creation of the world are discussed (9.16-11.9) as well as the origin of the figures of the upper world above (e.g. 14.1-23.17). The saving power of knowledge is presented (129.8-22). The ignorant are to be subject to destruction (128.8-14; 131.20-132.5). There is no explicit discussion of personal afterlife, although such may be present implicitly in the exhortation to save oneself and escape from matter (131.1-132.5).

The present heavenly realities include the perceptible world, which is the result of the fall of Sophia, and the aeons above (4.20-5.10; 9.16-11.9).

For its concluding elements, Zostrianos returns to the perceptible world and begins to preach to the elect (129.21-132.5).

The Apocalypse of Paul CG V,2 (ApocPaul)

Our next document, the gnostic ApocPaul, is a Christian apocalypse in which a small boy appears to Paul and exhorts him to awaken his mind and know what is hidden and thus come to the twelve apostles (19[13].10ff). Thereupon, the spirit takes Paul and brings him upon a journey through the heavens where he sees in vision the judgment and punishment of sinful souls until he finally arrives at the tenth heaven where he is greeted by his fellow spirits. There are elements of dialogue in the heavenly journey in that Paul witnesses a dialogue between the punishing angels and the accused soul (20[14].10ff) and in that Paul himself responds to the questions of the "old man" in the seventh heaven (23[17].1ff). But there is no dialogue between Paul's guide, the Spirit, and himself. It is difficult to date or locate precisely ApocPaul.

Paul is called to awaken his mind and know what is hidden and thus come to the twelve apostles (19[13].10ff). His ascent is probably a paradigm of salvation. In his ascent, Paul sees the fate of sinful souls, i.e., they are punished in the fifth heaven and cannot ascent to the highest heaven (22[16].2-12). Even he, Paul, cannot pass the "old man" in the seventh heaven unless he has the appropriate sign. The present heavenly realities include the lower heavens, which prevent one's ascent and in this respect are evil and through which one's soul must ascend to reach the tenth heaven.

Although there is no narrative conclusion, an idea of preaching the revelation may be implicit in Paul's desire to return to the world and "lead the captivity of Babylon captive" (23[17].13-17).

As a final example of this type, we mention I Jeu. As we shall discuss shortly, the first section of I Jeu is a gnostic dialogue without a heavenly journey, but after the lacuna following c. 32, a heavenly journey takes place in which the disciples question Jesus (c. 33, 39, 40). We shall discuss I Jeu in the following section. At this point, we also recall PS IV as a mixed type of apocalypse which contains both an appearance and dialogue and then later an otherworldly journey with dialogue.

In conclusion to this section, we may say that the above writings all show forth the characteristics of the definition of an apocalypse set forth in the Introduction. In addition, these apocalypses show forth the gnostic specifics of an emphasis on present salvation through knowledge and a cosmic dualism in which the lower heavens and/or their rulers are evil and only the transcendent realm is good. We have divided these gnostic apocalypses into two main types--those which do not have an otherworldly journey (I) and those which do (II). Of the sub-types, we note that, strictly speaking, there are no examples of the historical apocalypses either without (Ia) or with (IIa) an otherworldly journey. As we pointed out in the discussion, ApocAd, Melch (I) and ParaShem (II) do have phenomena that should be related to the historical type of Jewish apocalypses; but they cannot be considered, strictly speaking, historical apocalypses. There are representatives of the sub-type of cosmic apocalypses in the gnostic writings in that there are some references to the judgment of the world and/or evil cosmic powers both in those without (Ib: Melch, 2 ApocJas, GMary, NatArch, PS I-III) and those with (IIb: ParaShem) an otherworldly journey. The remainder of the gnostic apocalypses show an interest only in personal afterlife and can be considered representative of the sub-type of mystical apocalypses (Ic: ApocAd, Allog, SJC, ApocryJn, 1 ApocJas, ApocPet, PetPhil, PS IV; IIc: Zost, ApocPaul). Even those with a reference to the theme of judgment (Ib and IIb) should be associated here (Ic and IIc), since their view of salvation involves not a cosmic transformation but merely personal afterlife. In our presentation we have further distinguished those apocalypses with discourse from those with dialogue, and lastly we also noted a few examples of mixed types (Allog, I Jeu, PS IV).

Related Types

Among the many other tractates in the Nag Hammadi corpus, there are some related, revelatory writings whose study may be helpful to an understanding of the gnostic apocalypses. These writings include especially the gnostic revelatory dialogues and the gnostic revelatory discourses, which we shall treat. In addition, representatives of the following types are also present and will be introduced: Christian apocalypse, revelatory stele, and revelatory journey and epiphany.

Gnostic Revelatory Dialogues

Within the gnostic documents there is a small group of dialogues which contain all of the characteristics of the gnostic apocalypse with one notable exception. There is no account of the appearance or departure of the revealer and thus no clear presentation of Jesus as a transcendent mediator as in the gnostic apocalypses. Before we introduce them, it is necessary to consider briefly one other document from Nag Hammadi, *The Gospel of Thomas* CG II,2 (GTh), which has been discussed by scholars in relation to this category of revelatory dialogue. In itself, the GTh is not a revelatory dialogue; it is a collection of sayings (Koester, 1971a; Robinson, 1971). In it are gathered the sayings which the Living Jesus supposedly spoke to his disciples and which Didymus Judas Thomas had written down. Scholars have been divided as to whether the GTh is dependent upon the canonical Gospels (Grant; Schrage), partially dependent and partially independent of them (Wilson), or independent of them (Koester, 1971a). In any case, the GTh dates from the middle of the second century and probably derives from the East Syrian region (Koester, 1971b:127).

Thomas the Contender CG II,7 (ThCont)

The first example of a revelatory dialogue without an account of an appearance of the revealer is ThCont. ThCont purports to be a dialogue after the resurrection between Jesus and Judas Thomas, which Matthaios overheard and has written down. The tractate indeed consists of a dialogue throughout the first section, but then the questioning ceases and there follows a section which includes sayings material such as woes and blessings. The theme running throughout the tractate is ascetic, i.e., to flee the body with its passions and lusts.

Because of this noticeable shift in types of material within the document, scholars have proposed the use of sources in its composition. Turner suggested that the dialogue was prefixed to a homily with sayings type material. Perkins agreed that the dialogue was prefixed to a source, but identifies the latter as a paraenetic source. With regard to the genre of the tractate, Robinson in comparing it with the GTh suggested that ThCont was "more nearly in transition to the gattung of dialogues of the resurrected Christ with his disciples" than representative of the type of sayings-collection (Robinson, 1971:82). From a slightly different viewpoint, Perkins (chap. 4) compared ThCont with the other gnostic apocalypses with dialogue and suggested that the paraenetic source has been incorporated into an introductory section which followed gnostic literary conventions. However, since neither the appearance nor the departure of the revealer are recounted, perhaps one might say either that the source has not been completely assimilated to the genre gnostic apocalypse and instead remains a dialogue (although revelatory in content) or that the source has been developed into a revelatory dialogue (cf. Robinson and Rudolph). In any case, it seems that the issue deserves more detailed study. With regard to the date of ThCont, Turner has suggested that the sources of ThCont derive from the first half of the third century and that the redaction stems from the latter half of the same century (Turner: 5). It is questionable whether ThCont is even gnostic at all. Turner has stressed that the tractate does not present the gnostic myth of the pleroma or the cosmogony or the divine identity of the soul and thus could be considered merely as ascetic and dualistic. However, since even he admits that some gnostic features are present (227), it seems appropriate to include ThCont in this introduction until its gnostic status is clarified.

Salvation is ultimately escape from the body. It is dependent, however, upon knowledge of who one is and detachment from the body with its lusts and passions (e.g. 138.15-18). According to its eschatology, the souls of those who were not detached from the body will be judged and sent to Tartarus. Those who knew, were detached, suffered and continued in unity with the King, will attain rest and rule with the King.

There is no systematic presentation of heavenly realities, but it is presupposed that the King rules over the all. There is an interest in personal ruling with the King after separation from the body. On the other hand, the archon and celestial beings prevent the ascent of lustful souls. It is not clear that the archon and celestial beings are considered evil beyond this.

For its concluding elements, the recipients are to preach the revelation and suffer in so doing (144.39-145.8). There is the threat of persecution of the preachers of this word (144.39) and of the recipients (145.1-8).

The Dialogue of The Savior CG III,5 (DialSav)

The second example of a revelatory dialogue with no appearance of the revealer is the DialSav. The tractate contains a dialogue between Jesus and his disciples and the holy women. The time of the dialogue is not clearly after the resurrection. In the dialogue sayings attributed to Jesus are quoted (Doresse: 220-221). Further analysis of the document will no doubt clarify the relations among a collection of sayings of Jesus such as the GTh, revelatory dialogues such as ThCont and DialSav which incorporate sayings material, and a later work such as PS, which uses and reinterprets sayings material extensively and which exhibits all the characteristics of the revelatory dialogue including the appearance of the revealer (Robinson, 1971:79-85). The DialSav is also of interest because it contains symbolic episodes and visions (e.g. 134.24-135.7 and 136.17-20), which may have been independent (Puech). While aspects of the pleroma and the cosmogony are considered, the primary concern of the document is with the fate of the soul (Perkins: chap. 4).

The origin of the world is discussed (127.19-131.15) and can be considered as the place of deficiency (139.13-20). The souls that have known their consorts do not die (125.4-17), and the person who has known himself has already seen the place of pure light (132.6-19). The ignorant are to perish with the body (134.11-14). The works of femaleness are to be dissolved at the end (144.22-145.10), which probably include both matter and the archons. The disciples seek to understand not only how they came to this place of deficiency but also how they shall go (142.16-19) and are informed concerning the garments they shall receive when they come forth from the flesh (143.11-25).

The present heavenly realities include the evil archons through whom the Savior passed on his descent (120.20-25) and the place of light, the bridal chamber, to which the disciples will attain when they rid themselves of envy (138.10-20).

The First Book of Jeu (I Jeu)

Our next document, the I Jeu, opens with Jesus engaged with his apostles and disciples in a dialogue. There is a general reference to the fact that Jesus had come out of the light aeon in chapter 1 but no presentation of his appearance for this specific revelation. The first questions and answers are filled with gospel material. After a lacuna, Jesus continues with a discourse concerning the various aeons, their watchers, and emanations. The discourse reaches the twenty-eighth Jeu when another lacuna occurs. After this lacuna, Jesus and his disciples are portrayed as ascending to the fifty-fifth to the sixtieth treasuries (c. 33-38). The disciples question and learn about the treasuries, their places and dwellers, and they receive the name by which the dwellers will draw back so that they might reach the places of the Father.

The pieces, which together form the Bruce Codex in which the books of Jeu are found, date from the fifth century. Since the Books of Jeu are referred to in PS, they must stem from an earlier period, i.e., the beginning of the third century, and derive from the same circle of gnostics (Schmidt and Till: xxxff.).

Concerning the genre, Koester has suggested that I Jeu may be a further development of the sayings collection in its use of gospel material (Koester, 1971a:194 n. 122). From the viewpoint of gnostic apocalypses, Perkins has noted after the first lacuna (c. 33) the shift away from the dialogue with its gospel material and into the otherworldly journey motif (Perkins: chap. 10).

I Jeu presents an ordered treatment of the emanation of the Jeus and their aeons. According to Jesus in I Jeu, the life of his Father is to receive one's soul from the race of mind and to become knowledgeable through what he says and thus to be saved from the archon of this aeon (c. 2). Those who do not know are destined to destruction (c. 4). The journey through the treasuries is to provide knowledge about them but also to provide the name by which they will draw back and allow the soul to ascend to the place of the Father (c. 40). Above the evil archon of this aeon are the Jeus and treasuries. It is through them that the soul must ascend in order to reach the light.

The document ends with a prayer, rather than a narrative of the revealer's departure.

The Second Book of Jeu (II Jeu)

One final example of a revelatory dialogue in which there is no account of the appearance of the revealer is II Jeu. In it the Lord reveals to his perplexed disciples the mysteries to be received and the seals and apologies to be used by the soul in its ascent through the aeons. Actually the dialogue element is not prominent. There are only the question concerning the mysteries of the light treasury (c. 44) and the request concerning the mystery of the forgiveness of sins (c. 51). As a result, the document appears more as a treatise with a framework of a revelatory dialogue.

With regard to soteriology, the disciples receive the three baptisms of water, fire and Holy Spirit and the mystery of spiritual anointing (c. 45ff). The evil archons of the aeons retain those who have not received the mysteries (c. 51). The real concern of the document is in the departure of the soul from the body (c. 49) and the seals and numbers and apologies, which the soul will need, as it passes through the aeons (c. 52) to the light treasury. At present, the heavens are ruled by evil archons (c. 44), but more important are the pleromatic aeons through which the soul must pass (c. 52ff) to the light.

The recipients are strictly ordered to give the mysteries only to the children of light who have left behind the world and its gods and divinities (c. 43). However, this instruction occurs at the opening of the work rather than at its conclusion.

Gnostic Revelatory Discourses

Our next type is that of the revelatory discourse. In his study of the style of the gnostic revelatory discourse, Becker has identified three elements as constitutive of this scheme: self-predication, invitation, and promise. In the self-predication, the revealer identifies himself and often his essence and origin, as well as the situation of the cosmos which prompted his coming. The invitation or call to decision is a call from the divine realm into the world and either related to the calling subject or turned to the ethical demand. The promise is the blessing which awaits those who follow the call of the revealer. Often this is combined with a threat against unbelievers, so that together the promise and threat form a crisis-saying. The form of the saying may be a makarism plus "woe" saying (Becker: 54-55). Becker also noted these further features of the revelatory discourse. The discourses do not progress in a single, logical manner but rather follow a spiral, repetitious pattern. Secondly, they often use a rhythmic pattern which is marked by synthetic or antithetic parallelism of members. Thirdly, reflection or retrospective speculation is far from them (Becker: 56-58).

A number of the Nag Hammadi tractates, which we shall presently discuss, provide further material for the analysis of Becker. Since these revelatory discourses present an otherworldly mediator but do not involve a pseudonymous seer, they are not to be included in the gnostic apocalypses which we have studied. However, awareness of the revelatory discourses may shed light on the gnostic apocalypses. Further study may show that features from the revelatory discourse are also present in the speeches or dialogues of the gnostic apocalypses.

The Thunder: The Perfect Mind CG VI,2 (Thund)

The first example of this type is the work entitled the Thund. This tractate is a very distinctive document in the Nag Hammadi corpus. It is entirely a discourse of a revealing, evidently female, figure. There is no narrative element in the tractate. It is written in the first person style with many examples of the *egō eimi* formula. What is especially peculiar in the document is the revealer's identification of herself with opposites, e.g. "I am the first and the last, I am the honored one and the scorned one, I am the whore and the holy one" (13.15-18). After an initial self-predication there is a call: "Look at me, you who think of me, and hear me, you hearers" (13.6-7). Throughout the remainder of the tractate there is a spiral repetition of self-predication and calls (13.15-21.20). Finally, the Thund closes with a promise: those who become sober, i.e., who avoid passions or pleasures, will go up to their resting place, will find the revealer there, will live and not die again (21.20-30). Because of its nature, the Thund is very difficult to date or place, but it indeed confirms the analysis of Becker concerning the components of the gnostic revelatory discourse.

Trimorphic Protennoia CG XIII,1 (TriProt)

Another example of this type, the TriProt, is a tractate with three revelatory discourses of one female figure, in which she recounts her three descents into the world. In her first discourse, she identifies herself as Protennoia and Barbelo, presents the cosmogony and states that in her first descent she destroyed the bonds of the demons and provided the sons of light with an image (40.30-41.15). In her second discourse, she relates that her next descent was to announce the end of the present aeon and the coming of the aeon of light and that her descent nearly caused the destruction of the cosmos (43.5ff). In her last discourse, she asserts that in her final descent she appeared as the Logos, put on the clothing of the powers in her descent in order to fool them, taught the children of light about their brothers, and also put on Jesus and carried him away from the accursed wood (50.13-15).

In the discourses, sentences with the "I am" formula are very frequent. They and the other sentences of self-predication portray Barbelo as the origin of the All and the agent of salvation for the children of light. The gnostics are addressed frequently in the tractate and receive the call: "Hear me, you children of understanding; listen to the voice of the mother of your mercy, for you have been made worthy to receive the mystery hidden from eternity" (44.30-34). They receive the promise that if they enter the light they will receive glory, a throne, clothing, and baptism (45.13ff). The mythology employed identifies the tractate as Sethian, while the references to Jesus and Christ appear to be light Christianizations of a non-Christian document (Schenke).

Since there is a revealing figure but no pseudonymous seer, TriProt is appropriately classified as a revelatory discourse. It is interesting to note, however, that there are two responses from the unnamed gnostics to the discourse of Barbelo at 36.33-37.3 and 42.22-23. Further, each of the discourses is filled out with more speculative material which is less appropriate to the style of the revelatory discourse, e.g. the cosmogony in 35.3-20, the eschatology in 43.1-29, and the soteriology in 49.23-40. Perhaps both of these features, the answers and the more speculative material, are influences from the gnostic apocalypses.

The Second Treatise of the Great Seth CG VII,2 (GrSeth)

Our third example of this type, the GrSeth, is a Christian revelatory discourse given by a figure who later identifies himself as Jesus Christ, the Son of Man (69.20-22). The use of the first person singular and self-predication are repeated in varying terms throughout the tractate. The main focus is upon the revealer's coming into the world, his apparent death at the hands of the archons, and his return. But there is also a presentation that they, the gnostics, have been persecuted "not only by those who are ignorant but even by those who believe they are rich in the name of Christ" (59.22-26). But the gnostics are promised that they will be victorious in every occasion, since they possess a thought of the Father in an unspeakable mystery (60.3-12). The teaching of the archons is further said to be erroneous as well as the teaching of all those from Adam to Moses to the prophets to John the Baptist (60.13-64.12). The discourse closes with an invitation: "Rest now with me, my co-spirits, and my eternal brothers" (70.8-10).

Once again the presence of the revealer, addressing his hearers in the first person, but the absence of a pseudonymous seer mark the tractate as a revelatory discourse. It is noticeable that the typical calls to awaken, to hear, and to know are not prominent; nor are promises of life or rest to those who know the revealer. Rather, the invitation to rest and the promise of victory to those who suffer persecution bespeak the situation for which the discourse was composed, i.e., a situation of conflict with the orthodox church (those "rich in the name of Christ"; see Gibbons: 1ff.). This conflict probably marks the tractate as coming from a later period; the emphasis upon Seth would indicate a derivation from the Sethian stream of gnosticism.

The Concept of Our Great Power CG VI,4 (GrPow)

Our final example of this type, the GrPow, is a Christian revelatory discourse in which a revealing figure speaks in the first person singular but in which there is no "I am" formula. Since the addressees are not named, there are also no pseudonymous seers. However, the addressees receive the call to know how the one who has gone away came into being in order that they might know the one who lives to come into being (36.27-31). In the discourse itself there is a review of history, which divides the periods of revelation into three aeons. The first period is the aeon of flesh in which the revelation is made to Noah (38.21ff). Next is the psychic aeon in which a revealer appears to preach in parables and be handed over to the rulers, i.e., Christ, although he is not explicitly named (39.16-45.24). Finally, there are the aeon of judgment in which the cosmos is destroyed and the aeon of beauty to which the gnostics go (45.24ff). Those who belong to the revealer receive various promises. For example, in the context of the second aeon, those are proclaimed blessed who will know what has been spoken to them for they will know the truth that they have come to rest in the heavens (42.23-31). In the context of the third aeon, the revealer proclaims: "I will withdraw with everyone who knows me and they will go into the immeasurable light" (46.6-9).

It is difficult to date or place the GrPow, but concerning its type it is appropriate to locate it within the category of revelatory discourse, since there is a revealer but no pseudonymous seer or dialogue. However, the content with its review of history is more appropriate to the gnostic apocalypses and revelatory dialogues. There is even a set of questions at the beginning of the discourse, but in this case the revealer rather than the seer asks the questions: "Why do you not ask how you will be or how you have come to be" (37.2-5). Thus, GrPow may reflect a mixing of the types.

Christian Apocalypse

The Apocryphon of James CG I,1 (ApocryJas)

Among the Nag Hammadi writings there is one representative of the type Christian apocalypse, i.e., ApocryJas, which should be introduced here. This tractate is actually an epistle of James which contains an apocalypse, an account of a special revelation given to James and Peter after the resurrection (2.19-15.5). In this revelation the seers are exhorted to be filled with the Spirit; to endure persecution; to believe in the cross; to have faith, love, and works (8.11-14); to receive the Kingdom of Heaven through knowledge (8.24-27) and to be awake (9.33-35). After James and Peter witness the ascent of the Savior, the other disciples are informed, believe and are sent off to other places.

We have considered the ApocryJas here since it is disputed whether the tractate is gnostic or not. While some have noted the absence of the gnostic myth of the pleroma or the cosmos, they have yet considered it an example of gnosticism (Puech: 338) or semi-gnosticism (Brown, 1972:63-69); others prefer to see it as not gnostic (Van Unnik: 87; Perkins: chap. 5). Scholars have also noted that ApocryJas shows affinities with the early Christian writings *The Ascension of Isaiah* in the number of days between the resurrection and the ascension (550 for ApocryJas; 545 for AscenIs) and the *Epistula Apostolorum* in the stress upon the ascension of the Lord (Perkins).

The focus of interest is not upon cosmic destruction or cosmic salvation but upon present, personal salvation, the life attained by faith and knowledge (14.8-19). Woe is pronounced for those who have only seen the Son of Man (3.17-25) and for those who have not believed (12.35-13.1). Further, it is said that none of those who have worn the flesh will be saved (12.12-13). Concerning eschatology, Jesus reascends to where he came from and invites his followers to follow him there (10.22-30).

The heavenly realities are not described or emphasized and yet are part of the presentation. Jesus is the one who has come from there (8.37-9.4), who will reascend and who invites his disciples to follow him there (10.22-30).

Concerning the concluding elements, the Savior encouraged preaching (10.9-14) during the dialogue. The departure of Jesus here is his ascension to the Father, which is witnessed by James and Peter (15.5-28). After the other disciples are informed by James and Peter and believe, they are sent off to other places by James (16.2-8). Also, James and Peter are exhorted to endure persecution (4.37-5.35) during the dialogue rather than at its conclusion.

Revelatory Stele

The Three Steles of Seth CG VII,5 (3 StSeth)

Our next type is that of the revelatory stele. In this category we have the 3 StSeth, a tractate in which Dositheos reveals to the chosen ones the content of the three steles of Seth which he has read and remembered (118.10-19). The steles are in the form of prayers to the Father on the first, to Barbelo on the second, and to the first eternal one on the third stele. In these steles, Seth as the father of the immovable race praises the divine figures for saving him and his race and for revealing the word to him and petitions for further knowledge and salvation. The tractate concludes with an exhortation to the living to know that they have taught themselves about the boundless and to marvel at the truth and revelation in them (127.21-27).

While this tractate is clearly not a gnostic revelation in the sense of a revelation by an otherworldly mediator to a pseudonymous seer, the 3 StSeth should probably be examined in the context of the stele as a mode of revelation in Hellenistic and Greco-Roman literature.

Revelation Journey and Epiphany

The Acts of Peter and the Twelve Apostles CG VI,1 (AcPetTwAp)

The final related type is that of the revelatory journey and epiphany. The one example in this category, the AcPetTwAp, is not a revelation but a book of acts of the apostles. However, within it there is an appearance of the risen Lord. After the apostles travel by ship to the island of Gorg, the Lord appears to them first as a beggar selling pearls, then as a doctor, and finally as the risen Lord. Even then the apostles do not recognize the Lord until he identifies himself to them (9.11-15). In a dialogue then with the apostles, Jesus instructs them to teach those in the city who believe in his name, to give to the poor, to heal the sick who believe and to avoid making friends with the wealthy (10.1-12.13).

Clearly there are similarities to the genre of apocalypse in that there is a heavenly mediator, Christ, and there are pseudonymous seers, the apostles. However, the motifs of the earthly journey, appearance of the deity in human form and mistaken identity plus the difference in content suggest that one should look in the literature of the acts of the apostles and the literature of

Greco-Roman "apocalyptic" for proper determination of this type (see the paper of Attridge).

With ApPetTwAp we conclude our introduction to the related categories of revelatory literature to be found in the Nag Hammadi documents. It is clear that a full analysis of the gnostic apocalypses should take into account as well these other categories of revelatory literature.

GNOSTIC REVELATIONS	1.1.1 Vision	1.1.2 Epiphany	1.2.1 Discourse	1.2.2 Dialogue	1.3 Otherworldly journey	2. Otherworldly mediator	3.1 Pseudonymous seer	3.2 Disposition of recipient	3.3 Reaction of recipient	4.1 Theogony and/or cosmogony	4.2 Primordial events	5.2 Ex eventu prophecy	6. Present salvation by knowledge	8.1 Judgment of sinners or ignorant	8.2 Judgment of world	8.3 Judgment of otherworldly beings	9.2 Personal afterlife	10. Otherworldly elements: good and evil	11. Paraenesis	12. Instructions to recipient	13. Narrative conclusion
I Jeu			x	x	x	x		x					x	x			x	x			
DialSav	x		x		x	x		x					x	x	x	x	x	x			
ThCont			x		x	x		x					x*	x			x	x*		x	x*
ApocPaul	x	x*	x	x	x	x							x	x			x	x			x*
Zost	x	x		x	x	x	x			x			x	x			x*	x			x
ParaShem		x		x	x	x		x		x	x	x*	x		x		x	x		x	x
PS I-III		x	x		x	x	x	x		x*			x	x	x		x	x		x	x*
PS IV	x	x	x	x	x	x		x					x	x			x	x			
PetPhil		x	x		x	x	x			x			x				x	x		x	x
ApocPet	x	x	x		x	x	x	x					x	x			x	x		x	x*
1 ApocJas		x	x		x	x	x	x		x			x				x	x	x	x	x
NatArch		x	x		x	x	x	x		x	x*		x		x	x	x				x*
GMary		x	x		x	x	x						x	x*			x	x		x	x
ApocryJn		x	x		x	x	x	x		x	x		x	x			x	x		x	x
SJC		x	x		x	x	x	x		x			x	x			x	x			x
Melch		x	x		x	x				x	x	x	x		x		x			x	x
2 ApocJas		x	x		x	x	x	x			x		x			x	x	x		x	x
Allog	x	x	x		x	x	x						x	x			x*	x		x	x
ApocAd		x	x		x	x	x	x	x		x	x*	x	x			x	x		x*	x*

An asterisk indicates that the feature may be present

Manner of Revelation
1.1.1 Vision
1.1.2 Epiphany
1.2.1 Discourse
1.2.2 Dialogue
1.3 Otherworldly journey
2. Otherworldly mediator
3.1 Pseudonymous seer
3.2 Disposition of recipient
3.3 Reaction of recipient

Content: Temporal Axis
4.1 Theogony and/or cosmogony
4.2 Primordial events
5.2 Ex eventu prophecy
6. Present salvation by knowledge
8.1 Judgment of sinners or ignorant
8.2 Judgment of world
8.3 Judgment of otherworldly beings
9.2 Personal afterlife

Content: Spatial Axis
10. Otherworldly elements: good and evil
11. Paraenesis

Concluding Elements
12. Instructions to recipient
13. Narrative conclusion

SELECT BIBLIOGRAPHY

GENERAL

1972-1978 *The Facsimile Edition of the Nag Hammadi Codices.* Published under the Auspices of the Department of Antiquities of the Arab Republic of Egypt in conjunction with the United Nations Educational, Scientific and Cultural organization. Codices I-XIII. Leiden: Brill.

Bianchi, Ugo, ed.
1967 *Le Origini dello Gnosticismo: Colloquio di Messina, 13-18 aprile 1966.* Supplements to *Numen* 12. Leiden: Brill.

Doresse, Jean
1960 *The Secret Books of the Egyptian Gnostics.* New York: Viking.

Hennecke, Edgar
1963, 1965 *New Testament Apocrypha.* 2 vols. Ed. W. Schneemelcher. Trans. and ed. R. McL. Wilson. Philadelphia: Westminster.

Robinson, James M.
1974 *The Nag Hammadi Codices: A General Introduction to the Nature and Significance of the Coptic Gnostic Codices from Nag Hammadi.* Claremont: Institute for Antiquity and Christianity.

Robinson, James M., ed.
1977 *The Nag Hammadi Library.* San Francisco: Harper & Row.

Rudolph, Kurt
1969 "Gnosis und Gnostizismus, ein Forschungsbericht." *ThRu* 34: 121-175, 181-231, 353-361.

1971 "Gnosis und Gnostizismus, ein Forschungsbericht." *ThRu* 36: 1-61, 89-124.

1972 "Gnosis und Gnostizismus, ein Forschungsbericht." *ThRu* 37: 289-360.

1973 "Gnosis und Gnostizismus, ein Forschungsbericht." *ThRu* 38: 1-25.

Scholer, David M.
1970 *Nag Hammadi Bibliography.* Nag Hammadi Studies. Leiden: Brill.

1971-1975 "Bibliographia Gnostica, Supplementum I-V," 13: 2-15; 14: 312-331; 15: 327-345; 16: 316-336; 17: 305-336.

Wisse, Frederik
1971 "The Nag Hammadi Library and the Heresiologists." *VC* 25: 205-223.

1972 "The Sethians and the Nag Hammadi Library." Pp. 601-607 in SBLASP 2. Ed. Lane C. McGaughy. Missoula: Scholars Press.

SYNOPSIS

Attridge, Harold
1979 "Greek and Latin Apocalypses." *Semeia* 14: 159-186.

Collins, John J.
1979 "The Jewish Apocalypses." *Semeia* 14: 21-59.

Koester, Helmut
1971a "One Jesus and Four Primitive Gospels." Pp. 158-204 in J. M. Robinson and H. Koester, *Trajectories through Early Christianity*. Philadelphia: Fortress.

Parrott, Douglas M.
1970 "A Missionary Wisdom 'Gattung': Identification, 'Sitz-im Leben,' History and Connections with the New Testament." Ph.D. dissertation. San Francisco: Graduate Theological Union.

Perkins, Pheme
1972 "The Genre Gnostic Revelation Dialogue." Ph.D. dissertation. Cambridge: Harvard University.

Rudolph, Kurt
1968 "Der gnostische 'Dialog' als literarisches Genus." Pp. 85-107 in *Probleme der koptischen Literatur*. Wissenschaftliche Beiträge der Martin-Luther-Universität. Halle-Wittenberg: Martin-Luther-Universität.

1969 "Gnosis und Gnostizismus, ein Forschungsbericht." *ThRu* 34: 121-175.

Vielhauer, Philip
1965 "Apocalypses." Pp. 581-600 in Hennecke-Schneemelcher 2.

SURVEY

ApocAd

Text and Translation

Boehlig, Alexander and Labib, Pahor
1963 *Koptisch-gnostische Apokalypsen aus Codex V von Nag Hammadi im Koptischen Museum zu Alt-Kairo*. Wissenschaftliche Zeitschrift der Martin-Luther-Universität, Halle-Wittenberg, Sonderband. Halle-Wittenberg: Martin-Luther-Universität.

English Translation

Robinson, J. M., ed.
1977 *The Nag Hammadi Library*, 256-264.

Studies

Beltz, Walther
1970 *Die Adam-Apokalypse aus Codex V von Nag Hammadi: Jüdische Bausteine in gnostischen Systemen*. Habilitationsschrift Humboldt-Universität. Berlin.

Daniélou, Jean
1966 "Review of A. Boehlig and P. Labib, *Koptisch-gnostische Apokalypsen aus Codex V*." *RSR* 54: 285-293.

MacRae, George W.
1972 "The Apocalypse of Adam Reconsidered." Pp. 573-580 in SBLASP. Missoula: Scholars Press.

Schenke, Hans-Martin
1966 "Review of A. Boehlig and P. Labib, *Koptisch-gnostische Apokalypsen aus Codex V*." *OLZ* 61: 32-34.

Allog

Text

>*The Facsimile Edition.*

English Translation

Robinson, J. M., ed.
>1977 *The Nag Hammadi Library*, 443-452.

2 ApocJas

Text and Translation

Boehlig, Alexander and Labib, Pahor
>1963 *Koptisch-gnostische Apokalypsen aus Codex V.*

Funk, Wolf-Peter
>1976 *Die Zweite Apokalypse des Jakobus aus Nag-Hammadi Codex V.*
>TU 119. Berlin: Akademie Verlag.

English Translation

Robinson, J. M., ed.
>1977 *The Nag Hammadi Library*, 249-255.

Studies

Boehlig, Alexander
>1967 "Der jüdische und judenchristliche Hintergrund in gnostischen Texte von Nag Hammadi." Pp. 109-141 in *Le Origini dello Gnosticismo*.

Brown, Scott Kent
>1972 "James: A religio-historical study of the relations between Jewish, Gnostic, and Catholic Christianity in the early period through an investigation of the traditions about James the Lord's brother." Ph.D. dissertation. Providence: Brown University.

>1975 "Jewish and Gnostic Elements in The Second Apocalypse of James (CG V,4)." *NovT* 17: 225-237.

Melch

Text

>*The Facsimile Edition.*

English Translation

Robinson, J. M., ed.
>1977 *The Nag Hammadi Library*, 399-403.

SJC

Text and Translation

Till, Walter C.
>1955 *Die gnostischen Schriften des Koptischen Papyrus Berolinensis 8502.* TU 60. Berlin: Akademie-Verlag.

English Translation

Robinson, J. M., ed.
>1977 *The Nag Hammadi Library*, 206-228.

Studies

Krause, Martin
    1964   "Das literarische Verhältnis des Eugnostosbriefes zur Sophia Jesu Christi." Pp. 215-223 in *Mullus: Festschrift T. Klauser*. JbAC Ergänzungsband 1. Münster: Aschendorff.

Puech, Henri-Charles
    1963   "The Sophia Jesu Christi." Pp. 243-248 in Hennecke-Schneemelcher 1.

Schenke, Hans-Martin
    1962   "Nag Hammadi Studien II: Das System der Sophia Jesu Christi." *ZRGG* 14: 263-278.

ApocryJn

Text, Translation, Commentary

Giversen, Søren
    1963   *Apocryphon Johannis*. Acta Theologica Danica 5. Copenhagen: Prostant apud Munksgaard.

Kasser, Rodolphe
    1964   "Bibliothèque gnostique I: Le Livre secret de Jean." *RThPh* 14: 140-150.

Krause, Martin and Labib, Pahor
    1962   *Die Drei Versionen des Apokryphon des Johannes im koptischen Museum zu Alt-Kairo*. Abhandlungen des Deutschen Archaeologischen Instituts Kairo, Koptische Reihe, Band I. Wiesbaden: Otto Harrassowitz.

Till, Walter C.
    1955   *Die gnostischen Schriften des koptischen Papyrus Berolinensis 8502*.

English Translation

Robinson, J. M., ed.
    1977   *The Nag Hammadi Library*, 98-116.

Studies

Arai, S.
    1968-1969   "Zur Christologie des Apokryphons des Johannes." *NTS* 15: 302-318.

GMary

Text and Translation

Till, Walter C.
    1955   *Die gnostischen Schriften des koptischen Papyrus Berolinensis 8502*.

English Translation

Robinson, J. M., ed.
    1977   *The Nag Hammadi Library*, 471-474.

Studies

Puech, Henri-Charles
    1963   "The Gospel according to Mary." Pp. 340-344 in Hennecke-Schneemelcher 1.

Wilson, Robert McL.
    1968   *Gnosis and the New Testament.* Philadelphia: Fortress.

NatArch

Text, Translation, Commentary

Bullard, Roger A.
    1970   *The Hypostasis of the Archons.* Patristische Texte und Studien 10. Berlin: De Gruyter.

Layton, Bentley
    1974   "The Hypostasis of the Archons or 'The Reality of the Rulers.'" *HTR* 67: 351-394.

    1976   "The Hypostasis of the Archons, Part II." *HTR* 69: 31-101.

English Translation

Robinson, J. M., ed.
    1977   *The Nag Hammadi Library,* 152-160.

Studies

Fallon, Francis T.
    1978   *The Enthronement of Sabaoth: Jewish Elements in Gnostic Creation Myths.* Nag Hammadi Studies 10. Leiden: Brill.

1 ApocJas

Text

Boehlig, Alexander
    1963   *Koptisch-gnostische Apokalypsen aus Codex V.*

English Translation

Robinson, J. M., ed.
    1977   *The Nag Hammadi Library,* 242-248.

Studies

Brown, Scott Kent
    1972   *James.*

ApocPet

Text and/or Translation

Krause, Martin
    1973   "Die Petrusapokalypse." Pp. 152-179 in *Christentum am Roten Meer,* Zweiter Band. Hrsg. F. Altheim und R. Stiehl. Berlin/New York: Walter de Gruyter (hereafter *Christentum am Roten Meer*).

Brown, Scott Kent and Griggs, C. Wilfred
    1975   "The Apocalypse of Peter: Introduction and Translation." *Brigham Young University Studies* 15: 131-145.

Robinson, J. M., ed.
    1977   *The Nag Hammadi Library,* 339-345.

PetPhil

Text

> *The Facsimile Edition.*

English Translation

Robinson, J. M., ed.
    1977   *The Nag Hammadi Library*, 394-398.

Hyps

Text

> *The Facsimile Edition.*

English Translation

Robinson, J. M., ed.
    1977   *The Nag Hammadi Library*, 453.

Pistis Sophia

Text

Schmidt, Carl
    1925   *Pistis Sophia*. Coptica 2. Copenhagen: Gyldendalske Boghandel-Nordisk Forlag.

Translations

Mead, G. R. S.
    1921   *Pistis Sophia*. 2nd ed. London: Watkins.

Schmidt, Carl and Till, Walter C.
    1954   *Koptisch-gnostische Schriften I*. 2nd ed., rev. W. C. Till. GCS 45. Berlin: Akademie-Verlag.

ParaShem

Text and Translation

Krause, Martin
    1973   "Die Paraphrase des Seem." Pp. 2-105 in *Christentum am Roten Meer*. Eds. F. Altheim and R. Stiehl.

English Translation

Robinson, J. M., ed.
    1977   *The Nag Hammadi Library*, 308-328.

Studies

Wisse, Frederik
    1970   "The Redeemer Figure in the Paraphrase of Shem." *NovT* 12: 130-140.

Zost

Text

> *The Facsimile Edition.*

English Translation

Robinson, J. M., ed.
    1977   *The Nag Hammadi Library*, 368-393.

Studies

Sieber, John H.
1973 "An Introduction to the Tractate Zostrianos from Nag Hammadi." *NovT* 15: 233-240.

ApocPaul

Text and Translation

Boehlig, Alexander
1963 *Koptisch-gnostische Apokalypsen aus Codex V von Nag Hammadi.*

English Translation

Robinson, J. M., ed.
1977 *The Nag Hammadi Library*, 239-241.

GTh

Text and Translation

Guillaumont, A., et al.
1959 *The Gospel According to Thomas.* New York: Harper.

English Translation

Robinson, J. M., ed.
1977 *The Nag Hammadi Library*, 117-130.

Studies

Grant, Robert M. and Freedman, David N.
1960 *The Secret Sayings of Jesus.* New York: Doubleday

Koester, Helmut
1971b "'Gnomai Diaphoroi': The Origin and Nature of Diversification in the History of Early Christianity." Pp. 114-157 in J. M. Robinson and H. Koester, *Trajectories through Early Christianity.*

Ménard, Jacques-E.
1975 *L'Evangile selon Thomas.* NHS 5. Leiden: Brill.

Robinson, James M.
1971 "Logoi Sophon: On the Gattung of Q." Pp. 71-113 in J. M. Robinson and H. Koester, *Trajectories through Early Christianity.*

Schrage, Wolfgang
1964 *Das Verhältnis des Thomasevangeliums zur Synoptischen Tradition und zu den koptischen Evangelienübersetzungen.* BZNW 29. Berlin: Töpelmann.

Wilson, Robert McL.
1960 *Studies in the Gospel of Thomas.* London: Mowbray.

ThCont

Text and Translation

Krause, Martin and Labib, Pahor
1971 *Gnostische und Hermetische Schriften aus Codex II und Codex VI.* Abhandlungen des Deutschen Archäologischen Instituts Kairo, Koptische Reihe, Band 2. Glückstadt: Augustin.

English Translation

Robinson, J. M., ed.
    1977   *The Nag Hammadi Library*, 188-194.

Studies

Turner, John D.
    1975   *The Book of Thomas the Contender from Codex II of the Cairo Gnostic Library from Nag Hammadi (CG II,7): The Coptic Text with Translation, Introduction, and Commentary.* SBLDS 23. Missoula: Scholars Press.

DialSav

Text

                The Facsimile Edition.

English Translation

Robinson, J. M., ed.
    1977   *The Nag Hammadi Library*, 229-238.

Studies

Puech, Henri-Charles
    1963   "The Dialogue of the Redeemer." Pp. 248-250 in Hennecke-Schneemelcher 1.

I and II Jeu

Text and/or Translation

Baynes, C. A.
    1933   *A Coptic Gnostic Treatise Contained in the Codex Brucianus (Bruce MS96, Bod. Lib. Oxford): A Translation from the Coptic; Transcription and Commentary.* Cambridge: Cambridge University.

Thund

Text and Translation

Krause, Martin and Labib, Pahor
    1971   *Gnostische und Hermetische Schriften aus Codex II und VI.*

English Translation

Robinson, J. M., ed.
    1977   *The Nag Hammadi Library*, 271-277.

Studies

Becker, Heinz
    1956   *Die Reden des Johannesevangeliums und der Stil der gnostischen Offenbarungsrede.* FRLANT 68 (N.F. 50). Göttingen: Vandenhoeck.

MacRae, George
    1973   "The Thunder, Perfect Mind." Pp. 1-9 in *Protocol of the Fifth Colloquy of the Center for Hermeneutical Studies in Hellenistic and Modern Culture.* 11 March 1973. Berkeley: The Center for Hermeneutical Studies.

Quispel, Gilles
    1975   "Jewish Gnosis and Mandaean Gnosticism: Some Reflections on the Writing *Bronte*." Pp. 82-122 in *Les Textes de Nag Hammadi.* Ed. J. E. Ménard. Nag Hammadi Studies VII. Leiden: Brill.

TriProt

Text and Translation

Janssens, Y.
 1974 "Le Codex XIII de Nag Hammadi." *Muséon* 87: 341-413.

Translation

Robinson, J. M., ed.
 1977 *The Nag Hammadi Library*, 461-470.

Schenke, G.
 1974 "'Die dreigestaltige Protennoia': Eine gnostische Offenbarungsrede in koptischer Sprache aus dem Fund von Nag Hammadi eingeleitet und übersetzt vom Berliner Arbeitskreis für koptisch-gnostische Schriften." *ThLZ* 99: 731-746.

GrSeth

Text and Translation

Krause, Martin
 1973 "Der zweite Logos des grossen Seth." Pp. 106-151 in *Christentum am Roten Meer*.

English Translation

Robinson, J. M., ed.
 1977 *The Nag Hammadi Library*, 329-338.

Studies

Gibbons, Joseph A.
 1972 "A Commentary on 'The Second Logos of the Great Seth.'" Ph.D. dissertation. New Haven: Yale University.

GrPow

Text and Translation

Krause, Martin and Labib, Pahor
 1971 *Gnostische und Hermetische Schriften aus Codex II und VI*.

English Translation

Robinson, J. M., ed.
 1977 *The Nag Hammadi Library*, 284-289.

German Translation

Fischer, K. M.
 1973 "Der Gedanke unserer grossen Kraft (Noema); Die vierte Schrift aus Nag-Hammadi-Codex VI. Eingeleitet und übersetzt vom Berliner Arbeitskreis für koptisch-gnostischen Schriften." *ThLZ* 98: 169-176.

ApocryJas

Text and Translation

Malinine, M., et al.
 1968 *Epistula Jacobi Apocrypha: Codex Jung F. I^r-F. VIII^v* (pp. 1-16). Zürich and Stuttgart: Rascher.

English Translation

Robinson, J. M., ed.
 1977 *The Nag Hammadi Library*, 29-36.

Studies

Puech, Henri-Charles
    1963   "Gnostic Gospels and Related Documents." Pp. 231-362 in Hennecke-Schneemelcher 1.

Unnik, W. C. van
    1960   *Newly Discovered Gnostic Writings.* SBT 30. Trans. H. H. Hoskins. Naperville, IL: Allenson.

3 StSeth

Text and Translation

Krause, Martin
    1973   "Die drei Stelen des Seth." Pp. 180-199 in *Christentum am Roten Meer.*

English Translation

Robinson, J. M., ed.
    1977   *The Nag Hammadi Library,* 362-367.

AcPetTwAp

Krause, Martin and Labib, Pahor
    1971   *Gnostische und Hermetische Schriften aus Codex II und Codex VI.*

English Translation

Robinson, J. M., ed.
    1977   *The Nag Hammadi Library,* 265-270.

GREEK AND LATIN APOCALYPSES

Harold W. Attridge
Perkins School of Theology

SYNOPSIS

During the Hellenistic era and the first three centuries of the Roman Empire, numerous works circulated in Greek and Latin which claimed to present or to record revelations. Within this very loosely defined group of revelatory works several genres may be distinguished by their common formal or contentual features. At least one separate text and one of these distinct genres share many of the features which characterize apocalypses in Jewish and Christian literatures. Like their Jewish and Christian counterparts, these texts are narratives of alleged revelatory experiences which disclose a transcendent world and proclaim eschatological doctrine. The other genres of Greek and Latin revelatory texts listed here often share certain revelatory devices or elements of content with Jewish, Christian and Gnostic texts, although they cannot be considered as apocalypses.

The Apocalypses

The one text which stands virtually alone in this collection is the *Poimandres*. Although it is part of the *Corpus Hermeticum* and shares many doctrinal elements with other Hermetic texts, it is not, like other Hermetic works, simply a scholastic dialogue. Rather, it presents its doctrines of personal eschatology in a visionary form. It thus closely parallels the apocalypses listed under Type Ic in the general introduction.

A second group of texts also should be classed with Jewish and Christian apocalypses. These texts describe otherworldly journeys which were a traditional vehicle for presenting doctrines of personal eschatology. These texts are seldom independent works, as are their Jewish and Christian counterparts (Type IIc), but are parts of longer pieces, often philosophical works. In this case at least, there may have been some historical connection between Greek and Latin literary traditions and the later Jewish and Christian apocalypses (Dieterich).

Related Revelatory Texts

A very few Greek and Roman texts contain political eschatology, so prominent in many of the better known Jewish apocalypses. These texts are similar to Jewish works inasmuch as they stand at the periphery of Hellenistic civilization and represent a reaction to it. The most significant works, in fact, clearly depend on a tradition of Egyptian prophecy. Although the development of eschatology in these texts is relevant to the study of the political and cosmic elements in the eschatology of Jewish apocalypses, the literary form of these texts is that of oracular prophecy. They do not narrate mediated revelations.

Another major group of revelatory texts consists of dialogues on various esoteric subjects, especially speculative philosophy and mystical theology. These texts, especially in the *Corpus Hermeticum*, are also of interest for the study of eschatological beliefs in later antiquity (Festugière). However, their distinctive dialogue form distinguishes them from Jewish and Christian apocalypses. Closely related to them are the Gnostic revelatory dialogues.

Many of the texts in the first groups share significant formal and contentual features. One device which appears frequently as a mode of revelation is the epiphany of a revealer figure. This is an extremely common form throughout antiquity, both in literary and non-literary sources, independently of eschatological doctrine.

A major component of the corpus of revelatory literature in antiquity are the works concerned with occult science: astrology, astro-botany, alchemy, and magic. Here various revelatory formats were used indiscriminately. The significant features defining the genre are the types of subject matter and their arrangement. Although these texts usually lack interest in a transcendent world or in eschatology of any type, they provide further examples of the formal revelatory features which characterize apocalypses.

One final segment of this survey examines a few verse oracles. These are not usually narratives of revelations. They do parallel the eschatology of some apocalypses. Their form is, of course, the same as that of the Jewish and Christian Sibylline collections.

SURVEY

The Apocalypses

Type Ic: Apocalypse with Only Personal Eschatology

The Poimandres

The first tractate of the *Corpus Hermeticum* is probably the best known, and in many ways the most interesting. It displays an unusual combination of revelatory features which are used to present a combination of cosmogony, anthropology and personal eschatology.

The text purports to be an account of a vision by an unnamed mystic in which a revealer, Poimandres, appears and satisfies the mystic's desire to "understand reality and to know god" (1-3). He does this by showing the seer another vision which portrays the process of creation (405). This is accompanied by an explanation of the vision by Poimandres and a dialogue on the further stages of emanation and creation (6-11). There follows a detailed discussion of the creation and nature of man (12-23) and an eschatological section which expresses the ultimate aim of Hermetic gnosis as the divinization of the essential element in the human soul (24-26). At the conclusion of the vision, the seer issues an exhortation to mankind to awake from slumber and to attain the immortalizing gnosis (27-29). The narrator concludes with a hymn and a prayer (30-31).

The following revelatory features may be cited (numbers refer to the paradigm given in the Introduction to this volume):

1.1.1	Visions
1.1.2	Epiphany of Poimandres
1.2.2	Dialogue between Poimandres and the seer
2.	The otherworldly mediator, Poimandres
4.1	A detailed cosmogony, including a description of divine emanations
9.2.2	Divinization is the goal of life
11.	Paraenesis on the part of the seer, after
12.	Instruction from the revealer to be a "guide for the worthy"
13.	Poimandres "mingles with the powers" and departs

Type II: The Revelatory Journey

A common format used to deliver a revelation is that of a journey, either through the heavens or into the underworld. The motif of such otherworldly journeys is ancient and widespread (Bousset, MacCulloch). It would hardly be worthwhile to catalogue all its attestations. However, among all the examples of the journey motif certain instances stand out because of their use in texts which convey definite doctrines about personal afterlife. As noted in the general introduction to this paper, these texts are closely parallel to many Jewish and Christian apocalypses which also heavily accentuate personal eschatology.

It is possible to distinguish three types of text where the motif of the otherworldly journey is prominent. The first group (a) consists of philosophical texts. In the earliest example, the poem of Parmenides, there is no particular concern with eschatology. Eschatology is quite prominent in Plato, whose "Myth of Er" serves as a model for many subsequent uses of the motif, e.g. Cicero and Plutarch. The motif is also parodied in Lucian.

Another group of journey texts (b) record a descent to Hades. These texts include some of the best known literary examples of revelatory journeys--the Odyssey, Book XI and Virgil's Aeneid, Book VI. An account of a descent into Hades was also apparently used by Orphic and Pythagorean groups (Ganschinietz) to present their psychological and soteriological doctrines. Although such accounts do not survive, they were probably influential on the philosophical and literary productions of this type. What Orphics have left behind are tablets from the Hellenistic and Roman periods which describe for a particular deceased person what awaits him in the hereafter. This motif, too, is parodied in Lucian.

One final group (c) consists of several examples where an earthly journey provides the frame for a transmission of some special doctrine or esoteric lore. The texts in this third group are not apocalypses, but are discussed here because of their close similarity to the otherworldly journeys.

(a) Philosophical Revelations

Parmenides

The opening of Parmenides' philosophical poem on the nature of Being is a revelatory vision wherein the philosopher is conveyed on a chariot accompanied by the daughters of the Sun. He is brought before the goddess Justice, who greets him and promises that he will learn the Truth, not merely the opinions of mortals. The text dates from the sixth century BCE.

In common with apocalypses it has the following features:

1.1	A vision and
1.3	a journey
2.	An otherworldly revealer
10.1	Heavenly realms and
10.2	Beings

The text hardly constitutes an apocalypse. There is no eschatology, only metaphysics. The revelatory character of the poem may well be inspired by the forms and motifs of mystery religions. The revelatory features doubtlessly influenced the later philosophical revelations.

Plato, Republic 614B-621B

The Republic concludes with the Myth of Er, a Pamphylian, who, after being apparently slain, experienced a heavenly journey. He viewed the rewards of the just and the punishments of the wicked. He also learned of the cycle of rebirth, in which each soul chooses its lot in life. The focus here is not on the description of the heavenly realm, but on the moral that choice of the best life is the most important act a man performs (cf. 318C). Hence there may already be an adaptation of a type of story in which the emphasis was in fact on the personal eschatology. The dialogue probably dates to around 370 BCE.

In common with apocalypses it has the following features:

1.3	The journey of Er's soul
2.	A mediator, in the form of a spokesman for the Fates, plays a minor role.
3.1	Er is obviously a fictional character.
8.1	He views the post-mortem judgment of the wicked.

Attridge: Greek and Latin Apocalypses

9.2.2	He learns the doctrine of metempsychosis.
10.1	He views the heavens and
10.2	Meets the Fates.
13.	Er's soul returns to its body and he tells of his journey.

Heraclides Ponticus

The works of this fourth century (c. 390-310 BCE) Platonist survive only in fragments. In one of these, either *On the Things in Hades* or *On the Soul*, he relates the vision of a fictional Empedotimos, in which he experienced an epiphany of Pluto and Persephone, who instructed him in the truth about the soul. This psychology included a doctrine of astral immortality, which explained the milky way as a path of souls.

It is unclear whether this piece involved a psychic journey as did the previous piece, or whether it used simply the format of a revelatory vision. In either case, it stands in the tradition of philosophical revelation about personal eschatology.

It displays the following common features:

1.1.1	A vision and possibly
1.3	A journey of the visionary's soul
3.1	A fictional seer, who learns of the
9.2.2	Soul's immortality among the
10.1	Celestial regions

Cicero, Somnium Scipionis

In the last book of Cicero's *De Republica*, Scipio Africanus the Younger, the primary interlocutor in the dialogue, records a dream vision which he experienced in Africa. Scipio Africanus had appeared to him and prophesied the future career of the young man. Then his natural father, Paulus, appeared and, along with Africanus, showed the dreamer a vision of the heavens. They also reveal the path to celestial immortality for the souls of those who conduct themselves nobly in serving the state.

The dialogue was composed during the years 54-51 BCE. The dream of Scipio survives through the commentary on it by the fourth-century CE scholar Macrobius.

Again, this text is not simply the account of a psychic journey, but of a vision with the same results. Like the ultimate model for this type of account, Plato, this vision has an explicitly paraenetic aim. The text displays the following common features:

1.1.1	A vision involving a psychic
1.3	Journey by a
3.1	Fictional seer, who meets
2.	"Otherworldly" mediators, who deliver
5.2	*Ex eventu* prophecies about the seer's career.
9.2.2	They also teach him a doctrine of immortality in
10.1	Heavenly regions.
11.	The revealers exhort the seer.
13.	The dreamer awakes.

Seneca, Ad Marciam de Consolatione

In his attempt to console Marcia on the loss of her sons, Seneca recalls her father, Cremutius Cordus. At the end of the work (chap. 26), Cremutius is imagined to be addressing his daughter from the heavens. He tells her that he is free of life's woes and that from his lofty perch he can survey all of history. He indulges in a bit of Stoic eschatology, predicting that everything mortal will be subject to a catastrophic end. There will be a final conflagration in which even souls which have partaken of immortality will be changed back into their elements. The text displays the following common features:

1.2.1	A discourse by a departed soul which has
1.3	Travelled into the heavens.
3.1	The seer is obviously fictional. He discusses
9.1	Cosmic destruction and
9.2.2	Personal afterlife, thus offering
11.	Consolation to the bereaved Marcia.

Plutarch, De genio Socratis

In chapters 21-22 (589F-592E) of his dialogue on the *daimon* of Socrates, Plutarch includes the vision of one Timarchus. This young initiate in philosophy, contemporary with Socrates, wanted to learn the nature of the mysterious "sign" of the master. He consulted the oracle of Trophonius and in a state between waking and sleep he experienced a visionary heavenly journey. After viewing the ocean-like expanse of the heavens and the abyss of Earth or Hades, Timarchus meets a *daimon* who explains to him the geography of the heavens and who teaches him a psychological doctrine, the central feature of which is the definition of *daimon* as that part of the human soul which is linked to the stars. The text displays the following common features:

1.1.1	A vision of a
1.3	Heavenly journey involving encounter with
2.	An otherworldly mediator, a *daimon*, by a
3.1	Fictional seer, lead to his vision by
3.2	Curiosity. In his visionary journey he learns of
9.2.2	Astral immortality and the nature of
10.1	Heavenly regions and
10.2	The *daimons* who inhabit them.
13.	Timarchus awakes from his visionary trance.

Plutarch, De sera numinis vindicta

In chapters 22-31 (563B-568A), this dialogue on theodicy concludes with a lengthy tale, similar in many features to the Myth of Er. The protagonist, Thespesius, falls and apparently dies, but is revived in three days. In the meantime, his soul experiences a heavenly journey. During the journey he sees how souls ascend to the heavens after death. He learns from the soul of a kinsman about the system of post-mortem reward and punishment, which includes (chap. 31) the punishment of souls at the hands of descendants who had suffered on earth for their forbears' crimes. The vision thus reinforces the main doctrine of divine justice which the dialogue defends. The vision also includes several minor, but interesting, details: a description of the place of Lethe, where souls are "liquified" by pleasures and develop a yearning for reincarnation (chap. 27); a mixing bowl, the oracle of Night and the Moon, which is the source of dreams (chap. 28); and a prediction of the seer's own fate, and of the impending eruption of Vesuvius and the death of Titus (chap. 29). The following may be compared with features of other apocalypses:

1.3	A psychic journey, and an encounter with
2.	An otherworldly mediator, by a
3.1	Fictional seer, who is given
5.2	*Ex eventu* prophecies and instruction on
7.1	Post mortem judgment and punishment, and
9.2.2	A doctrine of metempsychosis
10.1	There is also a description of the heavenly world and
10.2	Its inhabitants.
13.	Finally the seer's soul returns to his body.

Lucian, Icaromenippus

Several satires of this humorist of the second century CE mock or parody the type of otherworldly journey which served as a revelatory device in the pieces so far considered. Lucian's satires were inspired by the satirist of the third century BCE, Menippus. The parodies, like the motif parodied, thus were present both in the Hellenistic and the Greco-Roman periods.

In the *Icaromenippus*, Menippus reports in a dialogue with a friend that he had recently attempted to learn what philosophy could not tell him. He discovered a means to ascend to heaven where he had an interview with Zeus and a dinner with the gods. Zeus delivers a condemnation of speculative philosophy, which Menippus returns to report to its practitioners.

Like many of Lucian's other works, this piece subjects both philosophy and traditional mythology to ridicule. The following features may be compared with those of apocalypses:

1.3	An otherworldly journey
2.	An otherworldly mediator (Empedocles, chap. 13)
3.1	A fictional seer (at least in Lucian's work)
3.3	Puzzlement as the motivation for the journey
8.1	Judgment on philosophers
10.1	Description of heavenly regions and
10.2	The Gods
13.	Return of the seer to tell philosophers

(b) Descents to the Underworld

Homer, Odyssey XI

This book develops what is, no doubt, an ancient epic motif. The hero, in order to gain direction for the remainder of his journey home, engages in necromancy (23-50). He summons the shade of the prophet Teiresias, who tells him what is in store for him on Ithaca and what he must do after overcoming the suitors of Penelope (90-151). Odysseus then meets with the ghosts of various other figures, his mother (152-224), other heroines (225-327) and various heroes from the Trojan War (387-567). Finally he sees several mythical or legendary figures who are being punished for their crimes (568-600).

This last section, more than the rest of the book, is appropriately described as descent into the underworld. It describes not the appearance of disembodied spirits, but scenes of judgment and torment in Hades. Such notions of judgment and punishment appear only here in Homer. Thus the passage has properly been seen as an interpolation, possibly from Orphic sources. However, the interpolation predates Plato, who refers to the scenes described as Homeric (*Gorgias* 525E). The following features may be compared to those of apocalypses:

1.1.2 Epiphanies of the departed
1.3 An implicit underworldly journey
2. An otherworldly prophet
5.2 Prophecy about the seer's fate
8.1 Judgment and punishment of the wicked
9.2.2 An afterlife, of sorts, is presupposed.

Orphic Tablets

These tablets, found in graves dating from the fourth through the second century BCE describe the surroundings in the nether world which the deceased is to find on his or her arrival. They also provide the deceased with a formula to repeat, which apparently would insure his post-mortem beatitude.

These texts cannot be considered apocalypses in any meaningful sense. They are included in order to illustrate one type of revelatory text with a very specific function. They may be related to the Orphic descriptions of the underworld which were written as mediated revelations and which had a more explicit and detailed eschatology.

Virgil, Aeneid VI

In the sixth book of the Aeneid, the hero Aeneas undertakes a journey to the underworld, which follows in many details the journey of Odysseus and which serves some of the same literary purposes. There are also, of course, many points of difference between the two epics.

Virgil's account is prefaced by the story of Aeneas' consultation of the Sibyl. This consultation involves a theophany of Apollo which sets the numinous scene (45-55). The Sibyl then prophesies the wars which Aeneas will have to wage in Italy. Then the hero, in the company of the prophetess, descends to Hades, where he views various souls in Tartarus (548-627), the palace of Hades (628-636), and the fields of Elysium (637-702). From his father, Anchises, Aeneas learns about the fountain Lethe and the doctrine of metempsychosis (703-751). Finally, Anchises shows him the souls of many of his renowned progeny (752-886).

The Aeneid was composed between 26-19 BCE and was left almost completed by Virgil at his death. The following features may be compared with elements of apocalypses:

1.1.2 Epiphany of Apollo
1.3 The otherworldly journey of Aeneas
3. The otherworldly guide, the Sibyl
5.2 *Ex eventu* prophecy of Rome's greatness and prophecy of Aeneas' own future
8.1 Scenes of post-mortem judgment, reward and punishment
9.2.2 A doctrine of metempsychosis
10.1 Otherworldly regions

Lucian, Nekyomanteia and Kataplous

Lucian, again parodying the motifs discussed in this section, produced two pieces involving a descent. In the *Nekyomanteia*, Menippus reports to a friend his descent into Hades. He went in order to satisfy his curiosity about traditional mythology and the values it implied, and to settle questions about which philosophers disputed. He travels to Babylon in search of a magus, Mithrobarzanes. With him he goes to consult Teiresias. He learns from the prophet the uselessness of speculative philosophy and the inferiority of mere material possessions. The following features may be compared with features of apocalypses:

1.3	The otherworldly journey
2.	The mediator Teiresias
3.1	The fictional seer, Menippus
3.2	His curiosity which motivates the descent
8.1	Judgment on the rich
10.1	Description of Hades and
10.2	Its inhabitants
11.	Paraenesis to lead the simple life
13.	Return through the oracle of Trophonius

In the *Kataplous*, or *Downward Journey*, a Cynic lifestyle is compared with more extravagant styles. The piece is actually a dialogue between Clotho, Hermes and Charon. The reaction of several types of people to the fact of death is compared. The man with attachments to the material world naturally does not react as well as the simple man without such attachments. This piece is obviously a more distant relative of the type of literary topos treated in this section. Both the *Nekyomanteia* and the *Kataplous* illustrate a secondary application of the motifs at home in the revelatory texts listed here.

(c) Related Journey Texts which are not Apocalypses (Exotic Voyages)

Euhemerus, Hiera Anagraphe

This travel romance, written at the end of the fourth century BCE, is remotely relevant to the study of revelatory genres because it uses some of the motifs common in those texts. The story relates the travels of Euhemerus to a distant isle, Panchaia, where he found inscribed on stelae the deeds of ancient kings, Ouranus, Chronos and Zeus. On the basis of this "discovery" he develops an historical explanation for mythology. The work only survives in fragments.

(Ps.) Plato, Axiochus

This pseudepigraphical work, dating probably from the first century BCE, discusses the immortality of the soul and concludes with a report from a magus, Gabryes. His grandfather had come across two bronze tablets which had come from the Hyperboreans. These tablets described the fate of the soul after death. According to this account, souls are subjected to the usual judgment and then if just, are sent to the northern celestial hemisphere; if unjust, to the southern.

This text does not actually describe a heavenly journey. It teaches a doctrine of astral immortality common to many of the philosophical revelations. Although there is no actual journey, and there is a distinct revelatory device, the "hidden tablets," the report by the exotic stranger functions in much the same way as the exotic earthly journeys of the preceding and subsequent pieces.

Plutarch, De facie lunae

The whole work is a dialogue narrated by Lamprias. In chapters 26-30 (940F-945D), one of the interlocutors, Sulla, tells of a story told him by an unnamed stranger. This myth teaches that

the moon is inhabited by souls which have left their bodies or
which have not yet been reincarnated. This eschatological myth
had been narrated to the stranger while he was on a journey to a
distant and fabulous isle where he met the "Chamberlains of Chronos."

Here the formal structures of the account are strikingly
similar to those of the previous piece. A doctrine of astral immortality is placed on the lips of an exotic stranger and reported
secondhand.

Related Revelatory Texts

Eschatological Prophecy

This first group of texts consists of one work in Greek,
the Potter's Oracle, which stands in a tradition of Egyptian
prophecy (cf. McCown, Lanczkowski, Smith). Other representatives
of this tradition from the Hellenistic period are the Demotic
Chronicle and the prophecy of the Lamb to Bocchoris.

One further work from this tradition survives in Latin
and Coptic, the apocalypse from the Asclepius. These texts are
listed in an order which approximates their probable dates of composition. That order can only be quite tentative, since there are
conflicting opinions about the dating of some of these pieces. In
any case, several pieces seem to have had a long life, during which
the eschatological time frame was apparently modified and the ancient prophecies applied to new situations. Thus the texts seem
to have been in circulation through much of the Hellenistic and
Roman periods.

In addition to the main representatives of Greco-Egyptian
prophecy with eschatological orientation, there is also a reference
here to some fragmentary works and to another Hellenized oriental
whose work incorporated apocalyptic elements, namely Berossus.

The Demotic Chronicle

This work survives in a Demotic papyrus of the third
century BCE, and the text probably dates to the same period.
Spiegelberg suggests a date under Ptolemy I. Meyer places it
somewhat later in the time of the revolts of native Egyptians under Ptolemy IV (221-205). In any case, there is a clear allusion
to the Greek rulers (col. II. 25). The text consists of a series
of "ancient" oracular utterances which are commented upon in a
pesher fashion. These comments record *ex eventu* prophecies of the
oppression of Egypt by the Persians and the Greeks. They also
predict a future ruler who will set things right. There is no explicit eschatology or concern with the supernatural. Thus the
work might more probably be seen as native Egyptian proto-
apocalyptic. In terms of the comparative pattern employed in this
study, the text involves:

1.4   Writing as the mode of revelation
5.2   *Ex eventu* prophecy of
7.1   Persecution, followed by
9.1   Transformation and Restoration under a good king.

The Lamb to Bocchoris

The second example of eschatologically oriented, yet
politically based, prophecy is the report of the oracle of the
Lamb to Bocchoris, which survives in a Demotic papyrus dating from

the reign of Augustus. The text may have been composed originally
during the Persian period (Koenen, 1970). However, dating in the
first century of Ptolemaic rule is just as likely (Moret). In
either case, the text probably underwent a redaction in Roman times.

The oracle has a frame story which recounts the delivery
of an oracle by a sacred lamb to one Pa·sa·n·horus, who reports
the oracle to the king, Bocchoris. After delivering the prophecy
the lamb dies, is buried, and then is venerated by the king.

The prophecy itself predicts an invasion of Egypt from
Syria, followed by 900 years of oppression. God will end this.
Cult objects which had been stolen from Egypt will be returned and
Egypt will be governed by proper laws.

Testimony to the prophecy is found in Africanus and
Eusebius, who report a somewhat different figure (990 years) for
the period of oppression. The different figure may represent an
adjustment of the eschatological timetable. The pivotal point is
now set in the second century CE, possibly at the beginning of a
new Sothic period.

The text has no particular concern with the supernatural
world. In the terms of the analysis of apocalyptic literature
used in this study, the text displays the following features:

1.2.1	An oracular discourse as the means of revelation
2.1	A mediator with some supernatural aspects
3.1	A recipient who seeks the oracle
3.3	Another recipient, the king, who reacts to the oracle with veneration
5.2	*Ex eventu* prophecy of
7.1	Persecution, followed by
9.1	Transformation and restoration

The Potter's Oracle

This text survives in three Greek papyri of the second
and third century CE. It is the one text of precisely this type
of eschatological prophecy which was probably composed in Greek
and which survives in Greek. The original composition dates
either to the fourth (Roberts) or, more likely, to the second
(Koenen) century BCE.

Like the Lamb, this oracle is set within a frame story
in at least two of the papyri. The texts are fragmentary but the
main line of the story is fairly clear. It tells of a visit by a
potter to a sacred island of Helios. The potter, possibly a manifestation of the potter and creator god Chnum, fires some ceramics
in an oven. Because this activity is sacrilegious, the pots are
pulled out and destroyed. The potter is brought before the king,
Amenophis, where he interprets the destruction of the pots symbolically and utters a prophecy. After his death, he is buried
in Heliopolis and his book of prophecy preserved.

The prophecy itself predicts Greek domination followed
by cosmic and social chaos. The sun will darken, the Nile will
stop flowing and the land will cease producing. War ensues with a
king from Syria. Finally the Greeks will destroy themselves and
Alexandria will be laid waste. A king will come from the sun, sent
by the "Great Goddess," and he will restore Egypt.

Koenen (1970) has analyzed the tradition represented by the three fragmentary texts and has suggested that the latest text (P. Oxy. 2332), which lacks the narrative framework, speaks primarily of cosmic renewal and not simply of national restoration. In comparison with other apocalypses, this text displays the following features:

1.2.1	Oracular discourse as the mode of revelation
2.	A possibly otherworldly figure, who in any case is
3.1	Fictional (=pseudonymous). He delivers an
5.2	*Ex eventu* prophecy of
7.1	Persecution, followed by
7.2	Eschatological upheavals,
9.1	Then Restoration under a divinely guided ruler.

The Asclepius "Apocalypse"

In the Hermetic dialogue called the Asclepius, there is a section of eschatological prophecy in which Hermes laments to Asclepius over the fate of Egypt. This section (chaps. 24-26 = CG. VI. 70-74), which survives in both Latin and Coptic versions, is unique in Hermetic literature. Various sources have been suggested, including Jewish (Nock) and Iranian (Reitzenstein). The piece, however, seems most at home in the native Egyptian tradition, from which stem the first three pieces in this collection. With this Egyptian tradition, the text mixes elements of popular philosophy, including Platonic imagery about God the Steersman, and Stoic language about cosmic cycles.

Dating is difficult. A fragment of the Asclepius survives in a Greek papyrus of approximately 200 CE (P. Mimaut, col. 18). The Asclepius as a whole was therefore probably written no later than the third century. The "apocalypse," whatever its sources, is probably an integral part of the whole composition. The peculiar combination of philosophy and eschatology suggests that. Parts of the "apocalypse," however, referring to Christian legal persecution of pagan religion, are probably fourth century additions.

The prophecy begins with a reference to statues by Hermes. Hermes then praises Egypt as the world's temple and laments its fate, when its native piety will vanish and its religious institutions will be suppressed (chap. 24). Barbarians will inhabit it and the gods will depart. Finally there will be cosmic and social catastrophe (chap. 25). The end of the world (*senectus mundi*) will be marked by "inreligio, inordinatio, inrationabilitas bonorum omnium." Then the divine "gubernator" will effect a cosmic restoration.

As in the last stage of the Potter's Oracle, there seems to be virtually no political reference in the eschatology which focuses almost exclusively on the cosmic realm. There is not any particular interest in the supernatural within these chapters of the Asclepius, although the whole work undoubtedly has this as its major interest. In comparison with other "apocalypses," this section of the Asclepius displays the following traits:

1.2.2	Dialogue between an
2.	"Otherworldly" revealer and
3.3	A recipient who weeps. The dialogue discusses
7.1	Eschatological persecution,
7.2	Cosmic upheaval and
9.1	Cosmic transformation and restoration.

Fragments

There are two further minor papyrus fragments of works similar to the Greco-Egyptian eschatological prophecies just mentioned. They are too badly preserved to enable us to say anything about their overall form. The main example, P.S.I. 982, of unknown provenance but from the third century CE, is of interest because of an apparent reference to the Jews as persecutors.

Berossus

Berossus, a Babylonian figure whose activity is described in a variety of terms by pagan and Christian sources, lived in the early Hellenistic period and wrote extensively in Greek on native Babylonian traditions. His literary remains consist only of fragments, one of which has a pronounced eschatological orientation. Such an orientation may well have dominated his historical work, which also treats cosmogony and primordial history.

The explicitly eschatological fragment (#21 = Seneca, NQ 3.29.1) predicts the destruction of the world by fire and flood, when certain astrological configurations occur.

This fragment cannot be considered as an "apocalypse," although its quasi-scientific, astrological eschatology may have some relation to native Mesopotamian eschatological speculation, important for apocalyptic theorizing.

Virgil, Fourth Eclogue

The fourth Eclogue, written between 45-37 BCE predicts the birth of a child in whose time the earth will enjoy a new golden age. The poem relies on some tradition of eschatological prophecy like that found in the Greco-Egyptian tradition.

Revelatory Dialogues

The revelatory dialogues surveyed thus far occasionally contained dialogue between a seer and a revealer. This feature was, however, regularly subordinate to oracular discourse or to the motif of the journey. In those cases where a journey account was incorporated within a philosophical dialogue, that environment had little impact on the formal features of the journey account itself.

In a certain group of texts, primarily those of the *Corpus Hermeticum*, it is the dialogue format itself which serves as the mode of revelation. The formal feature of the dialogue which renders it revelatory is the status of one of the interlocutors, who is usually a deity. On occasion other devices, such as the apocryphon motif, are also used. In addition, the subject matter of dialogues in this group consists of philosophical and theological themes deemed to be beyond the capacity of ordinary human knowledge.

The roots of the revelatory dialogue are in the dialogues of the philosophical tradition and in scholastic literature. In contrast to philosophical dialogues, the interlocutors here play a quite minor role. The focus is primarily on the words of the divine revealer. The interlocutor at most asks questions which define major topical sections in the revealer's discourse.

These texts also display a practical, even pietistic, orientation which is usually lacking in philosophical texts. Hence the dialogue often includes prayers and hymns not at home in the philosophical tradition. Despite these differences, there is at least one important philosophical text which foreshadows the revelatory pieces and their techniques.

Plato, Symposium (201D-212A)

Plato's great dialogue on love reaches its climax in the story told by Socrates of his discussion with a mysterious wise woman, Diotima, who explained to him the nature of love as a gradual attraction through various lower stages of the ontological ladder up to the highest and most abstract entities.

Diotima's discourse recalls in some respects the speech of the revealing goddess in the poem of Parmenides. Socrates does play some role in this dialogue, especially in its earlier stages. As it progresses, it becomes more simply a discourse by Diotima on the nature of love. The dialogue probably dates to 384 BCE.

Orpheus, Testament

The Testament attributed to Orpheus, in which he addresses his disciple Musaeus, consists of a discussion of theological questions, concerning the transcendent god and his relation to the cosmos. The textual transmission of this piece is quite complex. It now survives in three recensions, with Jewish and Christian interpolations. One form of the poem must date prior to the mid-second century BCE since it is used by the Alexandrian exegete Aristobulus.

Corpus Hermeticum

This is probably the most significant collection of revelatory literature from pagan antiquity. In form and content, it is quite distinct from most Jewish and Christian apocalypses, although it may well have some relation to the Gnostic dialogues.

Formally, many of the components of the Corpus are dialogues, usually between Hermes and Tat or Asclepius (I, II, IV, X, XII, XIII, XVII, according to the enumeration of the Nock-Festugière edition). In addition to the separate tracts, there are excerpts in Stobaeus. Many of these are very brief. Some of these have obvious elements of dialogue, involving Hermes and some interlocutor (IIA, IIB, IV, VI, VIII, XI) or Isis and Horus (XXIII-XXVIII).

Some tractates in the *Corpus Hermeticum* are in a slightly different form. XIV is apparently a letter; VII is a short exhortation and XVIII an epideictic discourse in honor of kings.

A detailed discussion of all the dialogues in the Corpus would not be particularly illuminating here. Most deal with a standard repertoire of topics involving the nature of God and of the created world, the place of man within that world, his relationship to God and the possibility of being reunited with him. There are three texts which are of particular interest and importance, the Asclepius, the Kore Kosmou and the Poimandres. These texts deserve separate treatment.

Dating the collection is difficult. There are attestations of the Poimandres and the Asclepius in Greek papyri dating from the end of the third century. These fragments provide a *terminus ante* for those two tracts at least. The other components of the Corpus also probably date from the same general period, the first few centuries of the common era. The Poimandres has been discussed at the beginning of this survey.

Asclepius

One segment of the Asclepius has already been discussed, the so-called "Apocalypse." The rest of the tractate is a long and rather rambling discussion of the basic themes of Hermetism. The tract is particularly noteworthy because it exemplifies the optimistic type of Hermetism, which evaluated the created world in a positive way as a manifestation of divine goodness and the means by which god might be known. The tractate treats the following themes (cf. Nock):

I. The unity, multiplicity and hierarchical arrangement of all things (1-7)
II. The functions of man, tending the earth and adoring god (8-9)
III. The dual nature of man as spiritual and corporeal; his duty to be pious; the rewards of piety, i.e., return to God; the punishment of impiety, reincarnation (10-13)
IV. The first principles, God, matter and spirit; the question of theodicy (14-16)
V. Matter and intellect (18-19)
VI. The sexuality and fecundity of the creator and of created things (20-21)
VII. The limited number of the pious, who are endowed with intellect (22)
VIII. Man-made gods (23)
IX. The "Apocalypse" (24-26)
X. Death, judgment, crimes and punishments (27-29)
XI. Time and eternity (30-31); digression on knowing God (33)
XII. Perfection of the cosmos (33-36)
XIII. Man-made gods (37)
XIV. Fate, necessity, and order (39)
XV. Final prayer and epilogue (40-41).

The following features might be compared with elements of apocalypses and other revelatory works:

1.2.2	The dialogue format
2.	The figure of Hermes, the revealing mediator
3.1	The fictional recipient, Asclepius
3.3	His questions, punctuating the dialogue
4.1	Metaphysics and cosmogony dominate the work (cf. sections I, IV, V, XI, XII, XIV above)
8.1	The doctrine of post-mortem judgment and punishment (cf. sections III, X)
9.2.2	Doctrine of metempsychosis and return to God (cf. sections III, X)
10.1	The divine world (cf. sections IV, V, VI, XI)

The Kore Kosmou

Among the fragments in Stobaeus which record dialogues between Isis and Horus, one is of special interest, both because it is of considerable length and because of its doctrinal content. This is Excerpt XXIII, The Maiden (or Pupil) of the Cosmos.

In its present form, this text consists of three main sections (Festugière):
   I. The Hermetic prologue. Isis describes the original state of human ignorance. She tells how Hermes revealed the true state of things and left his revelation in a secret writing (1-8).
  II. The revelation (9-63, 66)
      a) Organization of the celestial world (9-21)
      b) Organization of the inferior world, including the fall and punishment of souls in matter (22-52)
      c) Primitive anarchy and its transformation by Isis and Osiris (53-63)
 III. Aretalogy of Isis and Osiris who transform human life and return to heaven (64-69)
(IV.) A hymn is promised in the final paragraphs of the preserved text, but it is lacking in Stobaeus.

Within this cosmogonic framework there are several excursuses incorporating elements of various esoteric theories, including astrology and zoology.

Various theories of the original composition and subsequent redaction of this complex work have been proposed (Bousset, Reitzenstein, Ferguson), although all are open to criticism (Festugière). The main concerns of the work in its present form are fairly clear. Like other Hermetic tractates, it deals with the origin and nature of the cosmos and with man's place in it. Its metaphysical position is somewhat different from that of the preceding work. The world is still seen as an extension of the divine nature and goodness. However, it is also viewed as a place of punishment for fallen souls whose ultimate destiny is to escape and to return to the divine (41). The following common revelatory features may be cited:

1.2.2	Dialogue
1.4	The revelation is recorded in secret writings
2.	An otherworldly mediator reveals to a
3.1	Fictional interlocutor
4.1	Cosmology and cosmogony are prominent features
8.1	The cosmogony involves punishment of fallen souls
9.2.2	A doctrine of metempsychosis is taught.
10.1	The structure of the celestial world and
10.2	Its inhabitants is explained.

Orpheus, Sacred Discourses (Hieroi Logoi)

This poem or collection of poems of uncertain date survives only in fragments. Some of these (e.g. Kern, fr. 61) are in the format of an esoteric discourse.

Other Related Types of Revelation

Many of the revelatory texts in this survey involve an appearance by a revealer figure in a vision or dream. Accounts of this sort of appearance are quite common throughout antiquity. It would be possible to analyze such accounts form-critically, and some work has been done toward that goal (Wickenhauser, Hanson). It is hardly proper to speak of a genre of apocalypse in regard to most of these accounts, especially in regard to the brief notices widely scattered in literary sources. The longer, independent texts which utilize this motif are at least revelatory texts in a broad sense. For reasons of space, it is not possible to review them here.

Lack of space also prevents a review of manuals of occult science. Most manuals of astrology, alchemy and related pursuits dating from the late Hellenistic period through the end of antiquity were presented in some sort of revelatory format. They are of interest for comparison with the formal features of various types of eschatologically-oriented revelatory literature.

Oracles

Within the broad confines of revelatory literature, oracles stand apart as a distinct sub-genre. A written oracle is always a prophecy or proclamation which purports to be a statement through a medium. With few exceptions, it is couched in verse.

Oracles dealing with political, cultic and personal matters were a constant feature of Greek life from the classical period. Responses from oracular shrines were collected and circulated as early as the fourth century (Hendess, Parke), although such collections are not now extant. From the Hellenistic period survives one long and erudite literary piece in oracular form. In the Roman period, especially the second and third centuries CE, oracles with theological and philosophical interests were given by oracular shrines and were issued as literary compositions. Thus there is a clear trajectory in the use of oracles from their ancient function of providing practical advice on political, social and religious matters to a new function of revealing metaphysical truth.

Although in any form the oracle remains a direct, and not a mediated, revelation, the concerns of the later oracles parallel other revelatory literature from the same period.

Lycophron, Alexandra

This is a lengthy poem in tragic iambics, purporting to be the oracle of Cassandra to Priam delivered before the fall of Troy. It is a learned and frequently obscure piece of Alexandrian poetry. Most of it consists of prophecy of events of the Trojan war and its aftermath as these events are known from epic sources. Two sections toward the end of the poem are *ex eventu* prophecies of hellenistic military affairs. Dating of the poem hinges on the interpretation of these allusions. The two possibilities are around 270 or around 196 BCE. The earlier date seems somewhat more likely. The problematic sections are lines 1226-1280 and 1435-1450.

Chaldaean Oracles

These literary oracles on theological topics were composed in the late second century CE. They are in the form traditional for oracles, hexameter verse. They were especially influential among the neo-Platonists. Unfortunately, they survive only in quite problematical fragments.

Tübingen Theosophy, Theological Oracles

The Theosophy of Tübingen is a work of the late fifth century CE which attempts to show that Christianity was anticipated in pagan oracles. The collection of oracles in it is diverse, but some at least are attested from the second and third century on epigraphical sources. These indicate that theological oracles were being delivered by the ancient oracular shrine at Claros during this period.

SELECT BIBLIOGRAPHY

GENERAL

Berthelot, M.
1887 *Collection des anciens alchimistes grecs.* (= Alchimistes) Paris: Steinheil.

Bertram, G.
1966 "Erhöhung." *Reallexikon für Antike und Christentum* 6: 22-43.

Bidez, J. and Cumont, F.
1938 *Les Mages hellénisés.* (= Mages hellénisés) Paris: Les belles lettres.

Boll, F.
1914 *Aus der Offenbarung Johannis.* Leipzig: Teubner.

Bouché-Leclercq, A.
1879-1882 *Histoire de la Divination dans l'antiquité.* Paris: Leroux.

Bousset, W.
1901 "Die Himmelsreise der Seele." *Archiv für Religionswissenschaft* 4: 136-139, 229-273.

Collins, J. J.
1975a "Jewish Apocalyptic Against Its Hellenistic Near Eastern Environment." *BASOR* 220: 27-36.

Corno, D. del
1969 *Graecorum de onirocritica scriptorum reliquiae.* Milano: Cisalpino.

Deubner, L.
1900 *De incubatione.* Leipzig: Teubner.

Dieterich, A.
1893 *Nekyia, Beiträge zur Erklärung der neuentdeckten Petrusapokalypse.* Leipzig: Teubner.

Dodds, E. R.
1951 *The Greeks and the Irrational.* Sather Lectures 25. Berkeley/Los Angeles: University of California.

Fauth, W.
1972 "Orakel." *Der Kleine Pauly* 4: 323-328.

Festugière, A. J.
1944-1954 *La révélation d'Hermès Trismégiste* (= *La révélation*). 4 vols. Paris: Lecoffre.

Ganschinietz, R.
1919 "Katabasis." PW 10: 2395-2430.

Grant, F. C.
1953 *Hellenistic Religions.* (= Hellenistic Religions) New York: Bobbs-Merrill.

Hanson, J.
1978 "The Dream/Vision Report in Acts 10:1-11:18: A Form-Critical Study." Unpublished dissertation. Cambridge: Harvard University.

Hendess, R.
1877 *Oracula graeca quae apud scriptores graecos romanosque exstant.* Dissertation. Halle.

Hengel, M.
1974 *Judaism and Hellenism.* Eng. trans. of *Judentum und Hellenismus*, 2nd ed., 1973. 2 vols. Philadelphia: Fortress.

Holland, R.
1925 "Zur Typik der Himmelfahrt." *Archiv für Religionswissenschaft* 23: 207-220.

Hopfner, T.
1921-1924 *Griechisch-aegyptischer Offenbarungszauber.* 2 vols. Leipzig: Hässel.

1935 "Nekromantie." PW 16: 2218-2233.

Kern, O.
1922 *Orphicorum fragmenta.* (= Orph. Frag.) Berlin: Weidmann.

Lanczkowski, G.
1960 *Altägyptischer Prophetismus.* Wiesbaden: Harrassowitz.

Latte, K.
1939 "Orakel." PW 18: 829-866.

McCown, L. C.
1925 "Hebrew and Egyptian Apocalyptic Literature." *HTR* 18: 357-411.

MacCulloch, J. A.
1914 "Descent to Hades." *Hastings Encyclopedia of Religion and Ethics* IV. 648-654.

Parke, H. W.
1967 *Greek Oracles.* London: Hutchinson.

Pfister, F.
1924 "Epiphanie." PWSupp 4: 277-323.

Schwartz, J.
1977 "Le voyage au ciel dans la littérature apocalyptique." Pp. 89-126 in *L'Apocalyptique.* Etudes d'Histoire des Religions 3. Paris: Geuthner.

Smith, J. Z.
1975 "Wisdom and Apocalyptic." *Religious Syncretism in Antiquity.* Ed. B. A. Pearson. Missoula: Scholars Press.

1976 "A Pearl of Great Price and a Cargo of Yams: A Study in Situational Incongruity." *HR* 16: 1-19.

Wickenhauser, A.
1939 "Die Traumgeschichte des Neuen Testaments in religionsgeschichtlicher Sicht." Pp. 320-333 in *Pisciculi, Festschrift Dölger.* Eds. T. Klausner and A. Rücker. Münster: Aschendorff.

WORKS ON INDIVIDUAL ITEMS (in alphabetical order)

Asclepius, Latin Hermetic Tractate

Text

Nock, A. D. and Festugière, A. J.
    1945   *Corpus Hermeticum*. Latin text, French translation and extensive notes. Vol. II. Greek fr. p. 353-354. Paris: Les belles lettres (reprinted, 1960).

Krause, M. and Labib, P.
    1971   *Gnostische und hermetische Schriften aus Kodex II und Kodex VI*. Glückstadt: Augustin. Pp. 184-206.

Scott, W.
    1924   *Hermetica*. Vols. I and IV. Text and English translation, and notes. Oxford: Oxford University.

Translation

Dirkse, P. A. and Labib, D. M.
    1977   "Asclepius 21-29 (VI,8)." *The Nag Hammadi Library*, 300-307.

Studies

Doresse, J.
    1956   "Hermes et la Gnose: A propos de l'Asclepius copte." *NovT* 1: 54-69.

Krause, M.
    1969   "Aegyptisches Gedankengut in der Apokalypse." *Zeitschrift der Deutschen Morgenländischen Gesellschaft*. Supplementa 1. Wiesbaden: Steiner. Pp. 48-57.

Reitzenstein, R. and Schaeder, H.
    1926   *Studien zum antiken Synkretismus aus Iran und Griechenland*. Berlin/Leipzig: Teubner.

Berossus

Text

Jacoby, F.
    1958   *Die Fragmente der griechischen Historiker*, IIIC, No. 680, pp. 364-397. Leiden: Brill.

Studies

Schnabel, P.
    1923   *Berossus und die babylonisch-hellenistische Literatur*. Berlin: Peiser.

Smith, J. Z.
    1975   "Wisdom and Apocalyptic." *Religious Syncretism in Antiquity*. Ed. B. A. Pearson. Missoula: Scholars Press.

Chaldean Oracles

Text

des Places, E.
    1971   *Oracles chaldaiques*. French translation and commentary. Paris: Les belles lettres.

Studies

Dodds, E. R.
1961   "New Light on the Chaldaean Oracles." *HTR* 54: 263-273.

Lewy, H.
1956   *Chaldaean Oracles and Theurgy.* Cairo: L'Institut française d'archaeologie orientale.

Merlan, P.
1963, 1964   "Religion and Philosophy from Plato's Phaedo to the Chaldaean Oracles." *Journal of the History of Philosophy* 1: 163-176; 2: 15-21.

Cicero, Somnium Scipionis

Text/Translations

Keyes, C. W.
1928   *De republica, De legibus.* LCL 16. London: Heinemann (reprinted, 1970; Cambridge: Harvard).

Ziegler, K.
1958   *M. Tulli Ciceronis Scripta quae manserunt.* Fasc. 39. 4th ed. Leipzig: Teubner.

Studies

Boyancé, P.
1936   *Etudes sur le songe de Scipion.* With text and French translation. Limoges: Bontemps.

1942   "Sur le Songe de Scipion." *L'Antiquité classique* 11: 5-22.

Festugière, A. J.
1946   "Les thèmes du songe de Scipion." *Eranos* 44: 370-388.

Harder, R.
1929   *Über Ciceros Somnium Scipionis.* Schriften der Königsberger gelehrten Gesellschaft, geisteswissenschaftliche Klasse 6/3. Halle: Niemeyer.

Stahl, W. H.
1952   *Macrobius, Commentary on the Dream of Scipio.* New York: Columbia.

Traglia, A.
1951   *Il sogno di Scipione.* Text, Italian translation, commentary. Rome: Bonacci (reprinted, 1962).

Corpus Hermeticum

Text

Nock, A. D. and Festugière, A. J.
1945   *Corpus Hermeticum.* Critical text, introduction and French translation, extensive notes. Vols. I-II. Tractates I-XVIII, Asclepius. Reprinted, 1960.

1954   Vols. III-IV. Fragments. The introduction to each piece includes bibliographical data.

Scott, W.
1924-1936   *Hermetica.* Vols. I-IV. Texts, English translations, notes. The text is inferior to that of Nock. Oxford: Oxford University.

Studies

Betz, H. D.
1966 "Schöpfung und Erlösung im hermetischen Fragment 'Kore Kosmou.'" *ZThK* 63: 160-187.

Bousset, W.
1922 "Kore Kosmu." *PW* 11: 1386-1391.

Ferguson, A. S.
1936 in Scott, *Hermetica* IV.

Festugière, A. J.
1944-1954 *La révélation*.

Nilsson, M.
1950 *Geschichte der griechischen Religion.* Vol. II, 581-612. A useful general survey with further bibliography; reprinted, 1961.

Reitzenstein, R.
1917 *Die Göttin Psyche in der hellenistischen Literatur.* Heidelberg: Winter.

Tröger, K. W.
1971 *Mysterienglaube und Gnosis in Corpus Hermeticum XIII.* TU 110. Berlin: Akademie.

Demotic Chronicle

Text

Spiegelberg, W.
1914 *Die sogennante Demotische Chronik des Pap. 215 der bibliothèque nationale zu Paris.* Leipzig: Hinrichs.

Study

Meyer, E.
1915 *Ägyptische Dokumente aus der Perserzeit I, Eine eschatologische Prophetie.* Pp. 286-304. Berlin: Akademie der Wissenschaften.

Euhemerus, Hiera Anagraphe

Jacoby, F.
1957 *Die Fragmente der griechischen Historiker*, Ia, No. 63, pp. 300-313. 2nd ed. Leiden: Brill.

Vallauri, G.
1956 *Evemero di Messene.* Turin: University of Turin.

Fragments of Eschatological Prophecy

Text

Vitelli, G.
1925 *Papiri Greci e Latini.* Pubblicazioni della Societa Italiana per la ricerca dei papiri greci e latini in Egitto. VII. 760; VIII. 982. Firenze: Ariani.

Tcherikover, V. and Fuks, A.
1964 *Corpus papyrorum Judaicarum*, #520. Vol. 3. Pp. 119-121. Cambridge: Harvard University.

Study

Manteuffel, G.
1934   *Mélanges Maspero. Memoires de l'institut française d'archéologie orientale du Caire* II. 123.

Heraclides Ponticus

Text

Wehrli, F.
1953   *Die Schule des Aristoteles* 7. Fr. 90-96. Basel/Stuttgart: Schwabe (reprinted, 1969).

Studies

Daebritz, R.
1913   "Herakleides Pontikos." PW 8: 472-484.

Wehrli, F.
1968   "Herakleides Pontikos." PWSup 11: 675-686.

Wilamowitz, U. von
1932   *Der Glaube der Hellenen*, pp. 533-536. Berlin: Weidmann.

Kore Kosmou

see *Corpus Hermeticum*

Lamb to Bocchoris

Text/Translation

Krall, J.
1898   "Vom König Bokchoris." *Festgaben zu Ehren Max Budingers*. Innsbruck: Wagner.

Studies

Burchard, C.
1966   "Das Lamm in der Waagschale." ZNW 57: 219-238.

Koch, K.
1966   "Das Lamm das Ägypten vernichtet." ZNW 57: 79-93.

Koenen, L.
1970   "The Prophecies of the Potter: A Prophecy of World Renewal Becomes an Apocalypse." *Proceedings of the Twelfth International Congress of Papyrology*. Pp. 249-254. Ann Arbor: University of Michigan.

Moret, A.
1903   *De Bocchoris Rege*. Paris: Leroux.

Lucian

Text/Translation

Harmon, A. M., et al.
1913-1967   *Lucian*. LCL II, III, IV. London: Heinemann; Cambridge: Harvard.

MacLeod, M. D.
1972-1974   *Lucianis Opera*. Vols. I, II. Oxford.

Studies

Betz, H. D.
    1961   *Lukian von Samosata und das Neue Testament.* TU 76. Berlin: Akademie.

Caster, M.
    1937   *Lucien et la pensée religieuse de son temps.* Paris: Les belles lettres.

Helm, R.
    1906   *Lucian und Menipp.* Berlin/Leipzig: Teubner.

Herrmann, L.
    1969   *Lucien et le christianisme.* Cahiers du Cercle Ernest-Renan 61. Paris: Cercle Ernest Renan.

Lycophron, Alexandra

Text/Translation

Mair, A. W.
    1921, 1955   *Callimachus, Lycophron and Aratus.* LCL. London: Heinemann; Cambridge: Harvard.

Studies

Josifovic, S.
    1968   "Lykophron." PWSup 11: 888-930.

Momigliano, A.
    1942   "Terra marique." *Journal of Roman Studies* 22: 53-64.

    1945   "The Locrian Maidens and the Date of Lycophron's Alexandra." *Classical Quarterly* 39: 49-53.

Ziegler, K.
    1927   "Lykophron (8)." PW 13: 2316-2381.

Orpheus, Testament

Text

Denis, A.-M.
    1970   *Fragmenta Pseudepigraphorum Quae Supersunt Graeca.* PVTG 3. Pp. 163-167. Leiden: Brill.

Kern, O.
    1922   *Orphicorum fragmenta* 245-248, pp. 259-266.

Study

Walter, N.
    1964   *Der Thoraausleger Aristobulos.* TU 86. Berlin: Akademie. Pp. 234-261.

Orpheus, Sacred Discourses (Hieroi Logoi)

Text

Kern, O.
    1922   *Orphicorum fragmenta* 60-235, pp. 140-248.

Comment/Translation

Festugière, A. J.
    1944-1954   *La révélation*, I. 346-347.

Orphic Tablets

Text

Olivieri, A.
1915   *Lamellae aureae orphicae.* Kl. texte 133. Bonn: Marcus and Weber.

Verdelis, N. M.
1950-1951   "Chalkē tephrodochos kalpis ek Pharsalōn." *Archaiologikē Ephemeris.* Pp. 80-105.

Kern. O.
1922   *Orphicorum fragmenta,* Fr. 32, p. 104.

Translation

Grant, F. C.
1953   *Hellenistic Religions,* 108-109 (partial).

Parmenides

Text/Translation/Commentary

Kirk, G. S. and Raven, J.
1962   *The Presocratic Philosophers.* Pp. 263-285. Cambridge: Cambridge University.

Taran, L.
1965   *Parmenides: A Text with Translation, Commentary and Critical Essays.* Princeton: Princeton University.

Studies

Guthrie, W. K. C.
1965   *A History of Greek Philosophy.* Vol. II. 1-79, with bibliography. Cambridge: Cambridge University.

Mansfeld, J.
1964   *Die Offenbarung des Parmenides und die menschliche Welt.* Assen: Van Gorcum.

Mourelatos, A. P. D.
1970   *The Route of Parmenides.* New Haven/London: Yale.

Plato, Republic and Symposium

Text

Burnet, J.
1900-1907   *Platonis Opera.* Oxford: Oxford University.

Translations

Cornford, F. M.
1941   *The Republic of Plato.* Oxford: Oxford University.

Shorey, P.
1930   *The Republic.* LCL. London: Heinemann; Cambridge: Harvard (reprinted in *The Collected Dialogues of Plato,* Bollingen Series LXXI, 1961; New York: Pantheon).

Joyce, M.
1935   *The Symposium.* London: Dent; New York: Dutton (reprinted in *The Collected Dialogues of Plato,* 1961; New York: Pantheon).

Studies/Commentaries

Adam, J.
1938 *The Republic, with critical notes, commentary and appendices.* Cambridge: Cambridge University.

Else, G. F.
1972 *The Structure and Date of Book 10 of Plato's Republic.* Heidelberg: Winter.

Ferguson, J.
1957 *Republic Book X.* London: Methuen.

(Ps.) Plato, Axiochus

Text

Burnet, J.
1907 *Platonis Opera.* Vol. V. Oxford: Oxford University.

Translation

Blakeney, E. H.
1937 *The Axiochus on Death and Immortality.* London: Muller.

Study

Cumont, F.
1942 *Recherches sur le symbolisme funéraire des Romains.* Paris: Geuthner, 47-52.

Plutarch

Text

Cherniss, H. and Helmbold, W.
1968 *De facie lunae.* Plutarch's Moralia. LCL XII. London: Heinemann; Cambridge: Harvard.

de Lacy, P. and Einarson, B.
1959 *De genio Socratis, De sera numinis vindicta.* LCL VII. Plutarch's Moralia.

Studies

Betz, H. D.
1975 *Plutarch's Theological Writings and Early Christianity.* Leiden: Brill.

Corlu, A.
1970 *De genio Socratis.* Paris: Klincksieck.

Görgemanns, H.
1970 *Untersuchungen zu Plutarchs Dialog De facie in orbe lunae.* Heidelberg: Winter.

Hamilton, W.
1934a "The Myth in Plutarch's De facie." *Classical Quarterly* 28: 24-30.

1934b "The Myth in Plutarch's De Genio." *Classical Quarterly* 28: 175-182.

Meautis, G.
1935 *De délais de la justice divine.* Lausanne: Les Amitiés gréco-suisses.

Soury, G.
1942   *La demonologie de Plutarque, essai sur les idées religieuses et les mythes d'un platonicien éclectique.* Paris: Les belles lettres.

von Arnim, A.
1921   "Plutarch über Dämonen und Mantik." Amsterdam: Akademie.

Poimandres

see *Corpus Hermeticum*

Potter's Oracle

Text

Koenen, L.
1968   "Die Prophezeiungen des 'Töpfers.'" *Zeitschrift für Papyrologie und Epigraphik* 2: 178-209.

Studies

Dunand, F.
1977   "L'Oracle du Potier et la formation de l'apocalyptique en Egypte." Pp. 39-67 in *L'Apocalyptique*. Etudes d'Histoire des Religions 3. Paris: Geuthner.

Koenen, L.
1970   "The Prophecies of the Potter: A Prophecy of World Renewal Becomes an Apocalypse." Pp. 249-254 in *Proceedings of the Twelfth International Congress of Papyrology*. Ann Arbor: University of Michigan.

Smith, J. Z.
1975   "Wisdom and Apocalyptic." *Religious Syncretism in Antiquity*. Missoula: Scholars Press.

Seneca

Text/Translations

Basore, J. W.
1935   *Seneca's Moral Essays.* Vol. II. LCL. London: Heinemann; Cambridge: Harvard.

Rosenbach, M.
1969   *Seneca. Philosophische Schriften.* Darmstadt: Wissenschaftliche Buchgesellschaft.

Traglia, A.
1965   *La consolazione a Marcia.* Roma: Ateneo.

Theosophy, Theological Oracles

Text

Erbse, H.
1941   *Fragmente griechischen Theosophien.* Hamburg: Hansischer Gildenverlag.

Studies

Battifol, P.
1916   "Oracula Hellenica." *RB* 25: 177-199.

Nock, A. D.
    1928, 1972   "Oracles théologiques." *Revue des études anciennes* 30: 280-290 (= *Essays on Religion and the Ancient World*, Vol. I, 160-168).

Robert, L.
    1968   "Trois oracles de la Theosophie et un prophète d'Apollon." *Comptes rendus de l'académie des inscriptions*, 568-599.

    1971   "Un oracle gravé à Oinoanda." *Comptes rendus de l'académie des inscriptions*, 597-619.

Virgil

Text

Mynor, R.
    1969   *P. Vergili Maronis Opera*. Oxford: Oxford University.

Williams, R. D.
    1972   *The Aeneid of Virgil*. Text and Commentary. London: MacMillan.

Studies

Norden, E.
    1924   *Die Geburt des Kindes*. Leipzig: Teubner.

    1926   *P. Virgilius Maro. Aeneis*. Buch VI. Text, German translation, commentary. 3rd ed. Berlin/Leipzig: Teubner.

Translation

Fairclough, H. R.
    1916-1918   *Virgil*. LCL. London: Heinemann; Cambridge: Harvard.

APOCALYPSES AND "APOCALYPTIC" IN
RABBINIC LITERATURE AND MYSTICISM

Anthony J. Saldarini
Boston College

SYNOPSIS

The classic forms of rabbinic literature (Targum, Midrash, Mishna, Tosepta and Talmud) do not include separate literary works which may be identified as apocalypses according to the definition given in the Introduction to this volume. They do contain some of the characteristics of apocalypses outlined in the master-paradigm in the Introduction. The rabbinic writings contain eschatological themes such as judgment, punishment and life after death, but no mention is made of the medium of revelation nor are any descriptions given of otherworldly regions and beings. Statements of belief about the end with their consequences for life, rather than visions of the future and of other worlds, interest the rabbis.

No sure theory has been developed to account for the demise of apocalypse as a major genre in rabbinic literature, though Akiba's ban on books with biblical pretensions and the reaction against anything smacking of revolt after the end of the War of Bar Kosiba in 135 CE seems most likely (Saldarini, 1975). Gershom Scholem has proposed the thesis that the Jewish mystical literature is the heir to apocalyptic literature and it is to his thesis and the mystical writings we shall turn first

Jewish Mysticism

Rabbinic mystical traditions centered around the interpretation of the description of God's chariot in Ezekiel 1 and the story of creation in Genesis 1. Hence, the names *Merkaba* (chariot) mysticism and *Ma'aseh Bereshit* (The Story of Creation) for these mystical speculations. Since the speculation often included a description of the seven palaces of God in the seven heavens, it is also called *Hekalot* (palaces) mysticism. Narratives concerned with the practice of this mysticism, which was severly restricted, are found especially in m. Hagiga 2:1 and its Gemara in the Talmuds, b. Hag. 11b-16a, p. Hag. 2:1 (77b); also b. Shab. 80b, b. Ber. 7a, b. Hul. 91b, b. Meg. 24b, Genesis Rabba 2:4.

In this century, the study of Jewish mysticism has been pioneered by Gershom Scholem. He has pored through manuscripts, poorly printed editions and once-lost works to reconstruct both the development and the thought world of mysticism, early and late. Two of his theses interest us here and guide our treatment. First, Scholem hypothesizes that apocalyptic literature, which does not appear amid the Talmudic and later literature, was transmuted into Merkaba mysticism (1961: chap. 2). Second, though older scholars ascribed the composition of Merkaba literature to the geonic era, Scholem concludes to the contrary: "Even though it is quite possible that some of the texts were not edited until this period, there is no doubt that large sections originated in Talmudic times, and that the central ideas, as well as many details, go back as far as the first and second centuries" (1974: 14-15).

The mystical works are contained in a bewildering mass of manuscripts, fragments, uncritical printed editions and collections. In this study we will examine ten texts, most of which are considered to be early by Scholem (1965:5-7), and in addition, several others considered to be late, but nevertheless typical and available. All the mystical materials have descriptions of otherworldly regions or beings (10.1, 10.2). They commonly have an otherworldly journey (1.3), an otherworldly mediator (2.) and pseudonymity, usually Ishmael and Akiba (3.1). This literature also contains as part of the content of revelation (10.) secret and magical names of God and angels, prayers and instructions for accomplishing mysticism and warnings of dangers. The historical references usually associated with Jewish apocalyptic literature are muted and the involvement with the heavenly world is heightened. Even though the atmostphere found in the mystical literature is different from that found in the earlier Jewish apocalypses, some of the mystical writings retain the temporal interest in eschatological salvation found to be essential to the genre "apocalypse" in the Introduction. First, those mystical works which fit the definition of "apocalypse" will be presented and then for comparison and control other mystical works which differ significantly from apocalypses.

Apocalypses

Three works among the earlier mystical works and four among the later have the literary characteristics of apocalypses set forth in the master-paradigm. Four of the works are Type IIb, otherworldly journeys with cosmic and political eschatology; they reflect the tendency of mystical works to include an otherworldly journey and yet they retain the apocalyptic interest in the fate of the world and cosmos. The other works vary: the Hebrew Apocalypse of Elijah is Type Ia, "historical" with no otherworldly journey; Sefer Hekalot (3 Enoch) is Type IIa, "historical" with an otherworldly journey; the Ascension of Moses is Type IIc, "mystical" with only personal eschatology. They are treated as follows:

Early
  Hekalot Rabbati (parts) (IIb)
  Merkaba Rabba (IIb)
  Sefer Hekalot (3 Enoch) (IIa)

Late
  Hebrew Apocalypse of Elijah (Ia)
  Chronicles of Jerahmeel (IIb)
  Revelation of Joshua ben Levi (IIb)
  Ascension of Moses (IIc)

The presence of the genre "apocalypse" within mystical literature validates Scholem's thesis that Jewish mysticism is the heir to the older Jewish apocalypses. Mystical literature has many emphases, characteristics and a general atmosphere different from earlier Jewish apocalypses, but retains enough in common with them to be included within the genre "apocalypse." Mystical literature stresses techniques, prayers and hymns which aid the practice of mysticism, dangers facing the initiate and elaborate lists of secret names. The descriptions of the other world and its inhabitants exceed those found in Jewish apocalypses in number, length and detail. Yet some mystical tracts, such as Hekalot Rabbati, are apocalypses standing near the boundaries of the definition arrived at in this study.

What change in interest or mood caused the shift in expression from the apocalypses of 200 BCE-100 CE? The shift away from political activity after 135 CE (Saldarini, 1975) is one cause. The study of apocalyptic elements in rabbinic literature indicates that the idea of the resurrection and eschatological salvation gained wide acceptance by the end of the second century CE. It may be that many of the mystical writings which have a heavenly journey and description of the other world without an

explicit mention of eschatological salvation (required by the
definition of apocalypse developed in this volume) actually presume the reality of transcendence of death and life after death
and build on this belief in another direction. Certainly the
journey to the other world suggests that humans may enter there
not only on a temporary mystical pass, but also permanently. Finally, the strong emphasis on the study of Torah which became central in the second and third centuries CE may have moved the
rabbis away from speculation about future eschatological salvation
and into present visions of the heavenly world arrived at through
intensive study of the Torah (especially Genesis 1 and Ezekiel 1)
in all its implications and richness. The concrete, mundane concerns of rabbinic law may have led to the deepest mystical speculation just as the complex and desperate events of history led to
sweeping eschatological theories in earlier Jewish apocalypses.

Any attempt to trace the precise developments which lead
from the apocalypses treated in the section of Jewish apocalypses
and those found here among the mystical literature must remain
highly speculative. The review of history, found only in a third
of the Jewish apocalypses, is the feature most notably absent. The
otherworldly journey, popular in both apocalypses and mystical
literature, is the feature most present. The presence of Metatron,
especially in Sefer Hekalot (3 Enoch), indicates continuity with
the earlier Enoch traditions. Type IIc, "mystical" apocalypses
with an interest in personal eschatology, seems to lead to some of
the later works which just describe rewards and punishments and
which cannot be classified as apocalypses. Rather than see clear
lines of development, we must probably content ourselves with
following traditions which interact and interweave with each other
over several centuries to produce a rich variety of forms, some of
which remain close to apocalyptic literature and some of which
diverge more widely.

SURVEY

Three Earlier Apocalypses

Hekalot Rabbati

The Greater Hekalot is a long collection of materials,
some of which are included in other works as well. Often descriptions are given without the medium of revelation being described.
There are also collections of hymns, stories and warnings. The
work is difficult to characterize either as a whole or in its parts.
It is marginal to the genre apocalypse, yet it seems to have a

consciousness of cosmic transformation and the salvation of Israel such that it can be characterized as Type IIb. The judgment of Rome and the salvation of Israel are mentioned and the warnings about coming calamities seem to imply that they will be followed by salvation from God. G. Scholem and Ch. Wirszubski are preparing a critical edition from the many manuscripts, editions and citations in rabbinic literature. Here the edition of Wertheimer will be followed with parts of greater interest cited, apocalyptic sections first.

pp. 74-75
When a persecution begins, Nehuniah sends Ishmael to the Merkaba to find out the future. Ishmael's journey and what he finds out has the form of an apocalypse (the numbers refer to the paradigm given in the Introduction to this volume).

1.2.1	The prince of the presence spoke to Ishmael.
2.	The prince of the presence is the mediator.
(1.3)	Ishmael is sent down to the Merkaba.
7.1	Various Tannaitic leaders have been jailed.
8.1	Rome will be judged and punished.
10.2	Hadriel writes a record of Rome's evils.

pp. 79-82
This section seems to be a continuation of pp. 74-75. If so, the revelation to Ishmael remains the context and some new content is added.

7.1	Caesar persecutes the Jews and tries to execute Hananiah ben Teradion.
8.1	A substitution is effected and Caesar and many Romans are killed (thisworldly vindication).
9.2	Hananiah's life is saved (thisworldly salvation).
10.1	The Great Assembly in Heaven.

pp. 75-79
This story is found elsewhere, including Merkaba Rabba (to follow), and Jellinek (1967: 5.167).

1.3	Ishmael journeys to heaven.
2.	Seganzagel guides Ishmael; then Hadriel guides.
3.1	Pseudonymity: Ishmael.
7.1 ⎫	Ishmael sees what evils await Israel and that they are
7.2 ⎭	delayed only by the prayers of Israel.
(9.)	It is implied that Israel will be saved.
10.1	Hadriel shows Ishmael the heavens and a worship service there.
10.2	David (as Messiah), the kings of Judah, angels.

pp. 118-134

2.	Metatron instructs Ishmael about the Messiah.
7.1	Crisis, with the fate of the Messiah discussed.
9.	Israel is to be saved. The role of the Messiah.

Some other sections of Hekalot Rabbati have characteristics of apocalypses, but not the full form. For example:

pp. 67-74

10.	A collection of songs which enable the person to ascend to heaven.
10.1	Some description of the heavens.

pp. 90-100
1.3   Ishmael ascends.
10.   Instructions for the ascent.
10.1   Description of the seven palaces.
10.2   The names of the doorkeepers.

pp. 107-108
10.   Danger at mistaking the marble of the sixth palace for water.

p. 116
1.2   Akiba hears a voice from beneath the throne.
10.1   Order of prayers in heaven.
10.2   How Enoch was made into Metatron.

Merkaba Rabba

This collection contains material in the names of both Ishmael and Akiba. It may have originally contained the most ancient redaction of the Shiur Qoma, which later was transmitted as a separate work (Scholem, 1974:375). The story of Ishmael's review of the afflictions which will come on Israel, found in Hekalot Rabbati, is repeated here. The necessary features of an apocalypse are found here along with secret names, warnings and procedures for doing mysticism, oaths for controlling the angelic guide and prayers.

1.1.1   Vision of heaven (1a, 5b)
1.2   Sandalphon speaks to Ishmael (1a, 2b); voice in Aramaic (3a).
1.3   Tour of heaven (3a-b).
1.4   Tablets with narratives of affliction to come upon Israel (3a).
2.   Sandalphon; Prince of the Presence; Hadriel.
3.1   Pseudonymity: Ishmael and Akiba.
3.2   Ishmael and dispositions for the Merkaba (4a-b).
7.1   Afflictions that will come on Israel (3a-b).
9.   Treasuries of salvation; David as Messiah (3a-b).
10.   Secret names of God; warnings about using Merkaba; oaths for controlling otherworldly mediator.
10.2   Description of God (1a).
13.   Ishmael is able to remember Torah after he is enlightened by Merkaba (4b).

Sefer Hekalot or 3 Enoch

3 Enoch is the best known of the Hekalot among non-Jewish scholars because it is accessible in the critical edition by H. Odeberg. The name Sefer Hekalot is more accurate than 3 Enoch. Scholem (1965:7) asserts that Odeberg used a bad manuscript as the basis for his edition. Also, Scholem dates the book to the fifth-sixth century rather than the third. A new edition is being prepared by I. Grünwald. The contents of Sefer Hekalot are composite and represent a different trend than that found in Hekalot Rabbati and Zuttarti.

In contrast to these works, extensive sections are found dealing with eschatological judgment and salvation, along with the more usual descriptions of otherworldly regions and beings. Sefer Hekalot is the mystical work most thoroughly imbued with apocalyptic eschatology and so it is partly atypical of the main stream of mystical literature. Apocalyptic elements are:

1.2.2	Metatron sometimes instruct Ishmael in answer to his questions.
1.3	Ishmael is taken up to the heavens.
2.	Metatron is a guide and major figure.
3.1	Pseudonymity: Ishmael. Also Metatron is Enoch transformed.
4.2	Adam stayed near the garden after he was expelled and watched the Shekina and angels ascend and descend (chap. 5). Heaven contains unborn spirits (chap. 43).
5.1	Ishmael is shown a brief summary of Israel's past (chap. 45).
7.1	Persecution of Israel (chap. 44).
7.2	Eschatological woes (chaps. 44, 45, 48).
8.1	Judgment is passed by an elaborate court in heaven, complete with seventy-two princes of the world, a record book, and angels of justice, truth, mercy, destruction, etc. Very little is said of specific sins, groups or historical events (chaps. 26-33). Judgment and punishment for the wicked (chap. 44).
9.	The Messiah (chaps. 45, 48).
9.2.2	The spirits of the righteous return to heaven (chap. 43).
10.1	Extensive descriptions of the heavens.
10.2	Extensive descriptions of angels.

Four Later Apocalypses

Many works, difficult to date and usually placed from the sixth century to the Middle Ages, are collected in various anthologies and are grouped as minor midrashim. They hover between apocalyptic, midrashic and mystical literature. Though they likely come from a period beyond that covered by this volume, a few which are typical and accessible are presented for their comparative value. The first three, the Apocalypse of Elijah, the Chronicles of Jerahmeel and the Revelation of Joshua ben Levi, are related to one another.

Hebrew Apocalypse of Elijah

The Hebrew Apocalypse of Elijah (not to be confused with the Coptic Apocalypse of Elijah treated in the section on Christian Apocalypses) is also found in Greek and Latin fragments. Buttenweiser, who did a text and translation, discerns a core from 260 CE. Most recently, the Encyclopedia Judaica suggests a mid-sixth century date. The various stages of development and transmission of the work are not clear.

1.1.1	Elijah sees the things detailed in 8.1 and 9.1-2 below.
1.2.1	Michael speaks to Elijah on Mt. Carmel for most of the work and reveals the end.
1.3	The spirit of Yahweh takes Elijah to the ends of the earth where no creature can enter.
2.	Michael.
3.1	Pseudonymity: Elijah.
5.2	War of Rome and Persia predicted by *ex eventu* prophecy.
7.2	Woes at the end; Gog and Magog; destruction of the world.
8.1	Judgment on sinners.
9.	The Messiah comes to fight.
9.1	Jerusalem descends from heaven.
9.2	The good in the garden.
10.1	Otherworldly regions.
10.2	Otherworldly beings.

The Chronicles of Jerahmeel

The Chronicles of Jerahmeel tells the story of Jewish history from creation on. Chapters 12-21, a digression from the story of Adam, speak of heaven, hell, judgment. The Chronicles is a medieval compilation which reproduces earlier sources. Except for a final revelation to Joshua ben Levi, we are not told how information about the other worlds is obtained. In the final revelation (chaps. 20-21), the Messiah conducts Joshua to hell and it may be that only this section should be classified as apocalypse. The whole group of chapters is characterized by a midrashic form, comments supported by Scripture, a focus on the law and sages and a moralistic listing of sins. Its tone is very different from other apocalypses and it genuinely but barely falls within the definition of the genre.

1.3	Joshua ben Levi travels to heaven and then to hell (chaps. 20-21).
2.	The Messiah conducts Joshua to hell (chaps. 20-21).
8.1	Judgment on sinners (chaps. 13, 15, 16).
9.2.2	Israel is saved and lives in paradise (chaps. 13, 19).
10.1	Descriptions of the compartments of heaven and hell.

The Revelation of Joshua ben Levi

The Revelation of Joshua relates that the Angel of Death brought Joshua to see heaven and Joshua tricked him by jumping into paradise and refusing to leave. Joshua tours heaven and, accompanied by an angel and the Messiah, hell too. He sends back his observations to Rabban Gamaliel through the Angel of Death. (This is Version A; Version B is very brief, and has no setting other than, "Rabbi Joshua ben Levi says...." Version B is not an apocalypse.)

1.3	Joshua journeys to paradise.
2.	The Angel of Death conducts Joshua to paradise. The Messiah and an angel, Kipod, conduct him to hell.
3.1	Pseudonymity: Joshua.
8.1	Punishment for sinners seen in hell.
9.	In the fifth compartment of heaven, the Messiah weeps because he must wait before going forth to save Israel.
10.1	A description of the seven compartments of heaven and a brief description of hell.
10.2	A description of the inhabitants of heaven and hell.

The Ascension of Moses

The Ascension of Moses has many parallels to the Ascension of Isaiah and the Testament of Levi as well as to the second-century Apocalypse of Peter, Shepherd of Hermas and Sibylline Oracles, Book 2. The Zohar is also cited by name. The stages of development and date of this book have not been firmly established.

1.2.2	Moses asks questions of Metatron.
1.3	Moses journeys to the heavens and also to Gehenna.
2.	Metatron and also Gabriel and angel guardians of paradise.
3.1	Pseudonymity: Moses.
3.2	Because Moses was humble in dealing with Pharoah, God orders this tour of paradise. Also, Moses is transformed into an angel of fire so he can survive the journey.
8.	Repetitious accounts of punishments, many of which fit specific crimes (compare the Chronicles of Jerahmeel).

9.2	Moses sees the thrones of the saved in paradise.
10.1	Moses sees the seven heavens.
10.2	Moses sees various angels.

Mystical and Other Works Which are not Apocalypses

For purposes of comparison, seven earlier mystical works (according to Scholem's list) and two later revelations will be presented. In addition, reference will be made to some other texts of interest. They all lack the temporal, eschatological dimension of salvation and some of them lack otherworldly mediators.

The Visions of Ezekiel

This text, which was found in the Cairo Geniza, is a brief midrash on Ezek 1:1, especially the clauses "as I was in exile by the river Chebar, the heavens were opened, and I saw visions of God." The bulk of the narrative is a brief mention of the seven levels below the earth and the primal waters of creation followed by an extended description of the seven firmaments, their contents and inhabitants and the distances between them. As is common in midrash, Scriptural verses are cited as support for various statements, along with rabbinic authorities. In the firmaments are found the Torah, Jerusalem and the Temple, realities found in the Book of Ezekiel. In agreement with Ezek 1:1, the mode of revelation is a vision. The material is Hekalot mysticism, but the form is a mixture of midrash and mystical vision.

1.1.1	Vision as the manner of revelation. God opens for Ezekiel the seven levels below the earth (p. 106 in Grünwald's edition) and shows him the primal waters of creation, according to R. Isaac (p. 109). Also, God opened the seven firmaments (p. 111) and the waters of the River Chebar opened the seven firmaments to him.
10.1	Ezekiel sees the firmaments, their dimensions, chariots, waters, etc.
10.2	Ezekiel sees ministering angels, the Archon, the Beasts, etc.

Hekalot Zuttarti

The Lesser Hekalot is a brief collection of disparate materials loosely joined, including prayers of praise, warning of danger, secret names, the story of the four who entered paradise, an account of Akiba's journey to the heavens and of what is seen at the throne of God. Only parts have been published and the mss., mostly in difficult Aramaic, have not been edited. The published parts, used here, are from "an atrociously bad manuscript" (Scholem, 1965:6).

1.2	At three points (6a, 6b, 7a) Akiba hears revelation.
1.3	Akiba refers to his journey on high (6b).
3.1	Pseudonymity: Akiba.
10.	Warnings of danger in doing Merkaba and instructions on how to control otherworldly beings by oath.
10.1	A description of the approach to God's throne, with reference to Daniel 7 (7a-b).

Shiur Qoma

The mystical contemplation of the dimensions of God is a very ancient part of the Hekalot. Originally a section of Merkaba Rabba, it later became an independent work. Manuscript fragments are available and also excerpts incorporated into Hekalot Rabbati and Zuttarti as well as rabbinic interpretations of the Song of Songs (Scholem, 1965:36-42; Lieberman's Appendix: 118-126). The fragments in Musajoff have little narrative frame or setting.

1.1.1	Ihsmael saw God's throne and the Beasts (362).
1.2	Metatron told Akiba (32a) and Ishmael (34a; 36a) of God's measurements and names.
2.	Metatron.
3.1	Pseudonymity: Akiba and Ishmael.
10.1	Descriptions of the heavens.
10.2	Descriptions of God.

Ma'aseh Merkaba

Scholem (1965:101-117) gives a text of a Hekalot work which has no name, but which is one of several works known by the name Ma'aseh Merkaba in the Middle Ages. It contains a variety of observations, warnings, prayers, instructions for entering Merkaba and journeys to the heavens. It is therefore a collection rather than a unified work. It has a strong didactic flavor with both Akiba and Nehuniah instructing Ishmael about Merkaba mysticism and especially in the prayers which must be said. The firsthand experience of mysticism has here been transformed into a teaching to be transmitted to a disciple. Numbers refer to paragraphs in Scholem's text.

1.1.1	Nehuniah's account of a vision (#21).
1.3	Akiba recounts what he saw when he journeyed to heaven (#2, 9, 33).
2.	Various angels (#23-25).
3.1	Pseudonymity: Akiba and Ishmael.
3.2	Purity and holiness are necessary for the Merkaba (#1); fasting and prayer (#11).
10.	Prayers; warnings; names (passim).
10.1	Description of the heavens and their contents (#6, 9, 10, 21-26).
10.2	Description of angels, etc. (passim).

Tractate Hekalot

Scholem (1965:7) suggests that Masseket Hekalot is the latest of these early Hekalot texts. It has seven chapters containing mostly descriptions of God, the heavens and their inhabitants. Only at the end is the source of revelation given.

1.2	Ishmael says (at the end of chap. 7) that Akiba heard all this when he descended to the Merkaba.
10.1	Description of the heavens, throne, palaces, what surrounds God, etc.
10.2	Description of various kinds of angels.

Tosepta to the Targum of Ezekiel 1

Scholem uses the title above for this brief targumic passage (1974:375) in Aramaic. Greenfield (1973:xxviii) calls it

Hekalot or Ma'aseh Merkaba. It is an odd work in which the arrogant Nebuchadnezzar, who says that he will conquer the heavens, is told by the Holy Spirit how vast the heavens are and then how he will be punished in hell. Then Nebuchadnezzar is sent to hell and converses there with Sennacherib.

1.2.1	The Holy Spirit speaks with Nebuchadnezzar.
2.	The Holy Spirit is the mediator.
3.1	Pseudonymity: Nebuchadnezzar.
8.1	Punishment of Nebuchadnezzar and Sennacherib.
10.1	Description of heavens and hell.

Sefer Ha-Razim

Sefer Ha-Razim (The Book of Secrets) was recently assembled from excerpts in various manuscripts. Its seven chapters describe the seven heavens. The only narrative is in the two-page introduction. It is filled with theurgic and magical elements as well as the names of a great many angels. It may be dated to Talmudic times.

Introduction
1.4	Raziel gave the book of these mysteries to Noah.
2.	Raziel.
3.1	Pseudonymity: Noah.

Body of the Work
10.	Instructions, Magic, Secret names.
10.1	Seven heavens described in seven chapters.
10.2	The names of many angels.

The Assumption of Moses

The two common versions of the Assumption of Moses contain no apocalyptic features. However, a fragment is preserved in the Midrash Bereshit Rabbati of Rabbi Moses ha-Darshan and published by Jellinek. It is a midrash on Gen 28:17b (Jacob's Ladder). When Moses is about to die, God takes him up to heaven to see his reward and the future of Israel.

1.3	Moses is taken up to heaven by God.
2.	God.
3.1	Pseudonymity: Moses.
5.2	Moses sees the temple and Jerusalem both in the heavens and on earth. He talks with the Messiah son of David. God hints that he will scatter Israel and then gather them a second time.
10.1	Moses sees God's throne and heaven.
10.2	Moses sees God.

The Revelation of Moses

This is a brief text consisting of an account given by Moses to Israel of a previous journey to the heavens.

1.3	Moses journeyed to heaven.
8.3	After God judges angels, they bathe in a fiery river and are renewed.
10.1	Description of the fiery river.
10.2	Description of several angels.

Other Hekalot Literature

Four sources of early Hekalot literature will be briefly noted, though they are not relevant for our research.

1. I. Grünwald has published some Geniza fragments of Hekalot literature. Some of the material is from Hekalot Rabbati and Zuttarti and some from unknown works. Their fragmentary nature leaves their form in doubt.

2. Scholem has published a chapter concerned with physiognomy and chiromancy which was originally part of the Hekalot literature. One weak link between this text and apocalyptic ideas might be that the measurements of different bodily parts enables one to distinguish who is good and evil. Scholem (1969:177) suggests that the date of the text may be geonic.

3. Greenfield (1973:xxix) notes a dissertation by M. Beit-Arie (Jerusalem, 1966) unavailable to me. A tractate of hymns edited in this dissertation is said to be early Hekalot.

4. Sefer Yetsira (The Book of Creation) is, according to Scholem (1974:23) the earliest Hebrew text of systematic speculative thought. Statements are made about the structure and origin of the universe in the form of halaka, with no explanation. This work seems to represent a parallel, non-ecstatic trend in Hekalot esotericism.

Other Related Works

The *Seder Rabba de Bereshit*, which should really be known as the *Baraita de Ma'aseh Bereshit*, is known in two versions and dates from the Middle Ages. It is an elaborate cosmology with lengthy descriptions of the heavens, but it does not speak of the mode or source of revelation. The *'Ottiyot de Rabbi Akiba* (The Letters of Rabbi Akiba) exists in two versions and contains mystical speculation based on the alphabet. Other versions of the Alphabet of Rabbi Akiba belong to this class of mystical literature. Again, no attention is paid to any medium of revelation.

M. Buttenweiser (1901:33-45) surveys six later works and then lists a group of apocalyptic descriptions. The collections of midrashim listed in the bibliography contain many descriptions of the Garden of Eden, Gehenna, Judgment, Paradise, etc., but they lack mention of an eschatological crisis and of a mode of revelation. They are summaries or statements of belief rather than apocalyptic or mysticism.

Rabbinic Literature

The rabbinic corpus contains no extended passages which have the characteristics of the genre apocalypse. There are several eschatological passages which refer to the Messiah, resurrection or the world to come. For reasons of space it is not possible to review these passages here (see Saldarini, 1977).

SELECT BIBLIOGRAPHY

JEWISH MYSTICISM AND LATER LITERATURE

General

Altmann, A.
1942   "Gnostic Themes in Rabbinic Cosmology." Pp. 19-32 in *Essays in Honour of J. H. Hertz*. London: Goldston.

Bowker, J. W.
1971   "Merkabah Visions and the Visions of Paul." *JSS* 16: 157-173.

Buttenweiser, M.
1901   *Outline of the Neo-Hebraic Apocalyptic Literature*. Cincinnati: Jennings.

Davies, W. D.
1976   "From Schweitzer to Scholem: Reflections on Sabbatai Svi." *JBL* 95: 529-558.

Ebn-Schmuel, J.
1954   *Midrashe-Ge'ulah*. 2nd ed. Jerusalem: Bialik.

Gaster, M.
1893   "Hebrew Visions of Hell and Paradise." *Journal of the Royal Asiatic Society*. Pp. 571-611.

Greenfield, J.
1973   "Prolegomenon." Pp. xi-xlvii in H. Odeberg, *3 Enoch or the Hebrew Book of Enoch*. Reprinted; New York: Ktav.

Grünhut, L.
1898-1903   *Sefer ha-Likkutim*. Jerusalem (reprint, 1967).

Grünwald, I.
1974   "The Jewish Esoteric Literature in the Time of the Mishnah and Talmud." *Immanuel* 4: 37-46.

Horowitz, H. M.
1881   *Bet Eqed ha-'Agadot*. Frankfurt am Main: Slobotzky (reprinted, Jerusalem, 1967).

Jellinek, A.
1967   *Bet ha-Midrash*. 6 vols. in 2. Reprint, Jerusalem: Wahrmann.

Lieberman, S.
1965   "The Teaching of the Song of Songs." Pp. 118-126 in Scholem, 1965.

Maier, J.
1964   *Vom Kultus zur Gnosis*. Salzburg: Mueller. Pp. 112-148.

Musajoff, S.
1921   (also Musajeff; Musayov). *Merkaba Shelema*. Jerusalem.

Néher, A.
1951   "Le voyage mystique des quartre." *RHR* 140: 59-82.

Neusner, J.
1971   "The Development of the *Merkavah* Tradition." *JSJ* 2: 149-160.

Saldarini, A. J.
1975 "Apocalyptic and Rabbinic Literature." *CBQ* 37: 348-358.

Schiffman, L. H.
forthcoming "*Merkabah* Speculation at Qumran: The 4Q *Serekh 'Olat Ha-Shabbat.*" To appear in the *Altmann Festschrift*.

Scholem, G.
1961 *Major Trends in Jewish Mysticism.* New York: Schocken.

1965 *Jewish Gnosticism, Merkabah Mysticism and Talmudic Tradition.* New York: Jewish Theological Seminary.

1974 *Kabbalah.* (A reissue and revision of the *Encyclopedia Judaica* articles on "Kabbalah" and "Merkabah Mysticism.") New York: Quadrangle.

Séd, N.
1973 "Les traditions secrètes et les disciples de Rabban Yoḥanan ben Zakkai." *RHR* 184: 49-66.

Strugnell, J.
1959 "The Angelic Liturgy at Qumran--4Q Serek Šîrôt 'Ôlat Haššabbāt." VTSup 7: 318-345.

Townsend, J. T.
1976 "Minor Midrashim." Pp. 331-392 in *Bibliographical Essays in Medieval Jewish Studies: The Study of Judaism*, Vol. II. New York: Anti-Defamation League.

Urbach, E. E.
1967 "Mystical Traditions in the Period of the Tannaim." Pp. 1-28 (Hebrew section) in *Studies in Mysticism and Religion Presented to G. Scholem.* Jerusalem: Magnes.

Wertheimer, S.
1968 *Batte Midrashot.* 2nd ed. Ed. A. Wertheimer. 2 vols. Jerusalem: Ktab Wasepher.

Wünsche, A.
1907-1910 *Aus Israels Lehrhallen.* 5 vols. Vol. 3: "Kleine Midraschim zur jüdischen Eschatologie und Apokalyptik." Leipzig (reprinted, in 2 vols., Hildesheim: Olms, 1967).

Hekalot Rabbati

Text

Jellinek, A.
1967 *Bet ha-Midrash*, 3.83-108, 161-163.

Wertheimer, S.
1968 *Batte Midrashot*, 1.65-136 (best text).

Studies

Jellinek, A.
1967 *Bet ha-Midrash*, 3.xlv-xlviii.

Scholem, G.
1965 *Jewish Gnosticism*, 31-55.

Smith, M.
1963 "Observations on Hekhalot Rabbati." Pp. 142-160 in *Biblical and Other Studies.* Ed. A. Altmann. Cambridge: Harvard.

Merkaba Rabba

Text

Musajoff, S.
1921   *Merkaba Shelema*, 1-6a.

Scholem, G.
1965   *Jewish Gnosticism*, 6, n. 15.

Sefer Hekalot or III Enoch

Text

Musajoff, S.
1921   *Merkaba Shelema*, 8b-15a.

Odeberg, H.
1928   *3 Enoch or the Hebrew Book of Enoch.* Cambridge: Cambridge University (reprinted; New York: Ktav, 1973).

Studies

Buttenweiser, M.
1901   *Outline*, 9-15.

Greenfield, J.
1973   "Prolegomenon." Pp. xi-xlvii in Odeberg reprint.

Odeberg, H.
1928   *3 Enoch.* Introduction, commentary and translation.

Scholem, G.
1965   *Jewish Gnosticism*, 7.

Apocalypse of Elijah

Text

Jellinek, A.
1967   *Bet ha-Midrash*, 3.65-68.

Buttenweiser, M.
1897   *Die hebräische Elias-Apokalypse.* Leipzig: Pfeiffer.

Translations

Buttenweiser, M.
1897   *Die hebräische Elias-Apokalypse.*

Wünsche, A.
1907-1910   *Aus Israels Lehrhallen*, 2.33-38.

Studies

Buttenweiser, M.
1901   *Outline*, 30-32.

Denis, A.-M.
1970   *Introduction aux Pseudépigraphes Grecs d'Ancien Testament.* SVTP 1. Leiden: Brill. Pp. 163-169.

EncJud
1971   "Elijah, Apocalypse of." *Encyclopedia Judaica* 6:643. New York: Macmillan. (The entry is attributed to "Ed.")

James, M. R.
    1920   *Lost Apocrypha of the Old Testament*. London: SPCK. 53-61.

Chronicles of Jerahmeel

Dan, Joseph
    1971   "Jerahmeel, Chronicles of." *Encyclopedia Judaica* 9: 1345. New York: Macmillan.

Gaster, M.
    1899   *The Chronicles of Jerahmeel*. Translation from a manuscript with introduction. London: Royal Asiatic Society (reprinted with a 124-page Prolegomenon by Haim Schwarzbaum; New York: Ktav, 1971).

Revelation of Joshua ben Levi (A)

Text

Jellinek, A.
    1967   *Bet ha-Midrash*, 2.48-51.

Translations

Gaster, M.
    1893   "Hebrew Visions," 591-596.

Wünsche, A.
    1907-1910   *Aus Israels Lehrhallen*, 3.97-102.

Studies

Buttenweiser, M.
    1901   *Outline*, 23-24.

Revelation of Joshua ben Levi (B)

Text

Jellinek, A.
    1967   *Bet ha-Midrash*, 2.52-53.

Translation

Gaster, M.
    1893   "Hebrew Visions," 596-598.

Ascension of Moses

Text

Buttenweiser, M.
    1901   *Outline*, 19-21.

Translation

Gaster, M.
    1893   "Hebrew Visions," 572-588.

The Visions of Ezekiel

Text

Grünwald, I.
    1972   "The Visions of Ezekiel: A Critical Edition and Commentary." Pp. 101-139 in *Temirin: Texts and Studies in Kabbala and Hasidism I*. Jerusalem: Kook.

Wertheimer, S.
    1968   *Batte Midrashot*, 2.127-134.

Scholem, G.
    1974   *Kabbalah*, 379.

Hekalot Zuttarti

Text

Musajoff, S.
    1921   *Merkaba Shelema*, 6a-8b.

Scholem, G.
    1965   *Jewish Gnosticism*, 6, 127.

Shiur Qoma

Text

Musajoff, S.
    1921   *Merkaba Shelema*, 32a-44b.

Studies

Lieberman, S.
    1965   See general bibliography

Scholem, G.
    1965   *Jewish Gnosticism*, 36-42.

Ma'aseh Merkaba

Text

Scholem, G.
    1965   *Jewish Gnosticism*, 101-117.

Tractate Hekalot

Text

Jellinek, A.
    1967   *Bet ha-Midrash*, 2.40-47.

Wertheimer, S.
    1968   *Batte Midrashot*, 1.49-62.

Translation

Wünsche, A.
    1907-1910   *Aus Israels Lehrhallen*, 3.33-47.

Studies

Scholem, G.
    1965   *Jewish Gnosticism*, 7, 28 n. 18.

Tosepta to the Targum of Ezekiel 1

Text

Wertheimer, S.
    1968   *Batte Midrashot*, 2.135-140.

Sefer Ha-Razim

Text

Margolioth, M.
1966   *Sefer Ha-Razim: A Newly Discovered Book of Magic from the Talmudic Period.* Jerusalem: American Academy for Jewish Research.

Studies

Dan, J.
1968   "Sefer Ha-Razim: Margolioth's Edition." *Tarbiz* 37: 208-214.

Merhavia, H.
1967   Review of Margolioth. *Kiryat Sepher* 42: 297-303.

Margolioth, M.
1966   Introduction and notes to the text above.

OTHER HEKALOTH LITERATURE

Grünwald, I.
1969   "New Passages from Hekhalot Literature." *Tarbiz* 38: 354-372.

1970   "Remarks on the Article 'New Passages from Hekhalot Literature.'" *Tarbiz* 39: 216-217.

Scholem, G.
1953   "Hakkarat Panim We-Sidre Shirtutim." Pp. 459-495 in *Sefer Assaf*. Jerusalem.

1969   "Ein Fragment zur Physiognomik und Chiromantik aus der Spätantiken Jüdischen Esoterik." Translation and notes for the text in Scholem, 1953. Pp. 175-193 in *Liber Amicorum: Studies in Honour of C. J. Bleeker*. Numen Supplements 17. Leiden: Brill.

Stenring, K.
1970   *The Book of Formation (Sepher Yetzirah)*. Translation and notes. New York: Ktav (original, 1923).

Revelation of Moses

Text

Jellinek, A.
1967   *Bet ha-Midrash*, 1.58-64.

Translations

Gaster, M.
1893   "Hebrew Visions," 588-590.

Wünsche, A.
1907-1910   *Aus Israels Lehrhallen*, 1.127-133 (up to p. 61 of Jellinek).

Assumption of Moses

Text

Jellinek, A.
1967   *Bet ha-Midrash*, 6.xxii.

Studies

Buttenweiser, M.
1901   *Outline*, 22.

Other Related Works

Baraita de Ma'aseh Bereshit

Text

Séd, N.
    1965   "Une cosmologie juive du haut moyen-age: le Berayta du Ma'aseh Beresit." *REJ* 124(4): 23-123 (with translation).

Wertheimer, S.
    1968   *Batte Midrashot*, 1.3-48.

Studies

Séd, N.
    1964   "Und cosmologie juive du haut moyen-age: le Berayta du Ma'aseh Beresit." *REJ* 123(3): 259-305.

'Ottiyot de Rabbi Akiba (2 versions)

Text

Jellinek, A.
    1967   *Bet ha-Midrash*, 3.12-64.

Wertheimer, S.
    1968   *Batte Midrashot*, 2.333-465.

Translation

Wünsche, A.
    1907-1910   *Aus Israels Lehrhallen*, 4.168-269.

Studies

Buttenweiser, M.
    1901   *Outline*, 25-29.

RABBINIC LITERATURE

Saldarini, A. J.
    1977   "The Uses of Apocalyptic in the Mishnah and Tosepta." *CBQ* 39: 396-409.

PERSIAN APOCALYPSES*

John J. Collins
DePaul University

SYNOPSIS

The terms "apocalypse" and "apocalyptic" are very widely used with reference to Persian writings and many scholars have posited extensive Persian influence on the Jewish and Christian apocalypses. Yet the study of Persian apocalypses of the period 250 BCE to 250 CE is impeded by exceptional difficulties which may well be insurmountable. These difficulties derive from the manner in which Persian literature has been transmitted. The Zoroastrian scripture, the Avesta, consists of writings from diverse periods which were collected in the Sassanian period (221-642 CE). While the Gathas are believed to derive from Zarathustra himself, the other components of the Avesta (i.e., the Younger Avesta) cannot be dated with any precision. Worse, the Avesta as we now have it is only about one quarter of the original. Much old material undoubtedly survives in the Pahlavi books, but these, in their present form, date chiefly from the ninth century CE. The most important documents of Persian "apocalyptic" and eschatology belong to this Pahlavi literature. A few important passages in classical authors, most notably Plutarch (*On Isis and Osiris*, 47) provide some evidence for the earlier period, and there are eschatological references in the Gathas and Younger Avesta. By analogy and comparison with these earlier passages, some older eschatological traditions can be recovered from the Pahlavi literature, but any reconstruction of a literary form of "apocalypse" must be extremely tentative and hypothetical.

What follows here is merely an indication of the major sources which may throw some light on Persian "apocalyptic" of the period between Alexander and Constantine. In each case extensive

---

* I am indebted to Professor Carsten Colpe for assistance with the Persian material.

redaction critical work is necessary before the supposed "originals" of the Hellenistic and Roman periods can be reconstructed with any confidence.

The material reviewed here is almost all very late in its present form and several items (e.g. the Bundahišn and Dēnkart) are compendia rather than revelation accounts. Only two of these works, the Zand-ī Vohuman Yasn and the book of Arda Viraf can be classified as apocalypses in their present form (Types Ia and IIc respectively). The Zand is especially important since this type of apocalypse is otherwise virtually confined to Jewish texts, and both the form and motifs of the Zand could possibly (but not certainly!) be older than the oldest full-fledged Jewish apocalypses. The history of the Persian work is too problematic and uncertain to support any theory of historical influences, but we cannot assume that the "historical" type of apocalypse was either peculiar or original to Judaism. The Žamāsp-Namak and the Oracle of Hystaspes are both closely related to the Zand-ī Vohuman Yasn. Both, however, are prophecies by human beings and are not mediated by an otherworldly being. Both appear to envisage cosmic transformation, but do not explicitly address the fate of individuals. Their closest analogues in the Jewish literature can be found in the Sibylline oracles. Arda Viraf, Mēnōk ī-Xrat and Hadōxt Nask are important witnesses to the interest in personal eschatology in the Persian tradition.

The great compendia of apocalyptic ideas in the Bundahišn and Dēnkart indicate that apocalyptic eschatology played a prominent part in Persian religion and must have been attested in a far greater corpus of works than we now possess. Unfortunately, our present evidence is too fragmentary and indirect to permit a clear picture of the nature of Persian apocalypses in the pre-Sassanian periods. Yet, fragmentary as it is, that evidence cannot be totally dismissed in any review of the apocalypses of the ancient world.

SURVEY

Type Ia: "Historical" Apocalypse with No Otherworldly Journey

The Zand-ī Vohuman Yasn

This Pahlavi work is allegedly a "zand" or "interpretation" of a lost book of the Avesta, the Vohuman Yašt. The lost Yašt is also widely thought to have influenced the Oracle of Hystaspes and the Žamāsp-Namak, and possibly some non-Persian writings, such as the Egyptian Potter's Oracle. Significant portions of the Zand have been dated to the Hellenistic age by Reitzenstein, Cumont, Eddy and Widengren, but the ancient material and later glosses cannot be separated with definitive precision. The Zand also appears (1:1) to depend in part on the Stûtkar Nask of the Avesta.

According to the Zand, chapter 1, Zarathustra asked for immortality from Ahura Mazdā but was granted instead the "wisdom of all-knowledge." He then saw a tree with four branches, one of gold, one of silver, one of steel and one of mixed iron. Ahura Mazdā explained the vision on his request and explained the four branches as four kingdoms of which the last is ruled by the "dīvs" who have "dishevelled hair." These have been interpreted as the Greeks (Eddy). The fourth kingdom comes "when thy tenth century will be at an end, O Spitâmân Zaratûhst!" In the third chapter we find a more extensive account of this incident. (Tavadia [122] considers chap. 1 secondary. Boyce [49] thinks it possible that chap. 3 evolved under Babylonian influence and that the version in chap. 1 "is the more purely Iranian.") In the longer account, Zarathustra sees seven branches, and these are again interpreted as kingdoms. Again they conclude with the "dīvs" of dishevelled hair and the end of the millennium of Zarathustra. In chapter 4, Zarathustra inquires about the signs of the tenth century and the end of his millennium, and Ahura Mazdā replies by describing a long series of upheavals and disturbances, both political and cosmic. Chapters 7-9 prophesy what will happen "when the Zaratûhstian millenium will end and Aûsîtar's will begin" (8:8). Then "near the end of the millenium Pêsyôtan son of Vistâsp will appear" as a savior figure who will destroy the dīvs. The millennium of Aûsîtarmâh follows, when men will not even die because they "will be so versed in medicine" (9:12). Then at the end of this millennium "Sôsîyôs will make the creatures pure again and resurrection and the finalmost material existence will occur" (9:23). (Anklesaria's translation is used here. Other scholars use the forms Hušetar, Hušētarmāh and Šošiyans for the names.)

The Zand-ī Vohuman Yasn, then, shows close similarity to the apocalypses which we have classified as Type Ia (the numbers refer to the paradigm given in the Introduction to this volume).

Manner of Revelation
1.1.1 Zarathustra sees a vision of a tree with either four (chap. 1) or seven (chap. 3) branches.
1.2.2 There is also dialogue in which Ahura Mazdā responds to Zarathustra's questions.
2. The vision is interpreted by Ahura Mazdā.
3.1 The Zand is anonymous and refers to Zarathustra in the third person.
3.2 The revelation is occasioned by Zarathustra's request for immortality. In chap. 3 the vision is seen in a dream.

Content: Temporal Axis
5.2 The four, or seven, branches are interpreted as kingdoms and so provide an *ex eventu* prophecy of the periods of world history.
7.2 Chaps. 4-6 describe a series of political and cosmic disasters.
8.1 No wicked person will pass from the millennium of Zarathustra to the next (6:13).

9.1 The world is transformed in the millennium of Hušētarmāh and definitively after the advent of the Šošiyans.
9.2.1 The final transformation includes resurrection.

Content: Spatial Axis
10.2 Spatial symbolism plays virtually no part in the Zand, but the main enemies are described as "dīvs" or demons.

There is no narrative conclusion.

Related Works

The Oracle of Hystaspes

The Oracle of Hystaspes is one of the writings widely thought to be influenced by the lost Vohuman Yašt. References to the Oracle (or Oracles) are found in Justin, Clement, and Aristokritos but our main source is the Divine Institutions of Lactantius. The nature of the work is most succinctly expressed in Div Inst 7:15: "A wonderful dream upon the interpretation of a boy who uttered divinations, announcing, long before the Trojan nation, that the Roman empire and name would be taken from the world." This passage indicates the form of the oracle--a dream vision interpreted by a boy which finds its closest parallel in Daniel 2 as has often been noted. The essential content is political upheaval--specifically the overthrow of Rome--but it also referred to the destruction of the world by fire (Justin Apol 1:20).

Some further features of the oracle can be established from passages in Lactantius where Hystaspes is not cited explicitly but appears to be used. In Div Inst 7:16 there is a description of the signs of the end which shows several parallels with the Zand-ī Vohuman Yasn and, to a lesser extent, the Bundahišn. Several of these motifs have no parallels in the Judeo-Christian tradition. Further, the references in Clement (Stromata, 6:5) and Lactantius (Div Inst 7:17) to a "great king" have been interpreted by Hinnells (1973:144) as ultimately deriving from a Persian savior figure, probably Šošiyans. Finally, Aristokritos, in the passage which refers to Hystaspes, indicates that "the fulfillment would take place after the completion of 6,000 years." Also, Lactantius (Div Inst 7:14) says that six *saecula* would elapse before the reign of Christ. While this passage does not refer to Hystaspes, the coincidence with Aristokritos and with the general Persian interest in periodization must at least suggest the possibility that this periodization was found in Hystaspes too (see further, Colpe, 1970:88).

The Persian provenance of the Oracle was definitively established by Windisch. Recently Hinnells has related it more specifically to Zoroastrianism and suggested a date in the first (or possibly second) century BCE. Accordingly, the oracle is extremely important evidence for pre-Christian Persian apocalypticism.

The Žāmāsp-Namak

Closely related to the Zand-ī Vohuman Yasn is the Pahlavi Žāmāsp-Namak. This is a prophecy of the minister Žāmāsp to the king Vištāsp and describes the eschatological upheavals leading up to the advent of Pêsyôtan. Two further eschatological passages, on further disasters and on the restoration of the world, are considered secondary by Messina, Tavadia and Boyce. Benveniste has argued that this Pahlavi prophecy should be read as verse and so reflects an older form than the prose Zand-ī Vohuman Yasn.

This prophecy is also included as chapter 16 in the longer Abiyātkār ī Žāmāspīk which is poorly preserved in late Pāzand and Persian versions. This work included a treatment of creation and is closely related to the Bundahišn (Messina: 17).

The Bundahišn

The Bundahišn survives in two recensions, the Greater (or Iranian) Bundahišn (translated by Anklesaria) and the shorter "Indian" Bundahišn (translated by West). The Bundahišn is thought to have grown through several redactions, from the time of the Arab conquest down to 1178 CE (Boyce: 40). Despite the late date and complicated history, Boyce (41) considers that its contents may in part be pre-Zoroastrian and several scholars have held that it reproduces material from the lost Avestan Dâmdât Nask (e.g. Bousset, 1926:507; see Colpe, 1961:154).

The work is presented as a compendium of traditional teaching entitled "Zand-âkâsîh," or "knowledge of the Zand (or tradition)." It begins: "first, as regards the origination of Ôhr-mazd and the opposition of the Evil-Spirit; then, as regards the nature [of the earthly] creatures, from the original creation till the end of the final material-life."

The course of history is divided into twelve thousand years: "For three thousand years the creatures remained in the spiritual state--that is, they were unthinking, unmoving and intangible" (1:14). Then the Evil Spirit attacked Ahura Mazdā, but the two agreed to limit the time of conflict to nine thousand years: "Within these nine thousand years, three thousand years will pass according to the will of Ôhr-mazd; three thousand years [will pass] in the mingled state, according to the will of [both] Ôhr-mazd and Ahrî-man; and in the final contest [He ought to render] the Evil-Spirit useless, and He will withhold adversity from the creatures" (1:28).

The greater part of the work (chaps. 8-30) deals with an encyclopaedic range of matters which pertain neither to creation nor to eschatology. Eschatology is treated mainly in chapters 33 and 34. Chapter 33 describes the calamities which would befall Iran in each millennium, down to the advent of "Šošiyans, son of Zaratust" (33:34). Chapter 34 describes the "resurrection and final material life." The purification of the world is effected by the fire which "will melt the metal which is within the hills and mountains" and becomes "like a river." This fire is like warm milk to the righteous but like melted metal to the wicked. Šošiyans raises the dead and all humanity becomes immortal. The Evil Spirit is returns to the darkness and the dragon Gôchîr burnt by the melted metal. Then the world will be renewed and immortal.

The contents of the Bundahišn certainly include apocalyptic eschatology. However, the form of the work is that of a compendium. Unlike the Zand-ī Vohuman Yasn and the Žāmāsp-Namak, there is no description of the way in which these doctrines were revealed. Whether the Bundahišn is based on an older work, in which the manner of revelation was described, we cannot be sure.

The Dēnkart

The Dēnkart, like the Bundahišn, is a compilation which includes materials of varied ages, redacted by various authors at a late date. Important eschatological material is found in Book 7, which deals with the career of Zarathustra (chap. 8) the millennia of Hušētar and Hušētarmāh (chaps. 9, 10) and the advent of Šošiyans (chap. 11). In this last period, "the fiend and Ahriman are annihilated and the renovation for the future existence occurs." There are also some eschatological allusions in Books 8 and 9. Book 9, chapter 8, contains material from the Stûtkar Nask of the Avesta, which is also cited in the Zand-ī Vohuman Yasn. As in the Zand, chapter 1, the Nask is said to have related "the exhibition of the nature of the four periods of the millenium of Zaratūhst." The account of the four periods differs somewhat from the Zand, a warning that neither is likely to be citing the Avestan source verbatim.

The Selections of Zāt-sparam

Zāt-sparam was an author who compiled three series of selections from religious texts then extant about 900 CE (West, 1897:133). He deals with themes similar to the Bundahišn and Dēnkart 7, but appears to be independent of both. He describes the three great moments of world history: first, creation and cosmology, second, the career of Zarathustra and third the advent of the final savior and the renovation (Tavadia: 83). Eschatological matters discussed include "the future existence of the soul" and "Aūhrmazd's statement of the reasons why mankind are to have a bodily existence in their future state" (West, 1904:105).

The Pahlavi Rivāyat Accompanying the Dādistān-ī Dēnīk

This work is a compendium of information on a great variety of religious subjects which was prefixed to the ninth century Dādistān-ī Dēnīk. In chapters 23-24 it contains a discussion of the fate of the souls of the righteous and wicked and how they feel after death. Chapter 25 discusses "the time of the Renovation." Chapter 48 discusses the millennia of Hušētar, Hušētar-māh and Šošiyans and the Resurrection; chapter 49 discusses the immortals (including Pêsyôtan) who assist Šošiyans in producing the renovation of the world and chapter 50 deals with "Hell and the Ridge of Arakzûr" (Dhabhar: ii-iii; West, 1904:104).

Plutarch, "On Isis and Osiris," Chapter 47

The account of Persian religion by Plutarch acquires special interest for a study of pre-Sassanian materials since it can at least be dated, firmly, much earlier than any of the Pahlavi writings. If, as seems highly probable, Plutarch derived his material from Theopompus, then it can be dated to the third century BCE. The passage is, again, a summary which gives no indication of the way in which these doctrines were supposed to have been revealed. Like the Bundahišn, it begins with an account of "Horomazes" and "Areimanius." The course of history will follow assigned periods: "Theopompus says that according to the Magians, for three thousand years alternately the one god will dominate the other and be dominated, and that for another three thousand years they will fight and make war, until one smashes up the domain of the other. In the end Hades shall perish and men shall be happy; neither shall they need sustenance nor shall they cast a shadow, while the god who will have brought this about shall have quiet and shall rest, not for a long while indeed for a god, but for such time as would be reasonable for a man who falls asleep."

The relation of this eschatological schema to what we find in the Persian writings is problematic. It is possible that the six millennia followed by a decisive destruction of evil should be correlated with the last nine thousand years of the Bundahišn (1:28). Alternatively, it may be correlated with the six *saecula* of the Oracle of Hystaspes.

The brief account in Plutarch is of interest here chiefly because of its early attestation of the periodization of world history with an eschatological conclusion.

Type IIc: Otherworldly Journey with Only Personal Eschatology

Arda Viraf Nāmeh (or Ardāy Wīrāz Nāmag or Artāy Vīrāp Namak)

A very different type of revelation is recorded in the book of Arda Viraf. Viraf (Wīrāz) was a priest who drugged himself to release his spirit to explore the fate of the dead. The work describes his visions of heaven and hell which have often been compared to Dante's *Divine Comedy*. Viraf is assisted on his journey by interpreting angels. After seven days, the spirit of Viraf returns and relates his vision.

The book of Arda Viraf conforms to the type of apocalypse we have designated IIc--an otherworldly journey with no cosmic or political eschatology.

1.1.1	Visions and
1.2.2	Dialogue are included in the
1.3	Otherworldly journey.
2.	Viraf is accompanied by angels who answer his questions.
3.1	The narrative framework refers to Viraf in the third person.
3.2	The circumstances which led to the journey are described in the first two chapters.
8.1	There are lengthy descriptions of the fate of souls
9.2.1	after death, especially the wicked.
10.	The book is largely taken up with descriptions of otherworldly regions and beings.
12.	Viraf receives instructions from Ahura Mazdā to return to the material world and preach.
13.	The return of Viraf is described in chap. 3, before the account of his experiences on the journey.

In its present form, the book of Arda Viraf probably dates from the ninth century, but Boyce believes that it "has probably a very old kernel" since the name of its hero occurs in the Avesta. However, no early portions can be extracted with any confidence. The work is mentioned here merely to indicate the presence of this type of apocalypse in the Persian tradition. Bousset (1901:157-159) and Widengren (1975:126) find traces of a heavenly journey also in Vendidad 19 in the Avesta, and also in other Pahlavi texts.

Related Works

Hadoxt Nask

This Nask of the Young Avesta has only survived in a few fragments, but there is also a Pahlavi translation. It contains a discussion between Zarathustra and Ahura Mazdā on the fate of the soul after death--Zarathustra asks brief questions and the god replies at length. Here again we cannot be sure of the date but at least the original Nask must be pre-Sassanian. Widengren (1965:102-104) uses the Hadoxt Nask as evidence for the eschatology of "the earliest Zoroastrian community." Widengren also insists on the close relation between the ascent of the soul in ecstasy before death and the ascent after death (1965:86).

Mēnōk-ī Xrat

This work consists of the replies of the "spirit of wisdom" to "62 inquiries, or groups of inquiries, made by a certain wise man regarding various subjects connected with the Zoroastrian religion" (West, 1904:107). In its present form, the work dates to about the ninth century, but, again, it may contain old material. Chapter 2:110-197 deals with the fate of the righteous and wicked souls after death. The righteous soul passes over the Činvat bridge and is met by its righteous deeds and greeted by angels. The wicked soul is bound by a demon and led over the bridge. It too is met by its deeds and it is abused by demons.

SELECT BIBLIOGRAPHY

TEXTS AND TRANSLATIONS

Anklesaria, B. T.
    1956   *Zand-Ākāsīh: Iranian or Greater Bundahišn.* Bombay: Rahnumae Mazdasnan Sabha.

    1967   *Zand-ī Vohuman Yasn.* Bombay: Cama Oriental Institute.

Bailey, H. W.
    1930-1931   "To the Zamasp-Namak." *BSOS* 6: 55-85, 581-600.

Colpe, C.
    1961   *Die religionsgeschichtliche Schule.* "Der awestische Hadoxt-Nask," 117-139. Göttingen: Vandenhoeck & Ruprecht.

Dhabhar, E. B. N.
    1913   *The Pahlavi Rivāyat accompanying The Dādistān-ī Dīnīk.* Bombay: Trustees of the Parsee Panchayat Funds and Properties.

Gray, L. H.
    1947   "A suggested restoration of the Hadoxt Nask." *JAOS* 67: 14-23.

Griffiths, J. G.
    1970   *Plutarch: De Iside et Osiride.* Cambridge: University of Wales.

Haug, M. and West, E. W.
    1872   *The Book of Arda Viraf.* London: Trübner; Bombay: Government Central Book Depot.

Hinnells, J. R.
    1973   "The Zoroastrian doctrine of salvation in the Roman world: A study of the oracle of Hystaspes." Pp. 125-148 in *Man and His Salvation: Studies in Memory of S. G. F. Brandon.* Eds. E. J. Sharpe and J. R. Hinnells. Manchester: Manchester University.

Messina, G.
    1939   *Libro Apocallittico Persiano: Ayātkār i Žāmāspīk.* Rome: PBI.

West, E. W.
    1880-1897   *Pahlavi Texts. Parts I-V.* Sacred Books of the East. Part I contains the Bundahišn and Bahman Yašt; Part II, Mēnōk-ī Xrat; Part IV, "The Contents of the Nasks," and Part V, Dēnkart 7 and Zāt-Sparam. Oxford: Clarendon.

STUDIES

Abegg, E.
    1928   *Der Messiasglaube in Indien und Iran.* Berlin: de Gruyter.

Benveniste, R.
    1932   "Une Apocalypse Pehlevie: le Zāmāsp-Nāmak." *RHR* 104: 337-380.

Bidez, J. and Cumont, F.
    1938   *Les Mages Hellénisés. Zoroastre, Ostanes et Hystaspe d'après la tradition grecque.* Vol. 1: *Introduction*; Vol. 2: *Les Textes.* Paris: Les Belles Lettres.

Bousset, W.
1926   *Die Religion des Judentums in späthellenistischen Zeitalter.* Ed. H. Gressmann. Tübingen: Mohr (reprinted, 1966).

1901   "Die Himmelsreise der Seele." *ARW* 4: 136-169, 229-273.

Boyce, M.
1968   "Middle Persian Literature." *Handbuch der Orientalistik* 4/1, section 2. *Literatur* No. 1: 31-66.

Colpe, C.
1970   "Der Begriff 'Menschensohn' und die Methode der Erforschung messianischer Prototypen III." (On the Oracle of Hystaspes). *Kairos* 12: 81-112.

Cumont, F.
1931   "La fin du monde selon les mages occidentaux." *RHR* 103: 29-96.

Eddy, S. K.
1961   *The King is Dead.* Chapters 1-3. Lincoln: University of Nebraska.

Hinnells, J. R.
1969   "Zoroastrian Saviour Imagery and its Influence on the NT." *Numen* 16: 163-173.

König, F.
1964   *Zarathustras Jenseitsvorstellungen und das Alte Testament.* Freiburg: Herder.

Molé, M.
1967   *La Légende de Zoroastre selon les textes pehlevis.* (Dēnkart 7, with a partial translation of the Pahlavi Rivayat). Paris: Klincksieck.

Reitzenstein, R. and Schaeder, H. H.
1926   *Studien zum Antiken Synkretismus aus Iran und Griechenland.* Leipzig: Teubner.

Shaked, S.
1970   "Eschatology and the goal of the religious life in Sassanian Zoroastrianism." Pp. 223-230 in *Types of Redemption.* Supplements to *Numen* XVIII. Eds. R. J. Z. Werblowski and C. J. Bleeker. Leiden: Brill.

Tavadia, J. C.
1956   *Die Mittelpersische Sprache und Literatur der Zarathustrier.* Leipzig: Harrassowitz.

Widengren, G.
1965   *Die Religionen Irans.* Die Religionen der Menschheit 14. Stuttgart: Kohlhammer.

1975   "Iran and Israel in Parthian Times with Special Regard to the Ethiopic Book of Enoch." Pp. 85-130 in *Religious Syncretism in Antiquity.* Ed. B. A. Pearson. Missoula: Scholars Press.

West, E. W.
    1904   "Pahlavi Literature." Pp. 75-129 in *Grundriss der Iranischen Philologie*. II Band. Eds. W. Geiger and E. Kuhn. Strassburg: Trübner.

Windisch, H.
    1929   *Die Orakel des Hystaspes*. Amsterdam: Koninklijke Akademie van Wetenschapen.

INDEX OF WORKS DISCUSSED

Works	Discussion	Bibliography
Jewish		
Abraham, Apoc of	36-37	54-55
Abraham, Test of	42	56
Animal Apocalypse	31	51-52
Baruch, 2 (Syriac)	34-35	54
Baruch, 3 (Greek)	41-42	55
Daniel	30-31	51
Elijah, Apoc of	See Christian and Rabbinic sections	
Enoch, 1.1-36	37-38	51-52
Enoch, 1.91-104	45	51-52
Enoch, 1. Similitudes	39-40	51-52
Enoch, 2	40	55
Ezra, 4	33-34	53
Heavenly Luminaries	38	51-52
Isaiah, Ascen	See Christian section	
Isaiah, Trito-	29	51
Isaianic Apocalypse	29	51
Job, Test of	46	58
Jubilees	32-33	52-53
Levi, Test of	40-41	57-58
Moses, Test of (Assumption)	45-46	57
Patriarchs, Tests of 12	46	57-58
Qumran Scrolls	48-49	59
Sibylline Oracles	46-47	58-59
Weeks, Apoc of	31-32	51-52
Zechariah	29	51
Zephaniah, Apoc of	43	56
Christian		
Adam, Test of	100-101	120
Adam, Penitence of	100-101	120
Bartholomew, Book of Resurrection 8b-14a	82-83	112
Bartholomew, Book of Resurrection 17b-19b	94	112
Bartholomew, Questions of	81-82	111-112
Didache 16	101	120-121
Elchasai	75-76	109
Elijah, Apoc	99-100	119
Esdras, Apoc of	87-88	114
Ezra, 5	78-79	110
Ezra, 6	98-99	118
Hermas	74-75	108-109
Isaac, Test 2-3a	79-80	110-111
Isaac, Test 5-6	89	110-111
Isaiah, Ascen 3:13-4:18	101-102	112-113
Isaiah, Ascen 6-11	84-85	112-113
Jacob's Ladder	69-70	107
Jacob, Test 1-3a	80	111
Jacob, Test 5	89-90	111
James, Apoc of	92-93	116
John the Apostle, Mysteries of	93-94	117
John the Theologian, Apoc of	76-77	109
John the Theologian, Ques of (attributed to Chrysostom)	102-103	121
Lord, Test of	77-78	109-110
Mark 13	96-97	117

Works	Discussion	Bibliography
Mary, Apoc of the Virgin	88-89	115
Mother of God, Apoc of the Holy	91-92	116
Paul, Apoc of	85-86	113
Peter, Apoc of	72-73	107-108
Revelation	70-72	107
Sib Or 1-2	97-98	117-118
Sib Or 7	98	118
Sib Or 8	98	118
Sedrach, Apoc of	94-95	117
Thomas, Apoc of	100	119-120
Zosimus	90-91	115-116

Gnostic

Works	Discussion	Bibliography
Adam, Apoc of	126-127	150
Allogenes	127	151
Archons, Nature of the	132	153
Hypsiphrone	134	154
James, 1 Apoc of	132-133	153
James, 2 Apoc of	128	151
James, Apocryphon of	145-146	157-158
Jesu Christi, Sophia	129-130	151-152
Jeu, I	141-142	156
Jeu, II	142	156
John, Apocryphon of	130-131	152
Mary, Gospel of	131-132	152-153
Melchizedek	128-129	151
Paul, Apoc of	138-139	155
Peter, Apoc of	133-134	153
Peter to Philip, Letter of	134	154
Peter and the Twelve Apostles, The Acts of	146-147	158
Pistis Sophia I-III	135-136	154
Pistis Sophia IV	135-136	154
Power, The Concept of our Great	144-145	157
Savior, Dialogue of	141	156
Seth, The Second Treatise of the Great	144	157
Seth, The Three Steles of	146	158
Shem, Paraphrase of	136-137	154
Thomas the Contender	140	155-156
Thomas, Gospel of	139	155
Thunder, The	143	156
Trimorphic Protennoia	143-144	157
Zostrianos	137-138	154-155

Greek and Latin

Works	Discussion	Bibliography
Asclepius, "Apocalypse"	170	178
Asclepius, Tractate	173	178
Berossus	171	178
Chaldean Oracles	175	178-179
Cicero, Somnium Scipionis	163	179
Corpus Hermeticum	172-173	179-180
Demotic Chronicle	168	180
Euhemerus	167	180
Fragments of Eschatological Prophecy	171	180-181
Heraclides Ponticus	163	181
Homer, Odyssey XI	165-166	

Index   221

Works	Discussion	Bibliography
Hystaspes, Oracles	See Persian Section	
Kore Kosmou	173-174	181
Lamb to Bocchoris	168-169	181
Lucian, Icaromenippus	165	181-182
Lucian, Nekyomanteia & Kataplous	166-167	181-182
Lycophron, Alexandra	175	182
Orpheus, Test of	172	182
Orpheus, Sacred Discourses	174	182
Orphic Tablets	166	183
Parmenides	162	183
Plato, Republic 614B-621B	162-163	183-184
Plato, Symposium	172	183-184
Plutarch, De facie lunae	167-168	184-185
Plutarch, De genio Socratis	164	184-185
Plutarch, De sera numinis vindicta	164-165	184-185
Poimandres	161	185
Potter's Oracle	169-170	185
Ps.-Plato, Axiochus	167	184
Seneca	163-164	185
Theosophy, Theological Oracles	175	185-186
Virgil, Aeneid VI	166	186
Virgil, 4th Eclogue	171	186

Rabbinic

Baraita de Ma'aseh Bereshit	198	205
Elijah, Hebrew Apoc of	193	201-202
Enoch, 3 (Sefer Hekalot)	192-193	201
Ezekiel 1, Tosepta to the Targum	196	203
Ezekiel, Visions of	195	202-203
Hekalot Rabbati	190-192	200
Hekalot, Tractate	196-197	203
Hekalot Zuttarti	195	203
Jerahmeel, Chronicles of	194	202
Joshua ben Levi, Revelation of	194	202
Ma'aseh Merkaba	196	203
Merkaba Rabba	192	201
Moses, Ascension of	194-195	202
Moses, Assumption of	197	204
Moses, Revelation of	197	204
'Ottiyot de Rabbi Akiba	198	205
Sefer Ha-Razim	197	204
Sefer Hekalot (3 Enoch)	192-193	201
Shiur Qoma	196	203

Persian

Arda Viraf	213	215-217
Bundahišn	211	215-217
Dēnkart	211-212	215-217
Hadōxt Nask	213-214	215-217
Hystaspes, Oracles of	210	215-217
Mēnōk-Ī Xrat	214	215-217
Pahlavi Rivāyat	212	215-217
Plutarch, Isis and Osiris	212-213	215-217
Žāmāsp-Namak	210-211	215-217
Zand-Ī Vohuman Yasn	208-210	215-217
Zāt-sparam	212	215-217

www.ingramcontent.com/pod-product-compliance
Lightning Source LLC
Chambersburg PA
CBHW021809220426
43662CB00006B/240